The Python Killer

The Python Killer / Stories of Nzema Life

Vinigi L. Grottanelli

The University of Chicago Press
Chicago and London

Vinigi L. Grottanelli, a leading scholar in anthropology and African studies, is professor emeritus and former director of the Istituto di Etnologia of the University of Rome. The recipient of numerous honors, he was named an Honorary Life Member of the International Union of Anthropological and Ethnological Sciences.

The University of Chicago Press, Chicago 60637
The University of Chicago Press, Ltd., London

Printed in the United States of America

97 96 95 94 93 92 91 90 89 88 54321

Library of Congress Cataloging-in-Publication Data

Grottanelli, Vinigi L.
The python killer.

Bibliography: p.
Includes index.
1. Nzima (African people)—Folklore. 2. Nzima (African people)—Social life and customs. I. Title.
DT510.43.N95G76 1988 306'.089963 87-31426
ISBN 0-226-31005-1

For Isabella

Contents

Felix qui potuit rerum cognoscere causas

Virgil *Georg*. 2. 490

Acknowledgments

The idea of sharing for a while the life of a West African tribe derived from a long-held secret wish of mine to extend my experiences of that absorbing continent. I had long traveled and worked in Africa before and just after World War II, but always along its eastern reaches, from Eritrea, Ethiopia, and Somalia down to Madagascar, and I was well aware that its western regions held equally significant but widely different human realities. However, the decision to select the Akan of Ghana, and the Nzema in particular, as the next main subject of my studies did not originally result from my personal inclination. This choice was strongly influenced by the arguments of Prof. Meyer Fortes of Cambridge University, the leading authority on West African anthropology, during one of our many conversations over the years, when we were both serving on the International African Institute's executive council. Admirable scholar and unforgettable friend, Meyer Fortes is alas no longer with us. But I remain deeply thankful to him for his advice—probably the soundest I ever received from a colleague.

The opportunity came in the summer of 1954, when I was nominated to represent my country at a UNESCO conference on the problems of urbanization in Africa. It happened to be convened in Abidjan, Ivory Coast—a city less than two hundred miles away from Nzemaland. A timely grant from the Wenner-Gren Foundation for Anthropological Research, in New York, which I acknowledge with gratitude, made it possible for me, at the end of the conference, to fly from the Ivory Coast to Ghana and to devote a first few weeks to fieldwork among the Nzema.

In those days, Ghana retained the century-old name of Gold Coast and was still under British rule. The British colonial authorities that I duly approached after landing in Accra directed me to a competent and resourceful minister who was a Nzema himself and who, on the eve of independence, was preparing to become his country's president, dictatorial master, and charismatic leader to countless millions of Africans beyond the borders of the Gold Coast—Dr. Kwame Nkrumah. We both deliberately and wisely avoided political topics, on which we would doubtless have disagreed, so the two long conversations we had turned out to be of great practical use for the initial research project I had in mind. If Kwame Nkrumah, consistent with his general outlook, viewed in his own heart anthropology and its followers as relics of the imperialistic world that he was about to attack and destroy, he was polite enough not to show it. He listened attentively to my plans of study, he praised them, he provided detailed information and useful suggestions, and he wrote and gave me personal letters of introduction to local chiefs. Although his political triumphs and final disaster are now long in the past, I am endebted to Kwame Nkrumah for his assistance and encouragement on the eve of my fieldwork among his fellow countrymen.

Years had to elapse before I could resume and continue those initial contacts. The combined duties of curator (and later director) of a national ethnographic museum and of university professor made it impossible for me to leave Italy for the long periods required by anthropological field research. Difficulties were eventually overcome in 1960, when what came to be known as the Missione Etnologica Italiana in Ghana (MEIG) was instituted and officially sponsored by Italian authorities. From that year onward, usually accompanied by two or more collaborators selected among my junior colleagues, assistants, and advanced students, I was able to return to Ghana to spend the summer months among the Nzema—nine summers between 1961 and 1975.

This way of distributing research periods over an irregular series of years has been criticized by some as unorthodox. But when MEIG began to function, the luxury of sabbatical leaves had not yet been granted to members of Italian universities, so that the splitting was inevitable if fieldwork was to be carried out at all. It also offered advantages: the encouragement of a diachronic perspective that emphasized the observation of process and gradual cultural change; the repeated opportunity of checking, integrating, or correcting information collected in previous seasons; the occasional creation of friendships with local men and women visited year after year. Long intervals between the periods of research also facilitate physical resistance to climate and environment conditions of a country cheerfully named in the past "the white man's grave."

By the late 1970s and early 1980s, the two volumes of MEIG's standard work had been published. But I could not bring myself to discontinue altogether my visits to the people I had come to love and admire, and I returned to them on four more occasions, each time for the duration of a few weeks. However, the severe political and economic crisis that had hit Ghana induced me to shift my research to the neighboring areas of the Ivory Coast—the Grand Bassam region—where for generations a growing number of Nzema had created for themselves a second homeland under more prosperous and peaceful conditions.

I acknowledge my debt of gratitude to the Italian Ministry of Foreign Affairs, to the Consiglio Nazionale delle Ricerche, and to the University of Rome for the generous grants that for more than two decades made my research possible.

Finally, I wish to extend the warm expression of my thankfulness to the myriad of Nzema informants, assistants, and friends. They are too numerous to be mentioned here by name—kings and dignitaries as well as simple farmers, proud priestesses and humble housewives, diviners and fishermen, young and old. They accepted with kindness and dignity the foreign intruder I was, answered with unfailing patience my endless questions, related and explained to me the true stories contained in the following pages, and above all succeeded in making me feel at home in their midst. In doing so, they provided me with more than information on exotic custom and scientific knowledge; they guided me to attain a fuller comprehension of the meaning of human life.

This book is theirs as much as mine.

Vinigi Grottanelli

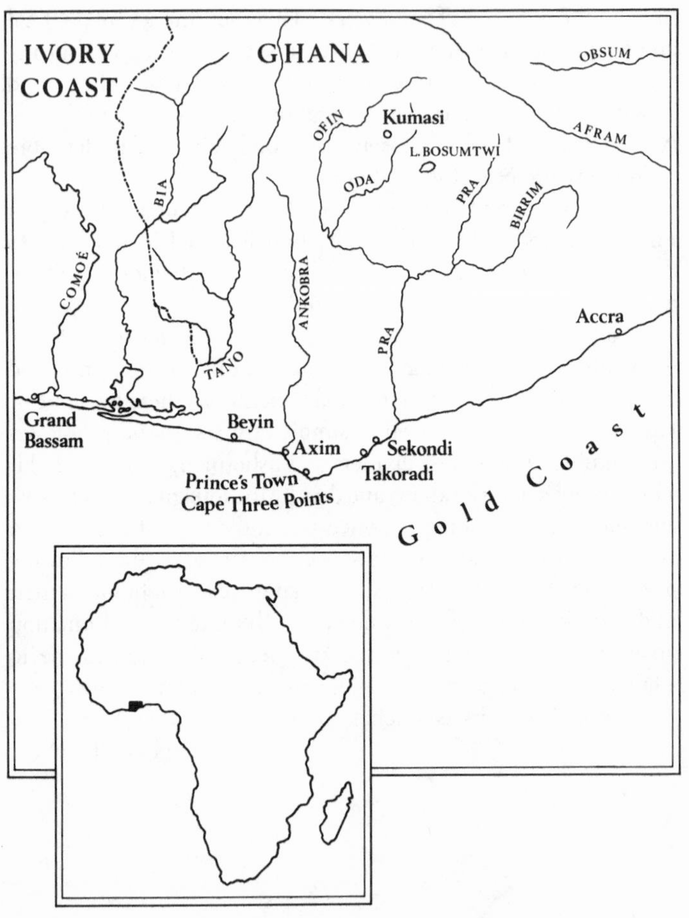
IVORY
COAST
GHANA
OBSUM
AFRAM
Kumasi
OFIN
L. BOSUMTWI
ODA
PRA
BIRRIM
BIA
COMOÉ
ANKOBRA
TANO
PRA
Accra
Grand
Bassam
Beyin
Axim
Sekondi
Takoradi
Prince's Town
Cape Three Points
Gold Coast

Introduction

This book is about the fundamental problems of life and death as experienced, judged, and solved by men and women of a little-known nation of West African farmers and fishermen. They are the Nzema, the southernmost branch of the great Akan linguistic family.

Their homeland is the long strip of tropical forest facing the Atlantic in the extreme southwest of Ghana, but for generations many of them have spilled across the political border into the neighboring areas of the Ivory Coast. In the Ivory Coast, the Nzema (or Nzima, as the name is often spelled) are commonly known as Apollonians—not, as a French author has imaginatively suggested, because of their fame of physical beauty but as a reflection of the first name given by Europeans to their country. Portuguese mariners sighted this part of the West African coast in the winter of 1470–71 and appear to have set foot on it for the first time on the day of St. Apollonia, February 9.

Past census figures are unreliable and obsolete, and the deliberate disregard of tribal divisions by African states since independence assures that future censuses will provide no further specific data concerning tribes. But the number of Nzema must by now far exceed my 1977 estimate of 100,000 (Grottanelli 1977–78, 1:15).

SOCIAL STRUCTURES

Nzema social structure is best explained in terms of two interlocking systems of institutions—segmentary and territorial. Like its better-known Akan neighbors—Fante to the east, Anyi to the west, Asante to the north—the Nzema nation is formed of acephalous, dispersed, matrilineal clans. There are seven Nzema clans, theoretically reputed to descend from as many female ancestors, and scattered all over the country. Their names are Adahonle, Alɔnwɔba, Azanwule, Ezohile, Mafole, Twea (pl. Ahwea, or Ndwea, also Ndweafoɔ, "dogs"), and Nvavile. Contrary to the rule obtaining among other Akan nations, Nzema matriclans are agamous, exogamy being obligatory only at the level of the minor descent groups or lineages into which the clan (*abusua*) is segmented.

Ancient and by now almost mythical migrations from an undescribed homeland in the north brought the ancestors of the seven clans to the gradual occupation of the present Nzema territory. The first clan or clan segment to reach a given locality and to settle in it founded a town (*suazo*) and claimed possession of the surrounding land. Thus it established a lasting ownership right in favor of all future generations. This proprietary right was sanctioned by the foundation of a "stool" (*ebia*), a seat and symbol of chiefly authority among all Akan peoples, and destined to remain the legitimate heirloom of the founding clan forever.

In this way the clan, according to tradition described as a migrant acephalous group, established both its territorial control and its administrative and political sovereignty in single areas of Nzemaland. Later arrivals, either segments of the same clan or of other clans, would ask the first occupants for a portion of their still unexploited land. Having obtained permission, they would settle down in their turn, acknowledging the sovereignty of the founders. In other words, they became subjects of that particular stool.

This process, still valid today despite the social changes of modern times, accounts for the fact that clans, deprived of unified organization in their present dispersed situation, do have their permanent territorial chiefs scattered throughout the country. A chief is called *belemgbunli* and addressed as *nana* (etymologically "grandmother"), but usually referred to by the name of his town followed by the suffix *-hene* (e.g., Anwiahene, Sanzulehene).

As in other Akan countries, there are paramount or state chiefs, also termed *belemgbunli* but more commonly known by the Twi title of *ɔmanhene*, and ceremonially addressed as *awulae* ("lord")—the chiefs of Eastern and Western Nzema, with capitals in Adoabo (Atuabo of the maps) and Benyinli (Beyin), respectively. Though formally ranking as kings and treated with deep respect, already under the British colonial administration, and even more in the independent republic of Ghana, these chiefs have had ceremonial prerogatives rather than political and administrative power.[1]

Wide geographical dispersion within the limits of Nzemaland and often beyond, combined with lack of central authority, has no doubt caused the decline in the functioning of the clans as efficient corporate bodies, in the same way as it led in the past to the abandoning of clan exogamy, enforced in other Akan nations. The socially significant characters and functions are thus devolved upon the lesser descent units in which each clan is subdivided, the lineages. These are also called *abusua* (pl. *mbusua*), but to avoid confusion between the major and minor group, a Nzema calls one's own lineage *suakunlu abusua* as distinct from the rest of the clan, *asalo abusua*. The lexical implications are meaningful: *suakunlu* is the inner chamber of a house, the private bedroom to which only close members of the family have access; *asalo* is the hall or entrance present in every house, where friends and strangers alike are received and entertained. Every person is by birth a member of his or her mother's lineage.

The lineage is thus the well-knit social unit within which members can safely trace their precise genealogical kinship relationship to all others, and in which land ownership is vested. The lineage head (*abusua kpanyinli*) is a male, not necessarily the oldest living member in terms of age but rather the leading representative of the lineage's senior branch in terms of female succession from the founder. He has control over legal matters, marriages, funerals, successions, emergencies, or important decisions concerning the lineage. Above all, he is responsible for the allotment of lineage land to members and the defender of all his kinspeople in land litigations with related segments of the same clan or with rival clans. He also defends the lineage's interests in controversies submitted to the local territorial chief.

There is also a female lineage head (*abusua kpanyinli raalɛ*), who has high moral authority, especially in the frequent litigations among lineage women and in decisions affecting controversial cases of succession. Over the decades and generations, mainly as a result of the geographical dispersion of its women married to men in faraway villages, the lineage is subject to periodical segmentation. Its average depth includes from five to eight generations; that is, its members reckon their common ancestry back to a female ancestor active from one to two centuries ago.

The intricacies of the kinship and affinity system would require a whole book, which has indeed been written (Grottanelli 1977–78). But for our present purposes it will suffice to summarize a few essential points.

THE SOURCES OF LIFE

The harmonious coexistence of matrilineal descent and paternal authority, characteristic of this society, can best be understood in the light of Nzema conceptions of the human being and his manifold composition. Elements forming human beings are both solid and liquid, durable and decaying, visible and invisible. At birth, children receive their bones from the mother, their flesh and blood from the father, their life principle or existential soul (*ɛkɛla*) from God. From the father they also receive a further element, the *sunsum*, or "personality soul." The Nzema see no contradiction between all this and their concomitant belief that children are sent to this world from Hades by the ancestors who dwell there.

At the end of the individual cycle, at death, the *ɛkɛla* (unless temporarily impeded by superhuman agencies) returns to God in the sky; the blood stops running; the personality is silenced; the bones remain in the grave for a long time.

This schematic pattern or, as the Nzema like to put it, this opposition of "the bones and the blood," does not coincide fully with its parallels among the other Akan peoples, notably the Asante. But it helps the Nzema to explain and justify their social system as entirely reasonable. The bones stand for structural solidity and duration, hence for the logical validity of matrilineal descent and grouping. Blood stands for vitality, strength, and personal growth, hence for the relevance of the father's role and authority in sustaining and guiding his children.

FAMILY, MARRIAGE, AND CHILDREN

As authority is vested in male members of the family, it is the mother's brother (*awuvonyi*), as the child's closest male adult relative within the lineage, who has jural rights over the child as well as lifelong duties of legal, moral, and financial support. The father (*egya*), though necessarily a stranger to the child's lineage, has complementary rights and duties toward the child. He must provide for the child's upkeeping and is responsible for the choice of his or her personal name. If the child is female, the father is the first to be approached by the girl's suitors, with the right to accept or reject their marriage proposals. Even more important, the children's "home"—where they are brought up and lodged in their infancy and to which they tend to return when old and lonely, widowed, or sick—is their father's, not their lineage's compound. In technical terms, matrilineal descent is balanced by patrilocal (and virilocal) residence, though I do not think that strong bilateral relationship is sufficient in our case to justify the definition of "double descent."

The difference between direct and collateral descent being ignored, basic kinship terms are used to indicate a far larger number of relatives than in our Western systems. For instance, the term *mother* (ɔmɔ) describes not only Ego's genetrix (biological mother) and all her sisters and half-sisters, uterine and consanguine, but also all lineage members whom Ego's mother calls sisters, all the father's sisters and half-sisters, the paternal uncle's wives, and the father's sisters' daughters. The reason for this last inclusion in the *ɔmɔ* group is that, should all Ego's father's wives and all his sisters die before him, it is one of his sisters' daughters who would be chosen to take care of the household, thus being from the start a potential future mother to Ego. Of course, this does not mean that, in his feelings and behavior, Ego does not fully appreciate the difference between all these women and his mother, "the one who brought me forth," or simply "my *real* mother," as the Nzema say.

Similarly, there are several distinct categories of individuals whom Ego considers and addresses as "father," "child," and so on.

There are eleven distinct forms of marriage (*agyalɛ*), including cross-cousin marriage, pawn marriage, "home" marriage (with a former slave or descendant of slaves, even if belonging now to Ego's lineage, a permitted exception), "excuse" marriage (of a man who remarries a former wife he had previously divorced), succession marriage (when a widow is accepted as wife by her late husband's successor), and Christian church matrimony. Somewhat unusually, the term *agyalɛ* is also used to refer to such unions as recognized concubinage, promissory infant betrothal, and "friendship" marriage, the formal union of a man (who may even be married) with a youth.

Polygyny is common, even among nominal Christians, though

most men appear to have one wife at a time. Bachelors and spinsters are rare. Divorce is frequent and easily obtained at the request of either partner.

Children are desired, with no preference for either sex. In many cases they are numerous, though infant mortality remains high to this day. They are brought up as a rule in their legal father's homestead until they reach the age of marriage, which by Western standards is very young, especially for females. The number of boys and girls in any compound is at times significantly influenced, however, by the widespread custom of *adanelilɛ*, the rearing and educating of children other than those of the married couple or—to put it more precisely—of the compound owner's wives. This popular sort of fostering in no way supersedes the adopted child's formal kinship links to parents and lineage kin. It is considered by the Nzema a highly honorable custom, useful to the children who benefit by it and praiseworthy to the person who accepts and rears them. It is only to a virtuous and respected man and his wives that parents will consent to entrust their children. In turn, the children profit by the experience of changing their environment at an early age and becoming acquainted with new people, sometimes of a different clan and usually in a new village. Understandably, the man who is asked to rear the child, or who volunteers to do so, is often a maternal uncle.

There is one notable exception to the desire of married people for numerous offspring, and it concerns the *bulu* and *amu* children. *Bulu* is the Nzema term for "ten": the tenth child brought forth by any woman, either by the same husband or by different men, is reputed unholy and unlucky, and must not be accepted. In the past, the infant was immediately smothered at birth; but as the British colonial authorities disapproved of this custom and even punished those who practiced it, in modern times other solutions were sought. These dangerous babies are at once either dispatched to some distant village and permanently entrusted to relatives or friends there, never again to be seen by their parents, or they are given to the Eikwe Catholic Mission in Eastern Nzema, where the kind German sisters made it known that they were prepared to accept and rear the "forbidden" babies. In any case, *bulu* children should not be kept by their mothers, as they are a menace to the *abusua;* if kept, some adult lineage member would be bound to die soon.

The same negative attitude is extended to the category of *amu*, children conceived by a mother not having previously passed at least three regular menses. They, too, must be destroyed at birth or permanently removed. The decision is or was taken as a safeguard for the integrity of the matrilineage, and accepted as legitimate in the past by society as a whole. But as the father's line was not supposed to be endangered by the baby's eventual survival, in recent times there has been an increasing tendency to oppose this practice. Cases have been reported of a father challenging his wife's *abusua*'s right to dispose of the forbidden child. Shortly before his wife's expected delivery, the prospective father would publicly pronounce a solemn oath—possibly the formal major state oath—declaring that, if after a given number of days after the infant's birth he did not see it alive and thriving, he would take legal action against his wife and her matrikin. This revolutionary attitude is one of the symptoms of modern changes in the better-educated layers of public opinion—influenced by European trends—tending to undermine if not abolish the age-old principles and privileges of the matrilineal structure.

PERSONAL NAMES AND SOCIAL ALLEGIANCES

Another sector of culture in which the interplay of maternal and paternal rights is patent, shedding light on the complexities of Akan social structures, is the system of personal names.

At first sight, the system seems simple. All Nzema men or women, including the many we shall meet in the life histories that follow, are commonly known in their social environment by either one single name or a couple of names—usually the given name preceded by the patronymic. But a more careful attention shows that this standard combination can be altered and replaced in a variety of ways. Not only do kings and chiefs adopt a totally new name on accession to their stool and priests and priestesses may add the name of their deity to their own, but ordinary farmers and housewives, irrespective of clan and lineage and territorial location, adopt different combinations of their traditional names. There is no exclusive or preferential reserve of personal names for any single descent group or geographical area. There are, on the other hand, some six or seven categories of such names according to preset circumstances of descent and birth and according to individual choice and allegiance.

A first category, automatically determined and maternally oriented, consists of what we would call serial birth names. A woman's first two children receive no such names. But if the first two born are male and the third is also a male, the baby will automatically be called Mieza; if a woman has three consecutive females, the third one will be Manza. If she brings forth five consecutive children of the same sex, whether male or female, the fifth will be Anlunli. On the other hand, if the first two children are male and the third a female, or vice versa, the third child will be called Kyɛndɔ irrespective of sex, and will be considered unlucky. At the end of the period of seclusion that follows delivery, a special blessing rite will have to be performed by the mother. The name Kyɛndɔ is not retained as a term of address for the child if the child survives.

Every child after the fifth, irrespective of sex, is known by a special name denoting the serial order of birth. The sixth born is Azane; the seventh, Asua; the eighth, Nyamekɛ; the ninth, Nyɔnra, the tenth, as already mentioned, Bulu; the eleventh, Eduku; the twelfth, Edunwio; the thirteenth, Edunsa. The list ends here, though cases of mothers having fourteen children or more are not unknown.

Serial names may be substituted by others in everyday use as the child grows up. But they often remain as familiar vocatives, or are chosen as "given" names in memory of some former bearer. Their social significance lies above all in their lucky or unlucky connotation. In contrast with the sad fate of Bulu, Nyamekɛ and Nyɔnra are hailed as particularly fortunate. They are said to be "pure and holy" children given directly by God, and are therefore exempt from the common risks carried over by all other children from Hades. They are jointly known as *nyangonle mmalɛ*, from the name of a special shrine erected for them in their father's compound. Provided that they observe certain taboos and wear the prescribed beads and that suitable libations and offerings are made every year at the shrine in their honor, the bearers of these two names are theoretically reputed to retain their holiness throughout their lives.

Twins (*ndalɛ*) are included in the category of *nyangonle mmalɛ* and are automatically given special birth names according to whether or not they are of the same sex. If they are the same sex, irrespective of whether they are both boys or both girls, the first born is called Ndakpanyi, the second Ndakyia. In the other case, the male is Ndabia, the female Ndabela. The next child born after a mother's twin delivery is always called Anlima.

The second type of personal names automatically assigned to every human being at birth is the set corresponding to the day of the week of the birth. The Nzema, and the Akan in general, long ago adopted the seven-day system; therefore, there are seven such names (*ɛkɛla aluma*, sing. *ɛkɛla duma*) for males, and as many for females. The male list, beginning with Sunday, is Kwasi, Kodwo, Kabenla, Kaku, Kwao, Kofi, and Kwame. The corresponding female series is Akasi, Adwoba, Abenlema, Akuba, Yaba, Afiba, and Ama. Linguistically, the double set corresponds fairly closely to its parallels in Twi (Christaller 1933, 599) and Anyi (Amon d'Aby 1960, 24).

The conceptual connection of this type of name with the life principle or soul is obscure to the Nzema themselves. It is said that *ɛkɛla* is "something like air." According to one opinion, it is a divine breath that touches the mother's body at the moment of conception, hence presumably determining the day of delivery nine months later. The use of the term *ɛkɛla* in a different context suggests a possible connection between a person's "soul name" and personal fate. The concept of good luck, or propitious fate, is in fact expressed by *ɛkɛla kpalɛ* or *ɛkɛla fufule* (lit. "good soul," "white soul"); that of bad luck, by *ɛkɛla ɛtane* or *ɛkɛla bile* ("bad" or "black soul"). Both are patently related to the God-sent breath and to the day of birth. Experience, however, has not failed to teach the Nzema that this correspondence works in the most erratic and unpredictable way, so that for the newborn child no day can be reputed luckier or unluckier than any other.

Children are usually called by their "soul name" only until they receive a "given" name, by which they will henceforth be known both within and outside the compound circle. In adult life, however, there are occasions in which the *ɛkɛla duma* is still preferred over other names. It continues to be used as a term of endearment and intimacy by relatives who have known the person from infancy, such as parents, siblings, and grandparents in both lines. It must be uttered by an enemy when pronouncing an incantation or curse against the person; otherwise an adversary's or a sorcerer's formulas are ineffective, or at least less effective. The soul name is also used during obsequies, when the women wail or sing dirges for the deceased.

A third predetermined type of name, assigned to everyone at birth and used throughout life, is the *ɛzɛ duma*, or patronymic. It precedes the soul name, and later the given name, as a genitive; for example, Aka, son of Eboyi, is referred to as Eboyi Aka. The patronymic is always the legal father's—not the genitor's—personal name. It may be omitted in colloquial speech, but must be uttered in formal and official circumstances; a person having no known patronymic, such as a love child whose father is unknown or uncertain, is always in a slightly inferior social position.

Fourth, and independent of the three categories just mentioned, a person's main name is the *dumadonlɛ* or "given" name, usually simply referred to as *duma*. It is chosen, and formally announced to the whole community, by the child's father, usually at a time when the baby begins to crawl and has cut the first two teeth, because this indicates "passing the grave," as the Nzema put it—that is, can be expected to survive.

If the child's paternal grandfather is dead, the choice of name rests entirely with the father. A first-born male will frequently be named after his father's father, a female after her father's father's sister or her father's mother. Following children will be named for their father's other classificatory fathers and mothers, or other patrilateral relatives. But if the baby's grandfather is still alive, the choice will be left to him, and the *duma* will then probably be drawn from those of an earlier generation. As there is no fear of necronyms—that is, no taboo against using dead people's names—and no objection to namesakes in general, a child can be named after a deceased or a living forebear. The name after dead ancestors does not imply the idea of reincarnation; this belief is followed by the Nzema only in exceptional cases, in contrast to the neighboring Anyi, for whom every conception allegedly results from an ancestor's reincarnation (Tauxier 1932, 225).

Varying circumstances may suggest quite different name choices. For instance, when a woman remains sterile for years and succeeds in conceiving only after recourse a *bozonle* ("fetish god"), her child may be named for that god, and throughout life that child will have ritual obligations toward the deity.

Again, if a baby is sickly, naming is postponed for months or even years, until signs of permanent recovery are visible. But if the parents decide not to postpone the event, or if the previous death of one or more of the baby's siblings induces the parents to fear for the present one's survival, a peculiar type of name will be given. For instance, the baby may be named after a socially inferior person or a worthless or despicable object. The most common one is Kanra ("slave"), or its equivalents (Wangala, Pepe, Abudu, etc.), referring to migrant laborers from the "uncivilized" north. Other such names are Fovolɛ (refuse heap), Ebinli (excreta), Kyɛkyɛkɔ ("pack and go," meaning "for all we care, you may go anywhere"), Ayile Ewie ("no more medicine"—i.e., we are tired of curing sick children), Azɛlɛ Ewie ("no more ground"—i.e., we have no room left in our cemetery), and the like. The rationale for the invention of such quaintly derogatory names, which is familiar to other peoples well beyond the Akan area, is that witches and other evil beings supposed to endanger the child's health and even life will refrain from causing harm if led to believe that even in the parents' eyes the child is no more than a worthless little creature.

The patrilateral orientation is revealed even more clearly by the institution of *nzabelano*, or honorary appellation. This fifth type is not strictly speaking an individual identification, nor is it used as a vocative in everyday life, so it can hardly be considered a "personal" name. It is only resorted to by men as a praise appellation on formal occasions, uttered in response to greetings or by strangers as an introduction on first meeting, and by elders at a funeral or other solemn or official occasion. Transmitted by father to son through the generations, the *nzabelano* appears to correspond to the Fante *egyabosom* (Christensen 1954, 77ff.) and to the Asante *ntoro*, some of the names being almost identical with those of the latter set. The Nzema, however, do not establish a close correlation between the father's spirit (*sunsum*) and the *nzabelano;* and still less do they consider the hereditary attribution of such a title as equivalent to the formation of a significant social unit comparable to the *ntoro* division of the Asante. That is, they don't somehow create a "submerged descent group" counterbalancing, as it were, the matrilineal *abusua*. Decades ago, both Rattray (1927/1954, 61–63, 318) and Danquah (1951, 12) already recognized the secondary role played by *ntoro* groupings in modern Asante society. Also, Busia (1954, 198) explicitly admitted that, "as practices connected with the *ntoro* have ceased to be generally observed, very few in Ashanti today have clear ideas about it." The corresponding Nzema concepts and practices have become obsolete to an even greater extent.

A sixth type is found in colloquial use; a fairly large number of Nzema are referred to and addressed by a nickname (*mgbayelɛ*) rather than by their official names. Nicknames fall into three classes. A first group corresponds to the double set of male and female soul names and is therefore predetermined for each person at birth and devoid of individual reference. The second group is similar in nature, except that each nickname of the series is attached to one of the frequently recurring bestowed names and birth names. The third class includes nicknames invented by a child's playmates, siblings, or other relatives, or even oneself.

Nicknames of the first two types are mostly meaningless words, the origin of which the Nzema are unable to explain. They either prefix or suffix the name (e.g., Ato Kwame, Kwame Ato) as an automatic appendix or instantaneous question-and-answer; their use is restricted to the small circle of one's kinsfolk and intimate friends, in a spirit of playfulness and endearment. But if assigned to important people—chiefs, lineage heads, et cetera—they can be rendered in drum language during ceremonies, to greet them when they make their appearance and to bid them farewell when they depart. The personage thus honored answers the musical greeting and is expected to make a small present (a few coins for a drink) to the drummers.

Nicknames of this third type are both linguistically and psychologically interesting to the anthropologist, as they express particular moods or feelings of the person who invents them or refer to the bearer's peculiar traits or habits. For instance, a lisping man or woman may be nicknamed Abɔlɔme (a tropical variety of lizard proverbially known for its flickering tongue); a child mocked by friends for being greedy will be called Aleɛkpole, "food gobbler"; and there are, of course, funnier ones.

In addition to these six categories of traditional names, the Nzema now have a further nontraditional but nonetheless socially meaningful set—Christian names or *ɛzɔnenlɛ aluma*, "baptismal names." In spite of repeated contacts with Europeans of various nations over the past five centuries, no consistent attempt to evangelize this nation was made before the early twentieth century; and these endeavors were hindered by local troubles, scanty connections with the outside world because of the absence of bridges, roads, and ports, and a scarcity if not total lack of preachers. Though the percentage of nominal Christians (mostly Catholics and Methodists) appears today to be on the order of 50–60 percent, the number of people actually bearing and using a baptismal name is by no means as high. In any case, it does not replace the previous traditional names but is combined with them, as everywhere else in Africa. For example, in the name James K. Andah, the middle initial usually stands for the patronymic and the last name is the *dumadonlɛ*; or it may be reversed, with the *ɛzɛ duma*, according to a recent fashion, being turned into a patrilineally transmitted surname or "family name," after the Western practice.

Even apart from its religious implications and from the rite of baptism, the possession of a Christian name appeals to progressive young men and women as a mark of literacy and modernity. A parallel though more limited trend is the equally recent adoption of Muslim personal names (in their modified Ghanaian version) following conversions to Islam. Many vital aspects of the Nzema's social allegiances and loyalties are thus reflected in their elaborate system of personal naming.

DEATH AND SUCCESSION

Death marks the day of the individual's utmost glorification. The deceased is cleansed, perfumed, dressed in the finest attire with all personal jewels and ornaments, laid in state for a whole day before burial, visited by a respectful crowd of kinsfolk and friends from many towns, and lamented and extolled in long funeral dirges. All this is important not only for those attending the funeral but also for the deceased, because it is known that until the moment of burial the spirit hovers over the death bed, and can still watch and listen. Cowries or coins, or nowadays even banknotes, are tied to the shroud, so that the deceased may pay the boatman for the ferry crossing the wide river separating *ewiade* from *ɛbolɔ*—this world from the next.

Sumptuous though the obsequies are for common mortals of both sexes, they are even more elaborate for a king or chief. They are simplified for people who die of unusual or "bad" deaths (*ɔtɔfoɔ*)—who are struck by lightning, crushed in the forest by the fall of a large tree, drowned, or murdered, as well as suicides and women who die in childbirth. Funeral rites for a small child are reduced to a minimum.

As everywhere, death calls for grief and mourning. But in the conception of the Nzema it is not considered a final defeat either for the deceased or the family. *Agyabe wu a, Agyabe de aze*, as the saying goes; "Agyabe dies, Agyabe is alive!" The deceased enters a new life, as we shall presently see; among the living, the deceased's place is promptly taken by a successor, and Nzema institutions ensure that such a replacement is fuller and more effective than succession in our own Western societies. As another consolatory proverb puts it, "The elephant dies, his remains are here."

The Nzema *koliagya*, usually translated as "heir," is a far more complex concept than that translation would imply. This person, who is usually (but not always) the one legally entitled to inherit the property of the deceased, is, more properly speaking, a successor in the full etymological sense of the term—a reliable substitute who replaces the deceased in kinship relationships and in social and moral obligations. Within the lineage, man succeeds man, woman succeeds woman; only children have no successors.

Both in preliterate times and in today's Ghana, in which writing exists (although the Nzema society is largely nonliterate), it is neither customary nor necessary to leave a written testament or an oral will nominating the heir or heirs; this task is accomplished by kinspeople. Officially, the choice of the successor is the responsibility of the lineage head after consultation with leading male elders. In practice, it is done by the lineage matrons assembled for the purpose after the burial.

A man's ideal successor is one of his classificatory brothers within the lineage, preferably chosen from the lineage's senior segment. In other words precedence and seniority are calculated according to primogeniture of the female apex of the heir's segment, not to the heir's personal age. In fact, it usually happens that the appointed person is younger than the deceased. The prospective successor of every lineage member thus tends to be known while both are still alive. But other considerations concur in making the final choice all but automatic.

If, owing to previous deaths within the lineage, one or more successors have already been appointed from the senior segment, A, the next choice is likely to fall on a member of the following segment, B, and so on. This gives representatives of all segments an equally fair chance of being called to succeed in turn. Thus, it may happen that a man's *koliagya* turns out to be one of his full uterine brothers. Furthermore, owing to the usual territorial dispersal or "fanning out" of lineage branches, the appointed successor often lives far away from the deceased's chiefdom, has no personal acquaintance with the family and social environment, and is therefore either unwilling or unsuited to accept the proposed succession. In view of such possible cases, the Nzema have wisely resorted to the habit of nominating not one but three successors for every man and two for every woman. This assures that at least one of them will consent to undertake the responsibilities as well as the advantages of the succession. And one of them—although perhaps not the first heir—may well turn out to be a member of the dead person's local segment, or indeed a full uterine sibling.

Personal qualities are also rightly taken into account. If the genealogically best qualified person is known to be in poor health, financially unreliable, or morally disreputable, that person will be disregarded in favor of a junior but more reliable sibling.

Finally, it may happen that all the classificatory siblings of the deceased (especially if the deceased was very old) have already died before him. In this case, uterine nephews or nieces take over, with preference to the eldest sister's children, and so on.

According to Akan mentality and legal custom, the *koliagya*, in male succession, is seen as the dead man's exact substitute. After the year of widowhood prescribed by custom, he automatically becomes the lawful husband of the deceased's wives. If the wives are old and sick, he may naturally waive his sexual rights, but must nevertheless provide their maintenance and assistance. In the traditional pattern, a man reaped few financial advantages: apart from inheriting the rights to cultivate the plots of land allotted by the lineage to the deceased, there usually was little personal money or other wealth to claim. As for the compound inhabited by the deceased, with all its buildings, furniture, and trappings, it is understood that it should be left to the widow or widows intact for their lifetime. Later, irrespective of matrilineal succession rules, it goes to the sons and daughters of the deceased, should they choose to remain or return there. In modern times, agricultural novelties such as the creation of cocoa farms or coconut plantations, regarded as personal property transmissible to one's successor, made the latter's economic position more enviable if the dead man had been an enterprising and successful cultivator.

In any case, the gatherings connected with obsequies are a fundamental event for the whole lineage. The complex web of all a deceased's ancient and current genealogical relations must be remembered and adjourned. Old claims and new interests must be reevaluated. And the ever-changing map of deaths, marriages, and births within the lineage must be redrawn, usually on the mere basis of elder members' memory and—except possibly in the families of chiefs—without the help of any written documents.

THE TIES BETWEEN THE LIVING AND DEAD

Death does not sever the manifold ties that deceased people had with the living in their lifetimes; ancestors, once individuals of flesh and blood and now pale though ever-present shadows in a mysterious but neighboring world, are the logical link between this earthly society and the so-called supernatural powers. Hades (*ɛbolɔ*) is the permanent and unchanging symbol of human life as it always has been and as it should go on being. The main concern of the silent, faraway crowd that lives there is that farms should go on being tilled in order to provide food for the living, that compounds built in the past should be kept in a good state of repair, that women should bring forth children so that lineages and towns multiply and prosper, and that social order and morals be respected.

Babies are constantly being sent to this world from Hades. This is an undisputable fact, the exceptions mentioned above confirming the rule, which is often expressed by saying that ancestors "bestow fertility" on women of their lineage. The expression is elegant but ambiguous, because it seems to indicate no more than a distant and indirect tutelary influence, whereas most people are convinced that babies do have their own mother in Hades proper. This woman is called Sama Abolowa, though opinions differ as to whether a single mythical woman of this name or several exist. Be this as it may, the existence of a mother who procreates children in Hades and sends them to the upper world (to obtain something for her up here, such as beads, ornaments, and gold, and bring it back to her) is a convincing explanation of why such a high percentage of babies and little children die. Sama Abolowa missed them and called them back to her.

Usually benevolent toward their descendants, ancestors sometimes appear in dreams to them, or in the form of ghosts, to advise and inform them; but they also expect to be remembered and honored with periodical libations and offerings. If offended by the behavior of the living, or simply displeased with them, they will not hesitate to punish them, warning them first by causing slight sickness, and if not duly appeased, sending a severe illness and death. In extreme cases, they become aggressive and are known to have attacked their relatives bodily.

One of these rare cases was reported to me in Axim on 23 September 1969. A young farmer from Andengle near Cape Three Points who was bathing in the sea was attacked and killed by a big shark. The unusual accident created a sensation, and at first popular opinion attributed it to the work of witchcraft. But the man's family was not convinced and sought a more authoritative explanation. A renowned diviner was consulted. In the course of the séance, which I attended, the oracle revealed that the young man had really been killed by the angry ghost (*nwomenle*) of a deceased senior brother, who had taken the form of a shark to wreak his vengeance.

With their lasting personal connection with their living kin, for good or for ill, the departed thus represent one vital sector of the manifold human forces constantly at work in influencing or determining the fate of mankind. Yet they are no longer wholly human; they can be reckoned as a class of those invisible powers that play an equally relevant role in shaping human destiny, usually (but not always correctly) termed in literature "supernatural beings."

DEITIES AND FETISH PRIESTS AND PRIESTESSES

The adjective *supernatural* is better justified when applied to the two deities that are the senior gods of the Akan pantheon, the Sky god and his spouse the Earth goddess. The former is known by two names, Ɛdɛnkɛma and Nyamenle. Whether these two terms refer to one or two gods can be the object of much debate and theological speculation for linguist, anthropologist, and philosopher (see Grottanelli 1967). To the modern Nzema, with whom we are here concerned, they are synonyms. From the very start, missionaries have chosen the name Nyamenle to indicate the God of Christianity; as a fair number of Nzema are or consider themselves Christian, this name is the one currently used. Nyamenle's spouse is called Azɛlɛ, which simply means "earth." Of the two, Nyamenle ranks first in seniority.

The divine couple is ontologically supreme but remote. Neither deity has or requires a clergy, shrines, or special places and occasions of private or public worship. Though they are sometimes invoked, and mentioned when pouring a libation, they are not the objects of a regular religious cult. This is offered, rather, to their innumerable "children," the *awozonle* (sing. *bozonle*), who live in ponds, boulders, conspicuous trees in the forest, reefs at sea, lagoons, and above all rivers and streams.

The *awozonle* are the everlasting (but strictly speaking not "eternal") representatives and inhabitants of Nature, an essential trait that has always made me hesitate to define them as "supernatural," as others generally do in similar contexts. They are invisible, but occasionally decide to make an appearance to mortals; so one knows that they are fully anthropomorphic, but bigger than humans. Some of them are male and some female, begetting children like humans. They have a frightening countenance and expression. Ignoring the learned critical objections of anthropologists to the concept and term *fetishism*, the anglophone Nzema consistently call these deities "fetish gods," their ministers "fetish priests," their main ceremonies "fetish dances."

Like the better-known *abosom* of Asante, the gods shun inhabited places and prefer secluded spots in the bush or in the waters. But they are fully informed of men's activities in villages and farms of their area. Some of them are considered tutelary deities of given lineages and towns. But much more often their attitude is one of reaction to, and punishment of, various sorts of human misbehavior. They are irritated by trespassers on their territory and by people arguing loudly and cursing. They dislike misers and liars, detect thieves, and take offense at people who break taboos, or who have sexual intercourse in the bush, especially near the gods' own abodes. In general, they hate all sorts of dishonesty, uncleanliness, and impurity, and they punish severely all those guilty of such sins, either of their own divine initiative or at the request of people who have been harmed. In a word, the *awozonle* can be described as the supreme guardians of social order and morals. Their retribution usually takes the form of some disease or accident, which may lead to death unless atonement is promptly made by the offender or sinner. Their unfailing action is so widely recognized and appreciated that the safest and quickest way to ensure the punishment of one's enemies is to denounce them (or to "give" them, as the vernacular expression goes) to one of the fetish gods, along with some small gift as kindly encouragement.

In what could be termed the official religious sphere, the qualified intermediary between mortals and the gods is the *kɔmenle*, the fetish priest or priestess (pl. *ahɔmenle*). At the same time, the *kɔmenle* is the mouthpiece and caretaker of a particular god, the guardian of that god's shrine, the medium who presents offerings supplied by petitioners, the interpreter of the *bozonle*'s commands and requests. Naturally, such a person is gifted with the rare privilege of "having an eye" (*ɔle ɔ nye*)—that is, of seeing the invisible. The *kɔmenle*'s profession is usually not a chosen one; in most cases it is a vocation imposed by the god, who selects future ministers either by causing them to fall into a trance in the course of *ahɔne*, or fetish dance meetings, or by repeated mysterious apparitions, or by sequestering them for days in a state of unconsciousness and keeping them secluded in the god's forest territory.

After a long and difficult apprenticeship, the fetish priest learns the techniques for contacting his personal and other gods at will, usually in the course of regular *ahɔne* performances, and for transmitting to them the appeals and requests of the faithful. When a *kɔmenle* reaches a state of authentic or simulated trance, the gods respond through the *kɔmenle*'s voice.

The gods have a variety of mysterious neighbors in their forest recesses. Some are age-old inhabitants of the forest, such as the tree-dwelling *ɛnwonzane*, resembling the *sasabonsam* of Twi-speaking peoples—spiteful hairy giants believed to harass lonely hunters and voyagers—or the more numerous *mmotia*, the mischievous dwarfs credited with an uncanny plant lore, who sometimes kidnap and confine mortals for weeks in their forest sanctuaries and impart to them the valuable secrets of herbalism and medicine.

Other invisible inhabitants of the wilderness are newcomers. This is the case of the *asonwu*, tiny noxious monsters who originally came from Anyi territory in the Ivory Coast. They are said to have invaded Nzemaland at the time of World War I (the Kaiser's war, as the Nzema call it). People became aware of their arrival because at the time they caused a major surge in serious maladies among the population and especially among the children, who died in great numbers. Precautions were taken. Competent soothsayers succeeded in establishing a contact with the hitherto unknown goblins and in discovering by what means they could be appeased. Special shrines—lattice platforms with thatched roofs—were set up for them in the forest. Year after year, appropriate offerings were made. The appalling tide of illnesses and deaths subsided a bit. But even today the *asonwu* have remained, continue to attack mortals, and demand to be pacified with repeated sacrifices. Unlike fetish gods and *mmotia*, the *asonwu* do not show themselves; only by looking at the earthenware figurines made in their image by expert potter-diviners who "have an eye" can we form a rough idea of their appearance. They are less anthropomorphic in shape than the *awozonle*; their features are decidedly monstrous; their stature is even smaller than that of the *mmotia*, less than one foot, according to the prevalent opinion.

They differ from the *mmotia* also on one fundamental point.

The traditional forest dwarfs acknowledge the sovereignty of God and respect God's will (although, as an informant once pointed out to me, "they do not go to church"). The *asonwu*, however, take no notice of Nyamenle, perhaps because they come from a foreign and heathen country; they move about and act of their own free will. Nevertheless, they have this in common with the gods of the Nzema: if, in an individual case, an *asonwu* is effectively identified before it has caused lethal effects, and if an appropriate course of worship is followed, the harmful being can be appeased and eventually turned into a protective force serving the interests of its former victim. This is what the white men call an ambivalent disposition.

The active intervention of superhuman forces into humans' lives is thus manifold and active from many directions. But no matter how strong the belief in these powers, the Nzema, like all other societies, acknowledge a universal truth: by their will and behavior, for good or for evil, human beings contribute to their own doing and undoing. Human forces, both constructive and destructive, are constantly at work in everyday life, and their combination or clash determines the outcome of man's endless struggle for life preservation, individual health, and social prosperity.

I deliberately use the term *forces* in this context because of—not in spite of—its vagueness and comprehensiveness. It covers a variety of covert actions, culturally conditioned reactions, mental attitudes, hidden feelings, magic manipulations, and mystical activities. These are conceptually distinct and customarily classified under different categories, but for our purposes they can all be grouped under a common denominator, as all of them—separately or sometimes jointly—can potentially or actually threaten human welfare.

I have elsewhere attempted to analyze in detail the whole range of these menaces and of the occult energies they can unleash (Grottanelli 1977–78). In the present introduction, only a few of them can be mentioned briefly.

TABOOS AND ILL WILL

Impurity, present in various forms and degrees but always hateful in the eyes of the gods, and dangerous in itself in its bodily as well as moral aspects, can be caused by the deliberate or unwitting infringement of a taboo (*kyibadeɛ*). Taboos, alimentary or behavioral, can be temporary or permanent, and are usually hereditary as matrilineal but more often patrilateral injunctions, or derived from a fetish god's command. Even more often, impurity may be a consequence of the improper use of sex. Male and female masturbation, rape, sodomy, lesbianism, bestiality, copulation with immature girls, common adultery, promiscuity on the part of married women, and incest are all deviations from the accepted pattern. But they are met with varying social reactions—from a sense of ridicule, or bland disapproval (as in the case of homosexuality), to stern condemnation and horror. Some go as far as causing the sinner's death through the intervention of a superhuman agency or the suppression of babies born as a consequence of the forbidden sexual act, as in the *bulu* and *amu* cases mentioned earlier, which always involve pollution (*evinli*). But the most heinous of all forms, involving not merely pollution but also *munzule* (abomination, scandal), is the adultery of a son with one of his father's wives, especially if this father is the son's real genitor and pater.

Another fairly frequent cause of sickness and impurity is *sipe*. This term, translated in Aboagye's dictionary (1968) as "an enmity," indicates a mixed feeling of grief, disappointment, anger, and resentment. It is experienced by a righteous person who through no personal fault has suffered occasional or lasting offense by near kin. The offense may, of course, lead to reprimands, litigation, or even blows, but *sipe* is not necessarily connected with any of these reactions; it lies deep in the offended person's soul, or, as some informants put it, "runs in his blood." It may not be outwardly manifested at all before it begins to affect the offender's prosperity or physical health; indeed, the more it is repressed and concealed, the stronger it becomes. The time and form of its action are unpredictable and independent of the will of the person in whose soul *sipe* resides. In most cases neither party may be aware that it is at work; an unconscious or oblivious offender's attention will be called to it only after taking the usual steps to ascertain the causes of persistent misfortune or some unaccountable ailment.

Once the cause is revealed, repentance and personal apologies are not sufficient to remove it. Appropriate "pacifying" actions of ritual nature are usually required to placate the offended person's resentment and thus to bring its effects to an end. If this is not done, at least in the most serious cases, death of the attacked person may ensue.

The most powerful and dangerous *sipe* is that of a father with regard to his children. People say that a mother's *sipe* may make her child sick, but a father's may kill. As another common saying goes, *sipe tɛla ayɛne*, "hidden resentment is stronger than witchcraft."

WITCHCRAFT

Of all the forces or invisible fluids emanating from human beings, the one that has just been mentioned, witchcraft, is the most dreaded and mysterious. Its Nzema name, *ayɛne* (pl. *nyɛne*) corresponds to Fante *anyɛn*, Twi *ayɛn*; as in these languages, it denotes primarily the occult power in the abstract, as well as the person endowed with it, in the majority of cases a woman. A synonym for "witch" is *bayivolɛ*, which again compares with Twi *bayi*, or *ɔbayifɔ* and Anyi *bayé*; the common Asante word for "male witch," *bɔnsam* or *ɔbonsam*, has no Nzema parallel.

Terminological similarities are matched by obvious analogies in beliefs concerning witchcraft, the circulation of which reaches far beyond the frontiers of tribe and state. It is worthwhile to remember, however, that, according to the widespread opinion registered by Debrunner (1961, 182), "The reputation of mystery with which popular superstition surrounds Nzima . . . strengthens the belief current in Ghana that all Nzima are witches." This fame is clearly exaggerated.

Witchcraft is an inborn spirit such as *sunsum* already present in some babies of both sexes when in their mother's womb, and that remains with them, as an indestructible part of their nature, throughout their lives. Unborn babies bring it with them from Hades; but the question of its original source remains a mystery that not only the average person but even the most learned soothsayers and priests are unable to clarify.

Witchcraft is contagious. It can be thrust upon others by means of an embrace or other bodily contact, or transmitted by succession (usually from mother to daughter, rarely from father to son), or even sold in a magic way. A person possessing it must pass it on before dying. It may be passed to another human being by the mere holding of that person's hand, or to some domestic animal such as a sheep or goat, which will then transmit it to the witch's successor.

Ayɛne people share with fetish priests and gifted diviners the rare faculty of preternatural sight; but an exclusive gift of theirs is the ability to fly. When witches set out to perform their evil deeds, they leave their body asleep and fly away in spirit. This happens usually at night and in utmost secrecy. If a witch happens to be sharing a bedroom with another person, the witch will first make sure that the roommate does not wake up by plucking a palm leaf from the thatch and silently placing it on the person's body; this will cause such sound sleep that waking will be impossible until the witch has finished the errand and has flown back to the bed or mat. During the absence of the spirit, the witch's body is immersed in deep slumber, incapable of standing or even sitting up in bed; attempts to wake the person are completely useless.

Witches' flight is often compared to that of bats. They fly low, just above the roofs of houses, where they occasionally perch to rest, flapping their invisible wings. They gather on treetops. Their cry can at times be heard in the darkness, approaching or fading away like that of night birds flying, *kyea kyea kyea* or *pea pea pea*; it means that the witch is just roaming about town without a precise aim. If, on the other hand, an *ayɛne* is on the way to perform some evil deed, the cry is different: *kyea kɔkɔkɔ, kyea kɔkɔkɔ, kyea kɔkɔkɔ*. This is a far more fearful omen; on the following morning, people will usually find out that some person in town has died during the night because of witchcraft.

The most fearful characteristic of witches is their "mystical" cannibalism. In everyday life, *ayɛne* people nourish themselves like ordinary mortals, but their favorite food is human flesh. They feast on it in the course of communal meetings, based on the pattern of *atoafɛlɛ* (a group of meal-exchanging friends in a village), each witch in turn providing a victim to be shared by those taking part in the gruesome banquet. The victim is chosen from the close kin of the individual acting in turn as host; it is usually a member of the witch's lineage segment—that is, a mother, uncle, sibling, or child if the witch is a woman, but possibly also a father or other close relative on the paternal side.

Not only lust for human flesh prompts witches to their evil

deeds; spite and envy are at the root of another typical *ayɛne* crime, the stealing of wombs from their luckier and more prolific kinswomen, especially if the witch is a *mota*, a person without issue. Greed for gain incites them to steal other people's property in a magic way; jealousy, vindictiveness, or sheer hate causes them to destroy their neighbors' crops, livestock, or other possessions. Their wickedness is matched by their cunning, and their crimes are sometimes difficult to detect owing to their power of metamorphosis. Of all animals, snakes are the ones into which they turn themselves more frequently; but a witch can also turn into an ant as tiny as the *ngyigyilira*, into a tarantula (*kyɛfonle*), or a millipede (*ezɔhɛla*); this last transformation is particularly dreaded, because the bite of a millipede-witch is reputed to cause leprosy. There really is no limit to the wicked things *ayɛne* can do.

It is true, on the other hand, that some people use their wonderful *ayɛne* powers for what are deemed "good" purposes. Ordinary people, to be sure, have little to say about these positive aspects, which consist mainly in the cleverness displayed by witches in the protection of their own children and in their ability to make money. It is believed that one or two enterprising Nzema men who left their homeland for such big cities as Accra and Abidjan obtained rapid career promotions thanks to their secret *ayɛne* nature. More sophisticated, literate informants have understandably been musing on the possible adaptation of witchcraft to modern conditions of life. Some have come to the conclusion that *nyɛne* should be credited with exceptional possibilities as inventors. In a delightful pamphlet on the subject published in Ghana, (Aboagye 1969, 22), the Nzema author stated that witches are capable of inventing airplanes, ships, trucks, and trains "in *ayɛne* way." Then he concludes with the following remark: "Truly, how wonderful *ayɛne* can be if used in performing good rather than evil deeds; whoever is gifted with it could do extraordinary things, such as not even Europeans are capable of."

ESTABLISHING CAUSES AND EFFECTING REMEDIES

Disturbances to social order and threats to individual integrity and welfare are thus traced back by the Nzema—as well as by countless other societies in Africa and beyond—to the host of possible factors I have mentioned: moral misconduct of the individual and of next of kin, grudges and inexpressed resentments of the person's relatives, oaths falsely sworn, the infringement of taboos, enemies' curses, ancestors' wrath, witchcraft and sorcery, punishment by deities and other superhuman beings, and the inscrutable will of the supreme rulers of creation, Sky god ("God" of the Christians) and Earth goddess, of which mortals are allowed to understand so little. In addition, a vague but alarming notion of such different causes as microbes, viruses, and the like, in which white men believe, has gradually been filtering into Akan conceptions in recent years, accounting for strange new orientations in their Weltanschauung.

The traditional beliefs I have attempted to summarize provide the anthropologist with a fascinating variety of subjects for investigation, interpretation, and comparison. But they acquire a far more vital relevance for the people themselves, who are not merely concerned with the theoretical nature and composition of the world, with the abstract conceptions of good and ill health, of fortune and misfortune, and of the reputed origins and causes of all these, but above all with the efficient practical procedures aiming at the safeguard of the individual's bodily and spiritual integrity.

Cosmological systems, mythological traditions, and eschatological hypotheses are essential and in themselves fascinating. But what are the ordinary person's practical problems, requiring immediate solutions? Kwasi's young sister may have died for some unaccountable reason, and there may be fear of further deaths in the family. Last year, some new pest all but destroyed the cassava on Kaku's farm, and he is anxiously thinking of how to protect the future crop. Afiba's first two babies were stillborn; how is she to ensure that the one she is now expecting will survive? Everybody has troubles such as these, or even more serious ones. What must be done? Obviously, and from their point of view very sensibly, the Nzema are not content with empirical, merely temporary remedies; they strive to ascertain the basic, real, and truly decisive causes of their ailments and misfortunes. I doubt that even to this day the most farsighted and best educated Nzema are able to trace a clear distinction between what could be called, using the terms of Murdock (1980), theories of natural and supernatural causation and their subcategories. But in every case remedies must be sought and applied; and even the ignorant housewife and the illiterate farmer know that all remedies are completely useless unless the true cause of the illness or accident has first been clearly understood and revealed. Competent advice must therefore be sought.

In the common cases of real or suspected illnesses, which are the most frequent events, the sick person will begin by recurring to a *ninsinli*, or herbalist, who, thanks to the knowledge initially imparted by the *mmotia*, or to personal empirical experience of herbs and roots, will prescribe the appropriate potions, ointments, fumigations, or enemas.

If remedies such as these have little or no effect, proving the case to be a serious one, it will be advisable to consult an oracle. In the majority of cases, this will be *adunyi*, the string oracle, which William Bosman noticed already in the 1690s in this part of the West African coast, and which Father Loyer diligently described in 1701. The manipulation of seven twined fiber strings or leather straps, each marked by an attached tiny symbol and defined by a corresponding name, will provide an unfailing response, as the spirit of *adunyi* descends upon and inspires the diviner. The soothsayer, though acting merely as the oracle's obedient mouthpiece, is usually at the same time a herbalist or healer, and is thus in a condition to prescribe the treatment in accord with the diagnosis.

But if the complaint or accident is a particularly grave one, or if explanation must be sought of a death or other misfortune seriously affecting the community, it will be advisable to interrogate the fetish gods themselves. This can be achieved by resorting to a *kɔmenle* and by organizing a public *ahɔne*, or fetish dance, under the *kɔmenle*'s guidance. Either at the priest's or priestess's compound, or if necessary at one of the influential gods' abodes in the forest, drummers are summoned, worshippers assemble along with the petitioners, the *kɔmenle* and assistants sing and dance, and the gods descend upon them and reveal the true causes of the disturbance.

These are the traditional solutions, but they are not the only ones. The fame of the white man's medicine has slowly been spreading among the Nzema in the course of the past few decades, so that modern-minded people will nowadays try to approach European doctors or their African pupils and followers. A decision of this sort will entail some difficulties for the average patient. Only a few dispensaries are scattered over the country and are not run by qualified medical personnel, and there is to this day in the whole Nzema country only a single small hospital with intermittent presence of a doctor, at the Catholic Mission at Eikwe. The old and severely ill living in outlying villages find it hard to reach. In very serious cases, a patient may have to be taken by truck to hospitals outside Nzemaland, in Axim or even Takoradi. But for the average person, even today, recourse to this type of treatment is not always a satisfactory experience. The European doctor and new Ghanaian followers may know a lot of strange things, and their medicines are sometimes powerful (though quite a few people are said to have died of them); but they do not bother to explain the really relevant matters. They will not tell you *who* sent the particular illness, and *how*, and *why* to you and not to somebody else, and *why* at this junction and not at some other time. They seldom let you speak, and if they do they hardly ever understand you or even listen to you properly. They usually complain that you have consulted them too late, when your case was already hopeless; or your sickness has been worsened by a *ninsinli*'s previous treatment, of which they know nothing but unfailingly disapprove. They only treat bodily diseases and are hopelessly indifferent to other kinds of misfortunes, troubles, threats, and sorrows that may of course endanger your health just as seriously.

But apart from the traditional solutions and those introduced by the white man, other ways of obtaining a diagnosis and treatment of their ills are open to the Nzema. One is the recourse to African diviners and healers of other nations. A small though statistically uncontrollable number of black migrants of non-Akan origin who specialize in magico-medical activities are either permanently settled in Nzemaland or visit it periodically. Some are peddlers of beads, miraculous drugs and herbs, and other wonderful things such as claws, bones, or entire skins or skeletons of unknown wild animals, of which they alone know the portentous virtues. Whether originating from the Northern Territories of Ghana or from other African states farther inland, such as Mali and Burkina Faso, they all come from the north and are known on the coast under the collective name of Ngɛnlamo (sing. Kɛnlamo)—that is, Muslims—though it is impossible to know how many of them are orthodox Muslims in the proper sense of the word. This question, at any rate, does not unduly concern the average Nzema, for whom the term *kɛnlamo* conveys at the same time the idea of a mysterious foreigner and a magician or doctor, hopefully credited with the exotic ability of performing wonders.

A substantially higher percentage of the population, however, seeks alternative moral and medical assistance with an equally foreign but far better organized healing group, the Twelve Apostles Church, more commonly known as Water Carriers (Nzema *awa asɔne*, "gourd church," or *nzule asɔne*, "water church"), a syncretistic pseudo-Christian sect stemming from the W. W. Harris movement.[2] This well-known West African movement, initiated by a Liberian "prophet" and originally aiming at a Christian revival along Wesleyan-Methodist lines, started with an uncompromising and initially successful antifetish campaign. But it gradually came to terms with traditional polytheistic beliefs and practices, and it degenerated into a "salutiferous" cult system. Among the Nzema, as in neighboring areas of Ghana and the southern Ivory Coast, priests and priestesses of the sect have adopted the practice of individual consultation with patients, combined with divining techniques, long-term treatment of the sick in the *awa* gardens, and the acceptance of corresponding fees.

The *awa* priest or priestess, called *ɛsɔfo* (cf. Twi *ɔsɔfò*), practices divination either by water gazing or by the casting of cowries. Both are plainly derived from techniques already widespread in traditional Akan or more generally West African soothsaying, but the first is clearly also linked with the symbolic virtues of water in Christian contexts. The constant display of crosses large and small, European-style candles, and conspicuous Bibles, which the *awa* ministers do not even pretend to read, are part of the original Christian orientation of the sect. Water also plays an important role in the Water Carriers séances, in the course of which long rows of patients—mostly women clad in white garments—shuffle and shake to the rhythm of gourd rattles, each of them supporting on their heads basins filled with blessed water. They hopefully wait not merely for the basin to overturn and for the holy liquid to soak their bodies but above all for the supernatural intervention that will cure their ailment or dispel their sorrows and troubles.

The present-day Nzema, in quest of a safe diagnosis and a

successful treatment of ills (mostly physical, but of course also mental and/or imaginary), have a choice among five different solutions. Two are traditional, two are relatively new but incorporating traditional elements, and one is what Westerners would term "scientific." Practically all the informants with whom I have discussed the criteria of their preference have admitted that each of the alternatives is worth considering and can eventually lead to positive results as well as failures. In fact, most of these people had, at one time or other, resorted to the various alternatives in turn without finding that any single one of them is so fruitless as to be discarded altogether or so safe as to be adopted permanently to the exclusion of all others.

This confusing situation is naturally not limited to the Nzema; with local variations, it is common to countless tribal societies in so-called developing countries. Referring to the whole of his country—but his remarks could be extended to the whole of West Africa—a distinguished Ghanaian scholar has written,

> Syncretic and spiritual churches that emphasise healing have mushroomed in Ghana, and the treatment of sick people is no longer the exclusive right of traditional healers and practitioners of scientific medicine but also the privilege of "prophets" and "brothers" of the spiritual church. . . . In Ghana disease is not only a physical phenomenon but also a social fact. The illness of an individual is often also the concern of the kin group. . . . In certain contexts traditional and scientific medicine offer different solutions to the problems that face a sick person, and the choice of one or the other or both may be influenced rightly or wrongly by what he believes to be the ultimate cause of his illness. Thus while the co-existence of different medical systems may give rise now and then to conflicts, it is clear that the problems that such co-existence poses are much more complex than this and need careful analysis. [J. H. K. Nketia, in Twumasi 1975, xv–xvi]

Professor Nketia's conclusions tally almost precisely with my own, apart from two remarks I should like to add. First, the situation is considerably more critical in an outlying rural area such as Nzemaland than in quickly developing, modernized urban milieus Nketia had in mind, writing in Legon or Accra. Second, the problems are by no means limited to the medical sphere; Ghanaians with whom I have long been acquainted regularly—and quite understandably—thought, spoke, and acted in terms of a wider and organically better structured sphere, including economic security, social welfare, and psychic harmony along with individual health as equally fundamental requisites for a bearable, full existence.

The basic ethnographic data condensed in the preceding pages are merely meant as a preliminary guide for readers not acquainted with the Akan society to which this book is devoted. This class of readers is bound to be a majority, because the Nzema are one of the few nations not only of the Akan group but of West Africa as a whole that have to this day practically been ignored in anthropological literature. The repeated visits I have paid to them over the last three decades, often assisted by some of my pupils and junior colleagues, have occupied, on the whole, well over two years of my life. Both during the periods of fieldwork and the long intervals between them, I have pondered the best way to make others share my knowledge and admiration for the unique sociocultural universe I was gradually discovering.

There are professional trends and academic conventions that cannot easily be overlooked. One of the basic and probably unavoidable ones, in anthropological studies, is the rule of generalization. The raw data assembled in the course of field research are later reexamined, evaluated, and compared not for the sake of their ephemeral significance but in the attempt to discover and establish the underlying general structures; in other words, those data are usually considered meaningful only insofar as they lead to a series of connected statements assumed to be valid within certain limits of time for the whole society studied. In conscious view of this end, the researcher is constantly looking for repetition of given events and patterns, as only once he has ascertained a certain degree of regularity in them can he attempt a synthesis of verified custom. His main task is to condense sociocultural data into what he assumes to be standardized behavior patterns or models, conveniently dovetailing into one another to form a coherent system.

Now, if it is the generalization as such that counts, the amount of specific detail used to illustrate it is a subsidiary matter for the individual anthropologist to decide. Some may consider it negligible. For, of course, minor everyday events recorded on the spot and later drawn from field notes, along with the host of minute facts engraved in the observer's memory, do not reflect orderly sets of rules and principles. Rather, they reflect raw chunks of life. They follow no systematic or even logical order. They introduce disturbing individual variants of the orthodox custom. They follow the course of casual circumstances in the life of the people studied and in that of the researcher, as the two intersect. Above all, they often concern sequences of collective behavior too intricate and extensive to be translated into the customary ethnological discourse.

Obviously, the requirements of theoretical synthesis come first, as some degree of generalization is the necessary shortcut by which we can achieve a consistent presentation of any culture, such that it may be understandable from the outside.

But surely, on the other hand, the tidy picture that emerges from this scholarly Procrustean process lacks the genuineness and captivating immediacy inherent in the real sequences of social events—the single and unique behavior cycles—that form the living substance of the observer's experience and the solid basis for all subsequent elaboration.

It is precisely to this too often neglected kind of field material—case histories—that I am turning in the present book. The twenty episodes presented here, all of them hitherto unpublished in English, are drawn from field notes taken down by me among the Nzema in 1970, 1971, and 1973. They concern what we would call dramatic situations—grave illnesses, accidents, and deaths—in the everyday lives of men and women of that nation, affecting the general theme in which I was interested in those days: the supreme and difficult art of keeping alive in a Third World society.

Many of the people involved I knew personally. A few of them had been friends of mine for more than a decade. So my information about their crises and problems was immediate and direct, provided by the people themselves and/or by their close kinsfolk and neighbors. In other cases, detailed reports were submitted to me shortly after the events by my Nzema assistants, and they could be checked, discussed, and completed in the course of later interviews with one or more of the interested parties. All the life histories relate facts that have really happened, even though their antecedents or "causes," as seen by my Nzema friends, may appear doubtful or downright fantastic to the Western reader. With two or three exceptions, dates, toponyms, and personal names are authentic, as I have seen no reason to conceal or alter them.

It is now time to let the stories speak for themselves.

1 / The Python Killer

On that clear morning of 2 May 1970, the first fishermen who walked to the Ngelekazo beach shortly after sunrise had a pleasant surprise. The sea was as calm as the Atlantic Ocean can be along the coast at the end of the dry season, and those who waded for a few yards beyond the foam of the breakers noticed that large shoals of fish were assembling in that direction. No time should be lost in setting out to cast their nets. They hurried to inform their colleagues, pushed their heavy black boats into the sea, and paddled out with all their strength, using the traditional precautions devised in order not to frighten the fish away. When they returned to the beach a few hours later, they dragged ashore in their long nets one of the largest catches of the whole season.

By that time, most of the population of Ngelekazo, including old people, women, and children, carrying their baskets and bags, had noisily flocked to the seashore with the intent of sharing, buying, selling, or merely admiring the announced wealth of fresh food coming in from the ocean. It was a long and laborious toil to drag the bulging nets ashore, even aided by strangers of all ages who cheerfully joined in. Excitement followed the appearance of the catch, and there was much shouting and bargaining. It thus took some time before people realized that a member of the fishing party was missing.

This was Ɛlea, a seventeen-year-old Twea boy from Negelekazo who had joined the adult fishermen at the last moment in hopes of receiving a small share of the fish that would be caught that morning. According to established custom, just as the men gradually dropped the long net into the sea, he had plunged from the canoe behind the net, making as much noise as he could, to prevent the fish from escaping seaward. As they knew he was a good swimmer and had safely played that same role on previous occasions, the men on the boats and on the beach had no reason to worry about him. It was only the next day, when nobody had seen him for twenty-four hours, that people realized something was amiss and began to suspect that he might have fallen victim to some accident.

In fact, the boy's body must have sunk under water without anybody noticing it and been carried away by a current. It was only found on the third morning after the accident, washed ashore during the night far from the place where Ɛlea had last been seen alive.

This was plainly a case of *ɔtɔfoɔ* death.[1] But the Twea people of Ngelekazo asked and obtained, with the hesitant assent of the chief and town elders, that the funeral and burial be carried out according to the usual pattern. Of course—as befits the obsequies of a boy or, more generally, of person who leaves no offspring—it would be in the quietest and most unobtrusive form.

A funeral provides townspeople with the foremost opportunity to assemble and discuss the circumstances of the death and its probable causes. But in this case, the inhabitants of Ngelekazo had not waited for the funeral gathering to debate these matters among themselves. The prevailing opinion was that Ɛlea's fatal accident had been caused by foul play. The boy was known to be in perfect health, and he was a sturdy and expert swimmer; therefore, his death by drowning could not be attributed to natural causes. Moreover, it was common knowledge that *ayɛne* (witchcraft) had for years been rampant in this segment of the Twea clan. The personal name of the suspected witch was not revealed to me at first, because these are delicate things about which people prefer not to speak openly; but my Ngelekazo informants, though aware that white men are often strangely skeptical about such matters, reported Ɛlea's case to me as a typical and obvious example of death caused by evil witchcraft. The rest, they confidently said, I would find out by myself. So I inquired further into Ɛlea's sad story.

Ɛlea was an abandoned boy. His father, an Ezohile farmer called Ɛholade Bulu, had died several years earlier. Ɛlea's mother, a Twea called Bɛnɛɛ, had remarried two years later and left with her second husband for the Ivory Coast, where they hoped to make a better living. Bɛnɛɛ had taken with her her only surviving daughter by the first marriage, a girl of fourteen named Elua. But she thought that Ɛlea, who incidentally did not get along very well with his stepfather, was old and strong enough to look after himself. So Ɛlea, by then almost fifteen, was left behind with no one to look

Watching the catch from the sea

after him and, what was worse, with no maternal uncle to whom he could turn for lodging and guidance. His nearest lineage kin in this part of western Nzemaland—the only part of the world he knew—were one of his maternal "grandmothers" (mother's mother's sister), Ama Agyakoma, and her daughter (technically a "mother" to him), Maneɛ. These two women lived together in Beyin, the old woman being a widow and Maneɛ divorced and childless. But apart from the geographical distance, Ɛlea knew them only slightly and disliked the little he knew of them. So, when his real mother settled down for good in the Ivory Coast, the boy went to live with his half-brother Kofi in Ɛlonyi, not quite two miles west of Ngelekazo, and had stayed with him ever since, until the eve of the fatal accident. The distance between the two villages was so small that it allowed the boy to come and go at ease and spend most of his time with friends in his birthplace, Ngelekazo.

Kofi was obviously the first person to approach and interview. The son of Ɛholade Bulu by a previous marriage (his mother is an Adahonle by the name of Amihyia Bozoma), he was an active and intelligent man of about forty, old enough to be a father to Ɛlea. He had traveled widely, working as a clerk for firms in Accra and serving in a foreign embassy in Abidjan for eight years. He spoke almost fluent English and moderately good French. Unmarried at the time, he led a bachelor's life in his late father's Ɛlonyi compound on the northern side of the main street. Usually he took his meals with his own mother in her compound on the southern side of the same street, because she was still alive and, since becoming a widow, preferred to go back to her own paternal home.

It took some time to contact Kofi, because he was often away on business. But when I succeeded in finding him in town one day, he proved to be a polite host and a most sensible informant. His half-brother's death, he said, was a sad event, but it did not present any mysterious problems. Of course, there were no witnesses to the accident, because the boy was alone out at sea. But the fishermen were not to blame for having left him behind when they took their boats ashore, as they were justified in assuming that Ɛlea would safely swim back by himself, as he had done on all previous occasions. Perhaps in the place where he dived there was a strong current or whirlpool, or possibly some big fish trying to escape the net knocked him down. Perhaps his strength simply failed him as he fought his way back through the breakers. Such accidents are, alas, liable to happen to fishermen.

I agreed. But, I asked, had there not been insistent rumors in town about other causes of the accident, causes of a totally different nature? Kofi scoffed at the suggestion. Indeed, he could not help hearing about the gossip, but, both as a Catholic and as a man of modern ideas, he did not believe a word of it. Why suspect witchcraft, even if such a thing exists, when the natural explanation of a death by drowning is so simple? Even if he did believe in these things, concluded Kofi, it would not be up to him to consult diviners or fetish priests to learn the truth. This was a matter that concerns the boy's *abusua* (lineage), not his.[2]

At the time I was living in Fort Apollonia, at the outskirts of Beyin.[3] The dead boy's surviving lineage relatives, as mentioned above, were settled in the same town, so there was no difficulty in contacting them. As soon as they heard that I wished to talk to them, Ama Agyakoma and her daughter Maneɛ politely called on me at the fort; but, as it turned out, they proved to be even more elusive than Kofi had been. Her grandson's untimely death, Ama Agyakoma said, had been a great shock to her, but it was the Lord's will. As far as they were concerned, there had been no question of seeking other causes, either by interrogating the *adunyi* oracle or by resorting to some fetish priest.[4] She and her daughter were Methodists and would never stoop to such superstitious practices. No, they had not even deemed it necessary to perform the customary rite in order to drag the drowned boy's soul out of the sea. That was that. Having nothing more to add, and having courteously but firmly refused the glass of whiskey the white man had offered them, the two women got up from their chairs, bowed slightly, took leave civilly, and departed.

Someone in Ɛlea's *abusua*, however, had not been satisfied with the naive explanation of the boy's death by sheer accident and had recourse to divination. This was Ɛlea's real mother, Bɛneɛ, the one who had brought him forth. Informed of her son's sudden death, she had at once come from the Ivory Coast to Ghana. After the funeral, and before she rejoined her husband in the lagoon area, she had visited Ɛzonle Kanra, the famed *ninsinli* (herbalist doctor and diviner) of Ngelekazo. This was confirmed to me personally by Ɛzonle Kanra himself. At Bɛneɛ's request, he consulted his *adunyi* strings in her presence and gave her the response: her son's drowning had not been caused by foul deeds or by any evil agency but by the very commonplace fact that the boy had taken too much food before diving into the sea.

For once, the pagan soothsayer agreed officially with the modern-minded, acculturated skeptic and with the Christian church attendants in giving a response of "death by natural causes."

Bɛneɛ was satisfied by the oracle's verdict, but the general public was not. Rumors about the presence of murderous witchcraft in that particular branch of the Twea clan continued to circulate in Ngelekazo, as well as in Ɛlonyi and Beyin; suspicions were almost unanimously directed against one woman of that branch, old Ama Agyakoma. It was murmured that by her sinister arts she had made one of her sons so weak and mentally dull that he was completely subjected to her will, unable to do anything of his own initiative. It was rumored that she had stolen her daughter Maneɛ's womb in an *ayɛne* way, thus making her permanently barren.[5]

A particular story about Ama Agyakoma had once created such a deep sensation that it was remembered and retold in a hush even now, though it had happened in her youth, perhaps thirty or forty years ago. One day, she had gone to the forest area north of the road between Ngelekazo and Beyin to collect palm nuts. She started climbing one of the oil palms, which bore several bunches of ripe red nuts, when a casual passerby stopped to give her a warning. At the foot of that very same tree was the den of a huge python, which villagers had for years been trying in vain to dislodge and kill. She did not mind the warning, but—as the man reported—she just laughed and laughed in the most uncanny way. And lo and behold! While she was at the top of the palm, the python came out of its lair and started to creep up the trunk after her. Any normal woman would have been frightened to death and would have screamed in fear. But Ama Agyakoma waited calmly until the huge snake twisted round her thighs and reached her waist; then she slashed at the monster with her cutlass with all her strength several times and killed it.

After this exceptional feat, Ama Agyakoma was carried to town in triumph, hoisted on people's shoulders. Drums were beaten in

Beyin in her honor. Surrounded by a cheering crowd, she was taken to the seashore to be ceremonially bathed, smeared with white clay, and dressed in a new white cloth. Even the *ɔmanhene*, king of Western Nzema, came out of his palace near the beach to congratulate her. But the very same people who were loudly praising and applauding the young woman were suspicious and afraid of her in their own hearts; only one who "had an eye," a powerful witch, could have emerged unscathed from such an exploit.

The sinister fame thus earned remained through the years and the decades, and when young Ɛlea succumbed to the fatal accident people had a fresh occasion to confirm their old fears. It is a well-known fact that witches are wont to exert their evil powers especially at the expense of the near of kin within their own lineage, and the old woman stood exactly in such a relationship to her unfortunate grandson. The rumor was discreet and anonymous; no one ever dared to come forth with a direct accusation that, in the absence of sound evidence, could be tantamount to slander. The respected *adunyi* oracle had failed to provide this evidence, so the more benignly inclined people were no doubt justified in believing and asserting that Ama Agyakoma was innocent of this misdeed, as well as possibly of all the others of which she had previously been suspected.

2 / *A Wife's Curse*

Kwao Babudu, an Adahonle fisherman from Ɛlonyi in Western Nzema, aged twenty-nine, died on 10 December 1970 near Twetwe Valevako in the Ivory Coast, after a short illness. His death was attributed to a curse by one of his two wives.

The sad event was reported to me only the following year, when, after an absence of several months, I returned to Fort Apollonia in Beyin, in southwestern Ghana. Beyin is very far from the place where Babudu worked and died, a small village on the Lahou Lagoon. But the sudden death of a strong and healthy young person naturally comes as a shock to his relatives and friends, urging them to find an explanation. It was thus from such people, including the two widows of the deceased, that I was able to obtain an accurate account of the facts that led to the fisherman's untimely end and followed it.

In 1967, having found out how difficult it was to make a living at home, Babudu decided to try his luck in the more prosperous Ivory Coast and moved to Ebunlu, a small village near Twetwe Valevako. There were several Nzema immigrants there, because the cost of living was low and fish were (and remain) plentiful in the nearby lagoon. He took his young wife with him, Asua from the Alɔnwɔba clan. A few months later, a child was born to the couple. But as babies so often do, the child died after a few weeks. At the end of the second year of their stay in Ebunlu, a series of angry disputes made Babudu realize that he had had enough of Asua. He took her back to their native town in Ghana, divorced her, and shortly afterward married a new wife. This was Ɛmenla, a young Nvavile woman from the same town, who had divorced her first husband after bearing two healthy children.

But the wedding festivities were scarcely over when Kwao Babudu was visited by his former parents-in-law. They came to beg him to forgive Asua, who—they assured him—still loved him dearly. They brought palm wine and "illicit gin" to pacify him, as they say in Ghana; they pleaded for more than an hour; they assured him that their daughter had promised she would never again quarrel with him. In the end, Babudu gave in; he remarried Asua. Shortly afterward, he once more made the long journey to the Ivory Coast, accompanied by his two wives, and the three of them settled down in his small compound in Ebunlu.

At first, their life was quiet and pleasant. Fish were plentiful. Relations between the two co-wives were friendly. They were both the same age, about twenty-five, had separate huts in the compound, but sometimes cooked and ate together. Babudu slept with each of them in turn on alternate weeks, so there was no question of jealousy at all. At the time of the events with which we are here concerned (December 1970), Asua was again in the first months of pregnancy; but then she had only been remarried to Babudu for a few months. There was an occasional squabble between Babudu and Asua, possibly derived from their earlier quarrels and divorce, but they soon patched it up every time.

The real trouble began one afternoon when Babudu, who was in the compound with Ɛmenla, suddenly ordered her to go and call Asua, who had just gone to visit a female neighbor in the village. As it became clear a few minutes later, the young man wanted to have intercourse with Asua then and there. When she got home and was told why she was being summoned, Asua flatly refused to comply—why, Ɛmenla (the source of information on this point) is unable to say, as she did not actually hear what they said to each other.[1] A violent quarrel followed, insults were exchanged, and to settle the matter Babudu gave his first wife a good beating.

Thereupon, Asua picked up one of her husband's cloths and rushed with it to the nearby stream. Some neighbors, alerted by the noise of the dispute and by Asua's shrill screams, came out of their huts, spied on her, and actually saw her dropping the cloth into the stream, called Tagba. They reported at once to Babudu, but by this time night had fallen. The following morning, the young man went to the stream and recovered his cloth. It had been thrown by Asua in the middle of the riverbed, under water, but the current had washed it ashore. When he came back with it, Babudu's friends advised him not to wear it again, but he took no notice of their advice. The next day, as soon as the cloth was dry, he wore it.

Under the circumstances, this was no doubt a serious imprudence on Babudu's part. Even if he preferred not to believe that his wife had acted with evil intentions (that is, that the casting of the garment had been accompanied by a curse against him and an appeal to the stream deity), to be on the safe side he should have consulted a fetish priest or an *adunyi* diviner on the matter. Better still, he should not have retrieved the cloth himself, but rather obliged Asua to do so and at the same time to withdraw the curse, if she had set one. But one thinks of such things afterward, when it is too late to change the course of fate.

Three days after wearing the cloth, on a Sunday evening, Babudu was suddenly taken ill. As he was going to the beach to fetch some fishing implement from his canoe, he fell down in great pain and was unable to walk back home. He had to be carried home. He had left the path to relieve himself, as he later told Ɛmenla, and had seen in the dusk a tall person—no doubt a *bozonle*—who at once hit him with a stick or a club. He was unable to describe the strange person in any detail, because the moment he was struck he fell down unconscious. After this, Kwao Babudu suffered from violent diarrhea and vomited a great deal. People began to fear for his life. The best local herbalist was called, who prescribed powerful medicines of pounded roots and herbs; his wives anointed him with these preparations and administered the potions and enemas. But the cure proved useless, and the patient's conditions worsened. At one point, Babudu was seen to make a strange gesture, placing his forefinger under his left eye and lowering the skin of his cheek. The gesture of the dying man, who was already unconscious, was understood to be really guided by the god who had attacked him. It was an ominous sign to all present and to Babudu himself, meaning "you shall see." At the very end, the young man was shaken by convulsive shivers, a symptom—according to Ɛmenla's account of these sad hours—that confirms beyond any possible doubt the presence of a hostile *bozonle*. Two hours later, Kwao Babudu died.

It never occurred to any of the informants to mention poisoning, deliberate or accidental, or some virulent form of gastroenteritis as possible alternative causes of Babudu's sudden sickness. When I later cautiously raised the question, it was quickly disposed of. Asua had done the cooking on the day Babudu fell ill, said Ɛmenla, but she herself had partaken of the food, as had others, including the Nzema fishermen who at the time were

Partial view of Nzulezo, western Nzema

sharing their compound, such as Ebukele, Kofi, and Durogyi. None of them had suffered any noxious effects that might be attributed to the food. She and Asua were in normal health that night and on the following days, and so were the wives of the other men, who had eaten the very same food. Incidentally, the three fishermen just mentioned were still in Ebunlu, in good health as far as Ɛmenla knows, but it was impossible to obtain their account of the events.

As soon as Kwao Babudu died, a telegram was sent from the local Ivory Coast station to his father, Mɛnla Kwao, in Ɛlonyi via the Beyin post office, and the telegram luckily reached him. Mɛnla Kwao was unable to go abroad himself, on account of his old age and of the cost of the expensive journey; but in the matter of two days, a few relatives arrived to Ebunlu from various towns in southern Ghana. These people included, for the Adahonle (the dead man's lineage), Babudu's mother, Adwo, the one who had brought him forth,[2] and her twin brothers, Ndakpanyi and Ndakyia.[3] For the Nvavile (Ɛmenla's lineage) came the girl's classificatory mother, Nyima. For the Alɔnwoba (Asua's lineage) no representative was reported to have come. At any rate, by the time these people reached Ebunlu, Babudu's burial had already taken place. According to custom, he had been buried in the morning immediately following his death; they took his body to the common cemetery that Nzema immigrants use jointly with the Blinya natives.[4]

When the newcomers from Ghana heard from the Ebunlu people the various reports about poor Babudu's sickness and death, they became very angry with Asua. Adwo, in particular, was furious, and her brothers had to restrain her from physically attacking her daughter-in-law.

Asua firmly denied her guilt, but the Adahonle people would not even listen to her. Directly after the eighth day's funeral obsequies they posthumously divorced the dead man from her. It was a brief ceremony, in which the leading part was taken by Ndakpanyi, one of Babudu's maternal uncles. In the presence of Asua and all the kinsfolk and neighbors who had attended the funeral, Ndakpanyi solemnly pronounced the state oath of Western Nzema, "*Bia anloanu nee Kranyabo*,"[5] and proclaimed that from that moment onward Asua was no longer the wife of the late Babudu. This was not only meant to be a formal condemnation of Asua's past behavior as a wife but the assurance that she would in no case be inherited as a wife by Babudu's heirs and successors; indeed, it creates an obstacle to her ever remarrying an Adahonle man in the future, even outside the circle of the lineage segment.

The next urgent thing to do was to release Babudu's *ɛkɛla* (soul), which was presumably held prisoner by the stream god who had caused him to die. A local priestess called Kyɛkyɛ, also known to practice divination, was entrusted with this task. She consulted her cowries to find out the exact place where the dead man's soul should be retrieved. Having done this, she allegedly performed the *ɛkɛla ɛhwanle* rite to restore the soul to freedom.[6] But, as following events were to show, either because of a mistake made by Kyɛkyɛ at the time or for some other unknown reason, her performance was not successful.

Once the funeral ceremonies were over, both Asua and Ɛmenla packed up their possessions and returned to Ghana. Asua went right back to Ɛlonyi, to await the birth of her baby, and settled there with her mother, Nyɔnra, in her uncle Ezane's compound.

Ɛmenla also returned to Ɛlonyi, but of course in a very different position. She was asked to stay at the compound of Mɛnla Kwao (Babudu's father) as long as she liked, at least for the first year of her widowhood. After this, she would have the choice of either accepting one of her late husband's successors, who according to custom would take her as his wife without the need of any ceremony, or of finding herself a new man. This was a fair and generous proposal, and Ɛmenla gratefully accepted it and settled down in her father-in-law's home. But in January 1971, about one month after Babudu's death, she fell ill. She had acute stomach pains and frequent vomiting, just like her late husband had suffered. As her parents-in-law could offer little assistance, she turned to her own Nvavile relatives in Ngelekazo, where wise old uncle Mɔkɛ Mieza provided the support and advice the young woman needed. One of her mothers, Aba, took her to a renowned Twelve Apostles priestess in Ɛkɛbaku, called Aya; uncle Mɔkɛ Mieza supplied money to cover the expenses of the trip and the treatment.

Interrogating her cup of holy water, Aya found out the cause of

Ɛmenla's complaint: she was being attacked by the same stream deity, Tagba, who had killed her husband. Ɛmenla was surprised. Why, she asked, should Tagba attack her, since for all she knew she had never done anything to offend him? And Tagba had his abode very far away, in a different country altogether, beyond the border. How could he have followed and found her here in Ghana?

Aya had the answers. Political frontiers, she explained, were a matter for smugglers, but did not concern gods, who took absolutely no notice of them. Besides, Tagba was being guided toward her, perhaps quite unwittingly, by Babudu's soul, whom he still held in his power. And how could she be sure she had never offended the god? When she was assisting her ailing husband in Ebunlu, day after day, night after night, was she sure she had never loudly reproached, possibly even cursed, the *bozonle* who was causing the poor young man so much suffering and indeed threatening his life?

Until the day when Kyɛkyɛ's first and plainly unsuccessful attempt would be more efficiently repeated, Aya promised she would do her best to cure Ɛmenla with her herbs and prayers. She kept her word. But, at first, there seemed to be no improvement. So, following once more uncle Mɔkɛ Mieza's advice, the girl went to Eikwe in eastern Nzemaland to try the white man's medicine. In early 1971, there was no doctor at the Eikwe Catholic hospital; the injections and tablets the German sisters gave her, says Ɛmenla, almost killed her, whereupon she returned to the Twelve Apostles "garden" in Ɛkɛbaku. It was there that I and my field assistants met her a few weeks later and were able to interview her, as she had nearly recovered from her illness. Her two children had been brought to her as soon as she was better, and she said she hoped to be in a position soon to look after them permanently.

As for remarrying, Ɛmenla had not made up her mind yet. One of Babudu's successors, a classificatory brother called Ɛlea, living in Takinta, let her understand that he would not mind to inherit her as a wife. But the young widow did not think she would accept him, not because the man was already married to another girl but because he was stingy. When she was very ill and appealed to him among other people for help, Ɛlea answered he liked her very much and would do anything for her, but—sorry—he would give her no money.

The last person interviewed in connection with Babudu's case was Asua, allegedly the party responsible for the young man's untimely death. She was an attractive, cheerful girl, rather proud of the six-month-old baby—Babudu's posthumous son—that she carried on her back, a fine healthy baby. Asua strenuously denied she had any responsibility for her husband's fatal sickness. She had no difficulty in admitting that there was some truth in the story of the cloth; but to say that she used it in order to curse Babudu by giving him to the *bozonle* was false and altogether fantastic. The truth was that, in the course of their quarrel that afternoon, her husband, in a rage, had thrown *her* own garments out of the house. By this he meant that, for the second time, he wanted to be rid of her, and this time for good. She had merely retaliated in kind. Babudu's cloth was an old one; it had no value whatsoever. It was only those spiteful neighbors who invented all this absurd story and planted the poisonous seed of suspicion into the minds of poor Babudu and of his clansfolk.

Asua sounded decidedly sincere and innocent. But, I asked, had she not been rather imprudent that fatal afternoon? How else did she expect her action would be interpreted? After all, everybody knows there is a *bozonle* in practically every stream, and people naturally jump to conclusions. "Ah," said Asua, "but it was late in the afternoon and already getting dark, and I never knew I was being spied on."

Could she tell me, quite confidentially, how that last fatal row with Babudu had really started? "Well," said Asua, completely ignoring the account previously given by her co-wife, "it was because of the fish. Babudu had given me and Ɛmenla a large quantity of fish to be smoked, and later he thought some of it was missing. It really was the river god who stole it," said Asua, "but Babudu refused to believe it. He suspected I had secretly been eating it myself or selling it to make illicit profits. So he insulted me and beat me. The god must have overheard the noise of the commotion from afar and taken it as an offense against himself. So he made Babudu sick and killed him."

Though several months had passed since that sad event, Asua was still afraid that her former affines, who continued to put the blame on her, would sooner or later try to poison her, or curse her by giving her to some fetish god. But she said her innocence would protect her. She may have been right, but at any rate she was being shielded from their revenge by a quite different reason, of which she was well aware though she did not mention it. Though Babudu's twin maternal uncles, Ndakpanyi and Ndakyia, belonged to a different clan from Nyɔnra, Asua's mother, having been brought forth by different mothers, they were half-brothers to Nyɔnra; they were begotten by the same father. Consequently, Asua was *awozoa raalɛ* to them, niece on the mother's side by extention, if not in the strictest sense. And, of course, no one would dare to put a curse on one's own *awozoa*.

3 / The Jealous God

Enɔ was a well-to-do Alɔnwɔba farmer from Nvelenu in Western Nzema, aged about sixty, who for agricultural and financial reasons had moved to a small village called Bɛlibɛtu on the right bank of the great Tano River, in Ivory Coast territory. His story was related to me in the course of many conversations by James E. Quarm,[1] one of my most reliable and intelligent Nzema informants, interpreters, and friends over the years. Quarm was bound to Enɔ by a long-standing friendship as well as by a close affinity as *meye adiema renyia*, because Enɔ had once legally married Quarm's full sister, Amoa Ekyi from Etikɔbɔ no. 1 (so called to distinguish it from another Etikɔbɔ far to the east). The premature death of this woman, a few years before, had not interrupted the close relationship between the two brothers-in-law, who went on addressing each other as *mezebia* (or, in Twi fashion, *akontagye*),[2] and continued on and off to assist one another in their farm work.

Indeed, Enɔ was connected by identical affinity ties to a vast number of other men, having had six wives in his lifetime. But Quarm prided himself in believing, probably quite justly, of having been Enɔ's favorite brother-in-law. At any rate, as we shall soon relate, Quarm happened to be the only witness when Enɔ met with his tragic end.

The complete list of Enɔ's six successive wives is tidily on record, with their personal names and clan membership, but need not be reported here in extenso. By his first wife, Aliba, Enɔ had had four children, one of which, named Nyɔnra Kpanyi, is still surviving; but by cruel fate none of the following five unions lasted more than a very few years—some barely months—and none of them produced any offspring. People not well informed might be led to suppose that this long chain of divorces resulted not just from bad luck but from Enɔ's bad temper or other defects of character. They would be mistaken. Eno was always a kind, well-mannered, generous husband: he proved it amply while he was married to

Quarm's sister Amoa Ekyi, his fourth wife. Amoa Ekyi had had several husbands before Enɔ and was no longer very young; it is suggested that she was not particularly good-looking and, worse yet, sickly. Despite this, Enɔ was extremely devoted to her, looked after her with loving attention, and during her chronic ailments provided her all the time with basinsful of medicines of all kinds. And yet it was she who in the end decided to divorce him. Quarm urged her strongly not to do so, warned her of the consequences of her ungratefulness, but she disregarded his advice. She was indeed punished for this; shortly after her divorce she died. After this, Enɔ married his fifth wife, a young girl this time, Nyamekɛ from Awiabo. But the match was a complete failure and lasted less than six months.

By this time, Enɔ was middle-aged and relatively wealthy, and he regretted that, having had so many wives, he had only succeeded in siring a single surviving son. So he married his sixth (and, as things turned out, last) wife, Evuka. This woman was an Alɔnwɔba from Etikɔbɔ no. 1, belonging not merely to Enɔ's clan but to his very lineage; but there was no infringement of the exogamy rule, the marriage being a *suanu agyalɛ*, a permitted "domestic marriage." In fact, as everybody knew, Evuka was the descendant of a female slave acquired long ago by one of Enɔ's matrilineal grandfathers. Consequently, she was adopted into the matriclan and was thus not a real "sister" to Enɔ.[3]

But as months and years went by, even Evuka did not become pregnant. Should Enɔ divorce once more, and try a seventh wife? His friends advised him not to do so yet, but first to consult a fetish priest. Enɔ followed the advice. He went to a local *kɔmenle*, who suggested that he should apply to a fetish god in order that his wife might conceive. The priest also provided the name of the deity that should be approached, a minor stream god of the forest area near Bɛlibɛtu.

This was in 1961. Seven years before, in November 1954, prophet Mabie, a follower of the famous prophet W. W. Harris from Liberia, had carried out his epoch-making tour of Nzemaland. His anti-juju and anti-fetish preaching had roused great interest and enthusiasm in Ghana at the time, and its effects were still felt throughout the area and in the adjoining Ivory Coast districts. Not only had the *asonwu* shrines been destroyed and

Offerings to a tree-dwelling deity

deserted on both sides of the border, but most of the traditional fetish cults had been temporarily discontinued or were being performed on a reduced scale. On the Tano River itself, where the worship of the great homonymous god had naturally been paramount, no god more than Tanoɛ was suffering from this new situation, and he was resenting it. And now the population, and possibly the gods themselves, came to learn that Enɔ was preparing to make offerings to a minor *bozonle* in Bɛlibɛtu rather than to Tanoɛ himself.

The potential dangers of this delicate situation probably escaped Enɔ's attention altogether; Quarm came to hear of them only later, through indiscretions of some neighbors. Enɔ had not said a word to him, even about the preparations of the sacrifice. Enɔ himself was a nominal Christian, and he knew well that his friend and brother-in-law had for years been and still was an active church member who took a leading part in Catholic services and even preached on Sundays when no priest was available. Enɔ did not dare to raise the subject. He knew only too well that Quarm would have disapproved.[4]

On the night of Sunday, 22 October 1961, returning home after a visit to common acquaintances, Enɔ and Quarm were quietly paddling along the western bank of the Tano River in the same canoe, Enɔ in front and Quarm sitting behind him. It was not raining, but it was a dark and moonless night. Suddenly, a rash movement by Enɔ caused the small canoe to capsize, and both men fell into the river. Quarm emerged at once, to find himself wading in relatively shallow water that did not reach higher than his chest. But to his surprise and dismay, Enɔ did not reappear, and despite all the calls and frantic efforts by Quarm no trace of Enɔ could be seen or heard. Quarm climbed ashore. Dripping wet as he was, he ran to call people, but not before he had stuck a branch into the river bank to mark the exact spot where the accident had occurred. People came from their hamlet, running with torches and shouting. They searched the whole place and downstream for hours, with no success. Only three days later was the body found, at the precise place where the canoe had capsized; neighbors praised Quarm for having marked the spot so accurately. The body was found afloat, swollen but otherwise intact, with no traces of crocodile bites, contrary to what people expected. Mud clung to the dead man's head, suggesting that he had sunk headfirst into the river and had somehow remained stuck in the muddy bottom among the weeds.

After long debates in the course of a palaver held by the local Alɔnwɔba clan members, it was decided that the funeral and burial would be those due to a person having died a natural death, not an *ɔtɔfoɔ* (violent and suspect death).[5] But the same people, considering that Quarm had been the only witness to the drowning, at once began to accuse him of having done nothing to save Enɔ; some even went as far as to accuse him of having killed Enɔ out of envy. Whether this invidious suspicion of theirs was supported by some oracle's response following the postmortem inquest, Quarm did not even stoop to consider. He had no trust in diviners, because he had too often been able to see through their tricks. All he did was bear with dignified patience the slander campaign waged against him, which amounted to a true defamation of character. His conscience was clear, and it was easy for him to point out to friends and foes that he, practically speaking, had much to lose, and nothing to gain, by his brother-in-law's demise.

Indeed, Quarm explained, several times during his lifetime Enɔ had offered him the free disposal of his farmland, where he grew every crop in abundance. Quarm had never accepted these generous proposals, because if Enɔ, who was a few years his senior, happened to die, his successors would promptly come from Ghana to take over his lucrative farms and plantations and would then probably lay claims on the plots on which Quarm had worked himself. Later, after his brother-in-law's death, Quarm congratulated himself for having resisted the temptation of those kindly offers. Enɔ's successors behaved, in fact, just as badly as he had foreseen.

The three Alɔnwɔba men chosen by the lineage matrons and nominated by the lineage assembly as Enɔ's successors and heirs were (1) Manlaba, a goldsmith from Grand Bassam in the Ivory Coast, (2) Ehɔnea from Ɛlonyi, and (3) Amu Ekyi from Bewia-Nvelenu, near Etikɔbɔ no. 2. The first heir never took the trouble of coming north to Bɛlibɛtu to collect the inheritance, but the other two did—not to continue and improve Enɔ's work on the farms, as honest successors should do, but in order to grab and exploit whatever property they could lay hands on.

Poor Enɔ, Quarm remembers, was exceedingly fond of the farms and plantations on which he had spent so many years of intelligent labor. Whenever we went to work on them together, Quarm said, Enɔ used to pour libation and say, "Let evil people never stay on this land." By this he meant, as if he had a gift of foresight, people inimical to himself and to his friend James Quarm. And now, indeed, the greedy successors have come and spoiled the property. Amu Ekyi made as much money as he could from the already existing crops. Then he abandoned the farms after barely one year, having arranged with Ehɔnea to leave some hired laborers from a nearby village to work on the land, which they did very badly. Out of respect for the dead man, Quarm's wife went on for a few years clearing the farms, weeding and sweeping under the cocoa trees and the coconut palms. But far from appreciating such devotion, Enɔ's heirs and their Alɔnwɔba relatives continued to spread wicked rumors against her and her husband. Quarm was so disgusted by their ungratefulness that he seriously considered leaving his own farm in the neighborhood and the Tano valley altogether, and retiring to Etikɔbɔ no. 1.

But how did he personally account, I asked, for Enɔ's strange death? The explanation offered by Quarm was twofold. First of all, he said, Enɔ must have been drunk when he fell into the river; this would account for his drowning in shallow water, where any sober man or even a child would easily have swum or walked ashore. The second reason, which in his opinion was by no means contradictory or even conflicting with the first, was the matter of the sacrifice Enɔ had in mind to offer the Bɛlibɛtu god on the following day. Tanoɛ, so long deprived of most of the customary offerings as a result of Mabie's preaching, was understandably incensed on learning that Enɔ was about to appease a subordinate, petty god of no importance without having first presented some gift to him. On the eve of the offensive sacrifice, he prevented it from being offered, by killing Enɔ.

The second explanation would account for the otherwise unexplainable fact that Enɔ's body was found, after three days, at exactly the same spot where it had sunk. In any normal case of death by drowning in a swift-running river, one would expect the body to be carried some distance downstream by the current. But if the sudden capsizing of the canoe and Enɔ's instantaneous death were caused by a superhuman agency, Quarm argued, the sheer violence of the god's action in pushing the body down would account for its remaining stuck in the same spot. Also, the strange fact that the body remained for days immersed in a river where crocodiles are swarming, without any of them devouring it or even biting it, would find an explanation: animals sense the presence of deities and respect their victims.

Tanoɛ's direct responsibility for the accident, at any rate, was more than just Quarm's guess; it was clearly revealed by a professional diviner, Nyɔnra Bakye, when the *abusua* kinspeople consulted him shortly after the funeral. Nyɔnra Bakye, a classificatory brother of Enɔ's, was a Muslim from Ɛbonloa, educated in Kamgbunli, the main Muslim center in Nzemaland. His verdict, which confirmed Quarm's hypothesis, was only indirectly brought to the latter's knowledge, because for reasons of principle Quarm would have refused to attend the pagan oracular meeting, even if he had been invited to it.

The story of Enɔ's death Quarm considered a significant proof of his conviction that you have nothing to fear from the fetish gods as long as you take no notice of them. The trouble arises, as Enɔ's fate showed, when you begin to worship them, letting them understand that you believe in them and fear them. But whatever a person's religious beliefs, a tragic event such as the one witnessed by James Quarm creates a deep and lasting impression. This impression was reflected in the personal oath that Quarm derived from it and used from that day forward on solemn occasions: *mɛ ka ɔ molɛ nɔɔzo*, "I swear on the Sunday night."[6]

4 / The Quarrelsome Rivals

When Ama Bomo came to Ngelekazo in 1968, she was a pretty young woman of twenty. She had already been married for a few years to a man in nearby Ɛlonyi, by whom she had two children, aged about three and one. When her husband divorced her, she decided to come and live with her "grandfather" (mother's mother's brother) Anubo Kodwo. This man had a socially outstanding position in Ngelekazo, being the *abusua kpanyinli* (head) of the Twea lineage, to which Ama Bomo belonged, and a close kinsman to the local chief Andualu Kwagya III, who had just been elected to the Ngelekazo stool.[1]

Her children being very small, she took them with her, according to custom. As the new chief happened to be temporarily alone, a few weeks after her arrival in town Ama Bomo moved over to his palace across the street, in order to cook for him and look after the compound.[2]

At the time, my friend Mɔkɛ Mieza was a "straw widower." His wife, Afo, had gone to Kumasi in Asante, or Ashanti as some people still say, for a five months' stay with a daughter of hers (by a previous marriage), who had just had a baby. Mieza, who had previously been a teacher at the Ɛlonyi school, knew Ama Bomo since she was a schoolgirl, and liked her. The two now being single, and living on the same street of a small town, had frequent opportunities to meet privately and began having an affair. From this relation, little Kabenla was born. But long before the boy's birth, with Afo's return from Kumasi and Ama Bomo's already noticeable pregnancy, the love affair between the latter and Mieza had come to an end.

Kabenla grew to be a beautiful baby, as a photograph kept by Mieza shows, and at the time of the events narrated here he was already toddling about and beginning to talk. He was never to reach the age of naming,[3] but had he survived, Mɔkɛ Mieza would no doubt have seen to this, choosing for him an appropriate name from his own father's lineage, according to tradition, because

Mieza was fond of the child and paid for his support. Even Afo, who at first had not taken the whole matter very well, had come to like the child. Mieza had been forced to tell his wife the whole truth about his affair with Ama Bomo; it had been the talk of the town, and Afo would soon have learned about it anyway. There had been some disagreeable arguments over it behind closed doors, but later Afo had been sensible enough to forgive her unfaithful husband, and allowed little Kabenla to come and play with the other small children in her courtyard.

Abandoned by her lover, Ama Bomo felt lonely. The company of the old men who came to the palace to talk business or just chat with the chief was hardly amusing for a young woman of her age. So she started another love affair with one of Mieza's former colleagues at the Ɛlonyi school, a young teacher from Beyin called Nwanyi.[4]

Alas, Nwanyi, too, was a married man. His wife, Amu, lived in Beyin with the children and was in the early months of a new pregnancy. When rumors about her husband's unfaithfulness reached her, Amu took a far less indulgent view of his frolics than Mieza's wife had done in a similar situation. What infuriated her most was that Nwanyi was spending on Ama Bomo every penny he earned, leaving her—his legal wife and an expecting mother—absolutely destitute. So Amu, having tried in vain to bring her husband to reason, decided she would at least teach her shameless rival a good lesson. She ground pepper and prepared fully,[5] walked briskly the one-and-a-half miles separating Beyin from Ngelekazo, entered belligerently the chief's palace, and attacked the unsuspecting Ama Bomo.

The exact text of the ensuing conversation between the two angry women is unfortunately not on record. But witnesses in Ngelekazo still remember the occasion with unconcealed amusement. Life in a small Nzema village tends to be rather dull, and lively little episodes like this one are a godsend to the villagers. It appears that the two rivals abused each other in the foulest language ever heard on the coast, soon came to blows, and tore at each other's eyes, hair, and clothes. Attracted by the hubbub, people assembled in the palace's courtyard to enjoy the fun, and eventually they strove to divide the two fighters. Among the onlookers was a priestess of the Twelve Apostles sect, an elderly matron called Adwoba, who managed to drag Amu to her own (Adwoba's) compound, or "garden."

But in her indignation at the unexpected attack, Ama Bomo did not give in. Disregarding in her rage the proclaimed holiness of a Twelve Apostles garden, which even nonbelievers in that sect are wont to respect as a sanctuary of sorts, she stormed her way into it, starting a fresh fight with her rival. When the townspeople at last succeeded in separating the two women, the priestess was fully justified in demanding that both contenders pay her a fee of ¢2.10 for the sacrilege.[6]

Ama Bomo complied, promptly producing the money. Amu, on the other hand, objected—not on principle, because she admitted it is right to atone for a sacrilege, but on the practical grounds that she just did not possess the ¢2.10. Indeed, as she pointed out, the whole fuss was over the fact that her husband was giving her no money at all.

Faced with this blunt reality, the priestess sensibly thought that the best thing was to claim the fee from the husband himself. But it dod not take her long to find out that Nwanyi had conveniently disappeared from the surroundings. Reconsidering the matter on the basis of these circumstances, Adwoba had to admit that there was something in Amu's point, and she did not press the matter any further. At this, Ama Bomo, considering that her rival who refused to pay was at least equally responsible for the litigation and the sacrilege, claimed her money back. Adwoba recognized that Ama Bomo had a valid point, and she generously refunded her money.

By this time, however, as the arguing and quarreling was still going on, the spirits present in the priestess's garden became really annoyed,[7] just as the other spirits in Nana Andualu Kwagya III's compound had been a few hours earlier; violent disturbance within the precincts of a chief's palace is quite as offensive as that in an *awa* priestess's garden. So they decided to take the shocking controversy in their own hands at last. They went into the matter among themselves, agreed that, although both women were responsible for the row, Ama Bomo was the one at fault in the first place, and made up their minds to punish her. For this reason they attacked her child.

Shortly after these events, little Kabenla showed the first signs of uneasiness by refusing to take his mother's breast. On the sixth day

Girl performing her domestic duties (pounding yams)

after the quarrel, shortly before dawn, while the child was sleeping next to his mother in the chief's compound, "something fell on him," as Ama Bomo put it to the child's father, whom she informed straight away. Mɔkɛ Mieza hurried to see his son and found him completely stiff in the body, with such a glassy stare in his wide-open eyes that not even water dropped into them could cause them to close.

At first they thought this could be a case of *anwuma*, which Europeans translate as "convulsions." They took the child around to Ɛzonle Kanra, the best herbalist doctor in town and a close friend of Mieza's, who tried without delay the "water-from-the-roof" treatment and used other appropriate medicines.[8] But as these had no effect, Kanra diagnosed that the sickness was not *anwuma;* it was probably being caused by some supernatural being.

This meant that special medicines should be sought in the bush and offerings presented to whatever god or other spirit was causing the ailment. Unfortunately, Kanra himself could in that period undertake none of these duties; he was in a temporary state of impurity (*evinlinu*) following the recent death of his brother Kɔlɔra, from which he could not yet be cleansed. In this condition he could not even consult the *adunyi* oracle to get a more precise diagnosis. So he advised Mieza to take his child to the other Ngelekazo *ninsinli*, James Kodwo.

Kodwo performed the *adunyi* divination and was thus able to disclose the real cause of Kabenla's sickness: the *nwomenle*, the ghosts protecting Adwoba's compound, were punishing Ama Bomo for her misbehavior. Kodwo took the sick child to his own compound and did everything in his power to cure him, including generous libations to the offended ghosts, but to no avail. Within a week, little Kabenla was dead.

It should be added that at the time Kodwo revealed a further cause for the child's illness, which had until then escaped the attention and the imaginative conjectures of the Ngelekazo people. Soon after her divorce, and before the affairs with Mieza and Nwanyi, Ama Bomo had had yet another lover in Ngelekazo. This man, aged about fifty and named Bile Kɔkɔlɛ, was not really a townsman; he usually worked in the Wassaw area, north of Nzemaland, and had only come to Ngelekazo for a short while as a guest of a half-brother of his (by the same father). Oddly enough, this Bile Kɔkɔlɛ was a bachelor all his life, and, though he was said to have had one or two concubines on and off, people murmured that he did not really like women enough to lead a normal married man's life.

But when he met Ama Bomo in Ngelekazo, he suddenly fell in love, and he made up his mind to marry and settle down at long last. For three or four months, he went on giving the young woman money and cloths. She encouraged him at first, and apparently promised she was prepared to become his wife. But later she changed her mind, decided she really did not like Bile Kɔkɔlɛ after all, and broke with him.[9] According to what Kodwo's *adunyi* oracle showed, Bile Kɔkɔlɛ was bitterly hurt by his mistress's behavior. When, shortly afterward, his brother died, he left Ngelekazo for good, and the compound where he had planned to settle with his future wife was now empty. But Bile Kɔkɔlɛ's hidden resentment, his *sipe*, remained, and the oracle assures that it contributed to the death of Ama Bomo's child.

5 / A Clear Diagnosis

The story of Nwia Boadi's death is a simple one, one that did not give rise to much comment and speculation in town at the time, unlike what happens in less transparent cases. This is clearly reflected in the first report of the sad event submitted to me as usual by one of my Nzema informants, which I quote verbatim: "Nwia Boadi had this kind of sickness called Hernia, or *ɛkolodo*, since about six years ago. On 17 August 1971 he went to the sea to catch fish with a cast net. In the sea he had troubles with that Hernia and came home. He was taken to Eikwe, from Eikwe to Sekondi hospital, where he was operated and died in the operation."

A simple ending to the life of a simple man in tropical West Africa, probably by now forgotten by most of his fellow countrymen and even clansfolk and neighbors, hence perhaps hardly worth being resuscitated in international literature. But I personally knew Boadi. Years before he died, more than once I had met him and talked with him on the beautiful white-sanded, coconut palm–lined beach of the Atlantic coast where he used to work. He had asked me to visit him in his village compound, where I had shaken hands and exchanged civil greetings even with his very old father, Nwia, who died long before him. When Boadi himself died, on 20 August 1971, I happened to be in Ghana, not far from his native village, and I attended his funeral obsequies. So I shall perhaps be forgiven for saying a few words about this humble man, an Ɛlonyi fisherman of the Twea clan, aged about fifty, the victim of a surgical operation or, as others think, of a curse by an anonymous neighbor.

Explanations and circumstantial details could probably have been obtained at once after Boadi's death, but at least in Ghana it is considered bad manners to ask questions during funerals, when, apart from being stricken with grief, people have many other practical things to worry about. So I allowed a few days to elapse before paying a call on the relatives of the deceased in Ɛlonyi.

When I revisited this town about a fortnight after the funeral, on

9 September 1971, the first person I found in Boadi's paternal compound was his widow, Asɔ. This young woman of the Alɔnwɔba clan, aged twenty-five, had conveniently shaved her head as a sign of mourning and was nursing her baby girl, whose head had also just been shaved, leaving odd tufts of hair on the sides and on top. Asɔ listened gravely to my condolences, but when I cautiously asked her for details about her husband's death, she burst out laughing. There was really nothing to add, she said, to what everybody already knew. On August 17, a Tuesday, after attending evening service at the Catholic chapel, Boadi took his *asawu* (cast net) and walked to the beach to catch some fish in shallow water. He returned shortly afterward, at sunset, feeling sharp pains in his stomach. She gave him a good *ɛzelalɛ* (enema) of red pepper, which had helped him greatly on previous occasions, but this time it did not stop the pains. He cried and moaned with pain throughout the night, and the next morning he was worse. So no time was lost. Boadi went to the main highway, waited for the first eastward-bound truck to arrive from Beyin, and boarded it. This was the truck belonging to Arisi, the one called All Is Vanity.[1]

A sick man cannot travel without assistance (Boadi almost needed carrying), so six people boarded the same truck to accompany and assist Boadi: Nyamekɛ, his brother (mother's sister's son); Kanra Ekyi, his sister (mother's sister's daughter); Nyanzu, one of the late Nwia's grandsons (Boadi's father's sister's daughter's son); Ndede Nyamekɛ, Boadi's half-sister by the same father; Nyasule Kwasi, representing the local branch of the Mboa Eku Society;[2] and, of course, Asɔ, his only wife at the time. The truck took them all to Eikwe, near the Catholic hospital of that little town.

When the Eikwe doctor examined Boadi, he said the man urgently needed an operation, but the water supply was not working at that time, so he could not operate. They all drove on to Axim by another bus, but as bad luck would have it, they were told that the local doctor was away. They took counsel among themselves, and, as Boadi's condition appeared to continue to be very serious, they decided to take him by ambulance to Takoradi-Sekondi, where there is a large hospital with white as well as Ghanaian doctors and nurses. At this hospital, they have strict rules; they did not allow the six people escorting Boadi to go upstairs with him into the ward. Only Nyamekɛ and Kanra Ekyi, after a long palaver, obtained permission to see him to his bed. Asɔ saw her husband alive for the last time on Thursday afternoon. She thinks he was operated on that same evening. On Friday morning, the hospital people told her he was dead.

While my friends and I were speaking with Asɔ, Boadi's mother, Ɛba, joined us and volunteered more information. Boadi's trouble, she told us, had always been with his testicles. They used to be inflamed, she remembers, since he was a boy of twelve or thirteen. This did not prevent Boadi from marrying thrice and begetting several children: four by his first wife, Afɔ, all of whom died, three in early infancy and one in his teens; two by his second wife, Alɛba, one of whom (a girl) was still alive. Asɔ became Boadi's third wife about four years earlier. She had previously married, at the age of thirteen, Mɔkɛ Ekyi of Ngelekazo, who divorced her after having begotten six children by her, five of which were still alive and in their father's care. By Boadi she had two more children, three-year-old Asua (her seventh-born, as the name shows), a boy, and the baby girl at her breast, Nyamekɛ (eighth-born).

In spite of her recent bereavement, Asɔ appeared to be in high spirits. She scoffed at the prospect of accepting any of Boadi's successors as a substitute husband; indeed, she said she had had enough of married life and of continuous childbearing. She would be content with continuing to live in her late husband's compound as long as they would have her there, to assist her aging second mother-in-law, with whom she was on excellent terms, and to bring up her last two children.

As to the real causes of Boadi's premature death, Asɔ seemed to take little interest. Repeating the almost stereotyped answer that we heard countless times, she remarked that the matter concerned the lineage of the deceased person, not her. All she knew was that, shortly after the funeral, inquiries were made by Boadi's kinsfolk with a renowned Twelve Apostles priestess in Beyin, Kanra Noma; but since Asɔ was still in a state of impurity resulting from her husband's death, she could naturally not attend the meeting. It was Ɛba who willingly supplied the information.

Kanra Noma, Kanroma for short, who divines by casting cowries, although (being a Methodist) she really gets her inspiration directly from God, saw at once that Boadi's death was not caused by

Fishing nets spread out to dry on Ɛkɛbaku Beach

hernia. Long ago, she said, Boadi had a quarrel with a neighbor over a coconut plantation. This person (whose name she did not mention, but the Twea people had no difficulty in guessing) "gave" Boadi to a god dwelling in the Eholaka area, less than two miles inland from Ɛlonyi, where the contended plantation was located. The god expected to be pacified by Boadi's kinsfolk with some offering. But they failed to do so, and he lost his patience at last, imprisoning Boadi's *ɛkɛla* in his bush domain, and causing Boadi to die. The Eholaka god was now still holding the soul in captivity, which made it imperative for the dead man's lineage people to perform the customary rite for the *ɛkɛla*'s deliverance. This matter was naturally no concern of Kanroma's, as she was a Christian, but Ɛba knew that arrangements were being made by her senior son, Kwao, for the rite to be performed in due course by Azira, a well-established priestess in town.

Kwao, the only surviving full brother of the deceased, lived in the adjoining compound, so we were able to make an appointment with him on the same day. He was sincerely touched by our expressions of condolence, as he had been very fond of his late brother; he regretted not having been able to assist him on those last two days, because he happened to be away from town. He took us to a corner of his compound to show us a well-kept *nyangonle* shrine, which, he said, would forever remind him of Boadi.[3] By a strange coincidence, he explained, both Boadi and their half-sister Ndede Nyamekɛ, also living in Ɛlonyi, were two *nyangonle mmalɛ* brought forth almost simultaneously by the two wives of their common father (Boadi being a Nyɔnra or "ninth born"). So he, Kwao, a senior brother to both his siblings, had erected the new shrine jointly dedicated to them, as the previous one dating back to their father's days was ruined beyond repair. This he had done only a year earlier, never suspecting that Boadi would die so soon.

On the subject of the Ɛhɔlaka god, Kwao not only confirmed his mother's report but was able to contribute firsthand information. Having gone out to the family farms in that area, just a few days after his brother's funeral, he actually *saw* the god. He was now unable to provide a precise description of him, because what he saw was a dim apparition at a considerable distance, on the border between the plantain farm and the bush. He returned home at once, shivering with lasting fright, and on the same evening he was sick, with symptoms similar to those that preceded and announced Boadi's death. He was "shaking," a sure sign of an attack by a *bozonle*. A sister of his, Asua Kɔkɔ, had to accompany and support him the next day when he went to Azira, the priestess, for treatment. This woman gave him a powerful medicine made from pounded herbs, with which he smeared his whole body according to her instructions, and he recovered. (Azira herself, whom I approached at a later date, confirmed her patient's account. She added that, in the course of *ahɔne*, she succeeded in establishing contact not personally with the god himself but with his wife, Azane Amenleba; the goddess told her that her husband was impatiently waiting to be appeased by Boadi's kinsfolk, and for this reason had appeared to the dead man's brother.)

According to Boadi's young widow, whom we visited a second time, Boadi had never mentioned to her, either before or during his fatal illness, that he had anything to fear from the Eholaka stream god or, indeed, from any other *bozonle*. This, Kwao explained, was because the story of the quarrel over the coconut plantation and of the consequent curse dated back to Boadi's youth. Asɔ was not even born at the time and could not have known anything about it. Kwao remembered that the matter had long ago been brought to the chief's court and settled, so Boadi himself could possibly have forgotten all about it. Nobody knew that a curse had been set on him by that wicked man, and that a fetish god was involved; therefore, it never crossed their minds that the god should be appeased at all. After all, Kwao concluded, it is not every day that a god waits almost thirty years before he strikes you.[4]

After the frightful warning personally addressed to him by the god, Kwao was the most anxious person in the whole lineage to have the *ɛkɛla ɛhwanlɛ* rite performed as quickly as possible. A date, Wednesday, 29 September 1971, was agreed on for this purpose. But as the day approached, difficulties arose. A sheep was required for the sacrifice, and no member of the local lineage segment possessed one. What was worse, between them they did not have the money to buy one, the average price of a sheep having gone up at the time to ¢20 or even more. There were still debts to be paid, the journey of Boadi and all his relatives to Eikwe, Axim, and Sekondi having been very expensive, especially the ambulance, as well as the transport of the body back to Ɛlonyi. The Mboa Eku Society's contribution had turned out to be less substantial than expected. My offer to contribute half of the sheep's price was gratefully accepted.[5] The corresponding cash was eventually placed into the hands of the responsible Twea lineage head. But putting together the other half of the sum still proved difficult for the family, so that to the best of my knowledge Boadi's *ɛkɛla* had to wait until 1972 before it was duly released by the fetish god.

In the interval, the legal matters regarding Boadi's succession had to be settled, and we were politely informed of them. Of the three classificatory brothers named to succeed, the first, Kaku, was unable to attend the funeral and even to come to Ghana at a later date, being busy with his fishing at Dwivo, west of Abidjan. The same was the case with the third successor, named Mieza, also reported to be working in the Ivory Coast. The second heir, however, the one "sitting on Kaku's knees," as the vernacular expression has it, was nominated in the person of Nyamekɛ, the same "brother" who had accompanied Boadi to the hospital. Although both Kaku and Mieza actually belonged to two different descent lines within the lineage, both senior to the segmented line of the deceased, Nyamekɛ descended from the very same grandmother. As there were several living classificatory brothers senior to him in the lineage order of succession, his nomination was a patent infringement to the theoretical rule. There was, however, some practical wisdom in this irregular choice, suggested by the assembled lineage matrons. The first legitimate successor was unable to return to Ɛlonyi, or unwilling to do so, for a possibly long period, as the *abusua* matrons and elders probably foresaw. Therefore, there was at least one man in town to look after Boadi's widow and orphans and to carry out the tasks interrupted by Boadi's death.

Nyamekɛ would, of course, be automatically entitled, with his co-successors' authorization and at no further cost, to take Asɔ as his regular wife. But he already had two wives living with him and did not wish to take a third one. This, as we already know, was in accord with Asɔ's declared intentions, so everybody was happy.

6 / The Wavering Christian

The case of Mozo Bile is an eloquent example of how a single mistake, even committed inadvertently and with the well-meaning intention of helping others, can lead to the sudden destruction of an otherwise fortunate, strong, and honest man.

Mozo Bile, a healthy and prosperous Twea farmer from Ɛlonyi in western Nzemaland, aged about fifty-seven, was one of the most respected members of that town's Catholic minority. Since his wife's death, he had decided to share his comfortable compound with Nyɔnra Amua, a full sister of his, begotten by the same father and mother, locally better known for short as Nyamua. An active and cheerful worker, he looked younger than his age, and, as he never had any serious health problems, his relatives and neighbors were surprised when in the brief space of barely three days a sudden illness caused him to die, on 7 February 1971. As we learned directly after the funeral from Kolɔra Kanra, a half-brother of the deceased, his death was attributed to an angry *bozonle*.

A farmer's ailments are logically connected with the events of agricultural life. It is therefore not surprising that Mozo Bile's troubles should have arisen from the manifold problems of cultivation. His lineage lands included a small isolated plot, which for a number of years he did not intend to exploit, so he allowed a neighbor—a middle-aged Ɛlonyi woman—to use it every year for planting her groundnuts. Along with the groundnuts, this woman also allegedly planted nine coconuts. These coconuts had not visibly begun to develop into green shoots by the time Mozo Bile claimed his plot back from her, starting a fresh coconut plantation on the whole extention of the land.

Even in the most favorable soil and climate conditions, it naturally takes several years before the coconut sprouts grow into real palms and begin bearing fruit. But when the time came and Mozo Bile was preparing to collect and sell the coconuts, his neighbor—by now an old woman—approached him once more, claiming the part of the crop deriving from the nine coconuts that, she insisted, she had planted herself in the first place. Mozo Bile would not hear of it. All the palms were his, planted and grown on his own soil; as he had generously lent her the plot free of charge, he expected, if not a show of gratitude, at least not to be pestered with new requests. The old woman disagreed entirely; she felt cheated and persisted with her claims. When at last she realized that Mozo Bile could not be convinced, she walked back to the plot near the lagoon to look for a last time at what she considered her own nine coconut palms. While doing so, she loudly complained of the injustice she was suffering. The fetish god of that lagoon, who is called Falabo, naturally heard her and listened carefully.

That very same day, Mozo Bile suffered a sudden fit. Neither he nor his sister, Nyamua, nor any of the neighbors who assisted him on that occasion could think of any explanation for this unexpected stroke; nor did they attribute much importance to it, because in the brief space of two days he recovered without any recourse to medical treatment. Soon he was his normal healthy self again. The incident was almost forgotten, and it was only several months later, following more serious events, that the true nature of its causes was revealed. On the spur of the old woman's laments and curses, Falabo had actually hit the owner of the coconut plot with his spiritual wand. But on second thought, having more carefully investigated the matter, the god decided to spare Mozo Bile, because he realized the man was a Christian and essentially an honest fellow.

Life had thus quickly resumed its peaceful course in the Ɛlonyi compound, when a new danger came to threaten its *abusua*. This time it was the turn of Agyeba, Nyamua's daughter, who in January 1971 fell seriously ill. Agyeba, a woman in her late twenties, well married and a mother of children, had no serious financial problems. But, like most Nzema women of her own and previous generations, she sought to earn some money entirely of her own. She had thus made an arrangement with a small group of townswomen to crack and collect coconuts in the groves near Ɛlonyi. The modest profit from this work should naturally have been shared between the various women, but it was murmured that with some pretext Agyeba managed to keep the money for herself. So, understandably, the other women resented her dishonesty and spoke badly about her as they walked to the bush together on the

Priestess with image of her goddess

way to their respective farms. A *bozonle* called Azanwoba overheard them and decided to punish Agyeba, who consequently fell sick. But after having been pacified with a sheep and other sacrifices by her relatives, Azanwoba forgave her and allowed her to recover.

Another crisis thus appeared to have been averted by the Twea people in town. But shortly after these events, Mozo Bile was again suddenly taken ill during the night with a fit similar to the one he had suffered four months earlier. Nyamua, sleeping in the room next to him, was awakened by his moans and gasps and rushed to call Kolɔra for help. The very next morning they hired a truck and drove the sick man to the dispensary at Etikɔbɔ no. 1. But the medicines from Europe did not help at all; Bile continued to suffer terribly. So they hurried to consult a local fetish priestess, who disclosed that the man was being attacked by a *bozonle*, but could suggest no useful treatment. In fact, on the third day Mozo Bile died.

The reason for the sudden sickness and the punishing god's identity were not revealed at the time by the Etikɔbɔ no. 1 priestess; they were revealed later, a few weeks after the funeral, by another *kɔmenle* whom Kolɔra Kanra and Nyamua consulted in the lagoon area. It was the same god, Falabo, who had twice attacked their late brother. The first time, as we have seen, Falabo had decided to spare Mozo Bile as soon as he had learned that the man was a good Catholic. This shows, as Kolɔra Kanra pointed out, that contrary to what foreigners think, the gods do not act rashly when someone asks them to punish or destroy an enemy. They first consider the matter in order to make sure that the request is justified. They examine the accused person's real position and discuss it among themselves. And Mozo Bile's position became more serious as a result of Agyeba's sickness.

When Agyeba was ill, her worried mother Nyamua at once approached the famous Ɛlonyi priestess, Azira. She could not have made a better choice; not only was Azira one of the most renowned and successful priestesses in town, and indeed in the whole of Western Nzema, but in this particular case she would surely request no fee for her diagnosis and advice, since Agyeba had recently become her own daughter-in-law. In fact, Azira, having identified Azanwoba as the *bozonle* who was attacking the young woman, explained that the latter's recovery required a sacrifice of twelve eggs, two hens, and a sheep, to be brought to the Azanwoba stream where the goddess has her abode.

These offerings were naturally to be provided by Agyeba's *abusua* kinsfolk. Nyamua was embarrassed. She knew she could easily manage the fowls and eggs, but she possessed no sheep, nor did she have the money to buy one. So she naturally appealed to her brother, Mozo Bile. At first, Bile refused to listen to her. Not only sheep were already very expensive at the time (up to ¢20 or even ¢25 according to size), but being a Catholic he was opposed as a matter of principle to offering sacrifices to fetish gods. But his sister did not give up. She reminded him of his obligations as a maternal uncle. Would he sit and do nothing while his own niece was dying? If Agyeba did die because of his indifference and avarice, the blame would be entirely his, and his name would be disgraced forever throughout Western Nzema and beyond. And how could he be sure that the cruel *bozonle*, whom he now refused to appease, would not in the end turn her wrath on him, too?

After much arguing, Bile gave in. No one will ever be able to tell us the extent of the painful internal struggle with his conscience that he suffered, torn between two conflicting loyalties, before he reached the decision. But he did buy the sheep. And having bought it, he thought he might as well join the kinsfolk who were going to slaughter it in the bush, and partake of the food; it is not every day that one gets a good mutton chop.

Azanwoba, the goddess, was pleased with the offerings, and she decided she would allow Agyeba to recover. But, as usually happens on such occasions, other gods in the surroundings were attracted by the food and flocked in, and among them was Falabo. Naturally enough, when this god came to know that the man he had spared a few months before, and who had never made any offerings to him, was now presenting his colleague Azanwoba with a sheep, he reconsidered the situation in a new frame of mind. Bile was not such a consistent Christian after all, so he well deserved the long-delayed punishment. So Falabo killed Mozo Bile.

Unlike his late half-brother, Kolɔra Kanra was not altogether a churchgoing Christian; and while giving us his accurate account of the reported events, he avoided committing himself openly to a judgment. On the one hand, he was sincerely sorry for his half-brother's fate, but on the other he did not conceal his opinion that the god had acted reasonably from his own point of view. At any rate, after poor Bile's funeral, Falabo was eventually pacified with another sheep in his turn, for fear that he may strike some other member of the family. As Falabo, being a lagoon *bozonle,* had no priest to speak for him in Ɛlonyi or in the neighboring towns on the coast, there had been some difficulty in finding the proper person to offer the sacrifice. Etia, an Ɛlonyi herbalist doctor known to "have an eye," finally presented the offering. Kanra had personally seen to this, and he had good reasons to believe that the sacrifice had been well accepted, because until the day we talked there had been no accidents, diseases, or other troubles affecting the *abusua* people.

So much about Kolɔra Kanra's report. As for Agyeba, Bile's niece whom we also interviewed because she had really been the cause of her uncle's death, she could add little on that subject. But she had plenty to say about her own affairs, as well as about the role Azira had had in these events.

Though not yet thirty, Agyeba had had two husbands. The first one was a young man from Bɔnyɛlɛ, by coincidence also called Bile,[1] by whom she had four children and many disappointments. The first child, a little boy named Eduku, was alive and well; but the second died at the age of two, at a time when Agyeba was suckling her third-born. When this baby showed the same symptoms of sickness that had preceded the death of its sibling, Agyeba feared it might be doomed to the same fate and rushed for advice to Azira. Agyeba was hardly acquainted with her at the time, but knew her to be the most authoritative fetish priestess in town. (It was on this occasion, incidentally, that she met Nyanzu, Azira's son, in no way imagining that he would later have such an important part in her life.) Azira listened attentively to what the young woman had to say, asked to see the sick baby, examined it carefully when it was brought to her, and then declared she had no treatment or medicine to suggest. She was no doctor, nor did she pretend to be; as a priestess, she could only convey to petitioners such diagnoses and prescriptions as were dictated to her by her tutelary deities or spirits. In fact, a few days later, having danced *ahɔne,* Azira was able to specify the rites and sacrifices required to save the baby's life.[2] But these entailed a considerable expenditure.

When Bile, the baby's father, worked out the figure, he refused to provide the money, alleging that he had little faith in Azira's remedies; and the baby consequently died.

Agyeba was grieved by this second loss, and her father, Boadi, was so indignant against his stingy son-in-law that he decided to divorce her from Bile. In this he had his daughter's full support. But it so happened that at the time Agyeba was pregnant once more.[3] She preferred to wait until the new baby was born before she left the husband she had come to hate. The baby, a little boy, was eventually named Wangala, a despicable name that no doubt shielded it from the attacks of hostile spirits.[4] The child remained alive and in perfect health. Soon after the boy's birth, Agyeba finally divorced Bile, and a few months later married the above-mentioned Nyanzu, whom she had been meeting with increasing frequency since that first encounter. Nyanzu was a nice young man with no regular job, who did odd bits of work here and there when he got a chance,[5] but in any case he was conveniently looked after by that affluent mother of his, Azira.

Interesting and instructive though Agyeba's biographical data may be, it is not with them we are here concerned but rather with the role this young woman unwittingly had in determining her maternal uncle Mozo Bile's death.

Agyeba's version of the facts that led to the *bozonle*'s attack on her health differs slightly from that provided by Kolɔra Kanra. It is true that at the time she had been cracking and trading coconuts in association with a girlfriend of hers. During this period they had both borrowed money from Agyeba's stepmother, Aya, Boadi's second wife. (Boadi had divorced Nyamua over ten years earlier.) When the copra was dried and properly stacked, and the girls finally collected their earnings, Agyeba at once refunded the money Aya had lent her, but her girlfriend failed to do so, falsely alleging as an excuse that Agyeba had not given her any share of the earnings. Aya was naturally furious, and the girl, in the attempt to justify herself in the eyes of Aya and of other townswomen, went on telling them, "Agyeba has taken all my money."[6] Repeated by women talking among themselves in the bush on the way to their farms, this lie was overheard, and at first believed, by Azanwoba, the fetish goddess in the stream where many Ɛlonyi women go to fetch water.

So one day, about a year earlier, Agyeba said she suddenly began feeling cold and dizzy, and fainted. Her mother Nyamua, who fortunately was with her at the time, realized that this was a serious case. At once she went to look for her daughter's mother-in-law, the main authority in town. Azira was far away from town on that day, working on her farm, but hurried home as soon as she heard the news, and examined her daughter-in-law. As soon as she could assemble the drummers, she began dancing *ahɔne*. Though Agyeba had witnessed the dance countless times, and occasionally even taken a minor part in it, she could not possibly describe from direct experience what happened in this particular performance, as on that day she was lying feverish and unconscious on her mat in her husband's compound. But she had repeatedly been told about it by her mother, Nyamua, who was naturally present, anxiously waiting to hear what the gods would reveal about her daughter's fate.

In contrast to the majority of Nzema priests and priestesses, who as a rule "speak" for a single god, Azira had two supernatural patrons. One was Kɔkɔ, the ghost of a fabulous priestess of olden days; the other was Ayisa, a female *bozonle* from a stream near Tanoɛzo in the lower Tano Valley. They would come to her whenever she needed them; she only had to pour a libation to them, or alternatively to dance *ahɔne*. It would take them about two hours to come, she reckoned, but she was not sure of the exact time, because she had no watch. Kɔkɔ, being a ghost, normally resides in Hades. (But she never revealed to Azira where Hades, *ɛbolɔ* for the Nzema, really lies; so Azira always admitted she was totally ignorant on this point.) Ayisa dwells in the bush. Kɔkɔ was usually the first to answer the priestess's summons, and would beckon to Ayisa coming after her; in turn, Ayisa was often followed by one or more other fetish gods, who came as her retinue. In this particular case, as Nyamua observed, it was Ayisa who manifested herself, because she knew it was a problem involving another god.[7] When Azira reached a state of trance during *ahɔne*, it was Ayisa who revealed both the origin of Agyeba's sickness and the sacrifices required to cure it. As soon as these were offered, Agyeba recovered. If Uncle Mozo Bile had put his trust in Azira, instead of asking to be taken to the Etikɔbɔ no. 1 dispensary, said Agyeba, who had a great admiration for her mother-in-law, he would certainly still have been alive. Alas, he was a Christian, and he paid dearly for his convictions.

A last detail should be mentioned. Kolɔra Kanra, on the night before his brother's funeral, as he was "going to the latrine" on the beach, saw Mozo Bile's ghost walking along the seashore. He recognized Mozo Bile beyond any possible doubt not only by his features dimly distinguishable in the moonlight but by the cloth the ghost was wearing, identical to his own, and of a rare pattern. As Kanra, his heart beating fast, started to walk back from the beach to his compound, the *nwomenle* seemed to follow him, treading slowly in the same direction, but keeping a distance between them. This was much to Kanra's relief, because he said that if his late brother's ghost had touched him, or even come close to him, it would have meant that he too, Kolɔra Kanra, was doomed to die within a short time. Then the apparition vanished. As far as I know, this was the last that was seen of poor Mozo Bile.

7 / The Rich Uncle's Coconuts

Bɔsɔ Bebu is remembered by everybody in Western Nzema, because he was one of the wealthiest and most reputed farmers in the country. He was born in the early 1880s in Ɛlonyi, of a Nvavile mother, Ama Tanoɛ, and a Twea father, Bɔsɔ. People who knew him only slightly added the patronym Bɔsɔ to his given name as a sign of respect and to distinguish him from other Bebus in the area, but to his near of kin and his friends he was just Bebu. He was reared in his father's compound, as the eldest of a series of about five or six siblings.[1] But when he reached the age of marriage, as the paternal compound was a crowded one, his father thought it advisable to build a new compound for him in the same town. There was no difficulty in finding a convenient plot, because the Twea are the original founders of Ɛlonyi and hence the traditional owners of most of the land. Furthermore, Bɔsɔ belonged to the lineage holding the Ɛlonyi stool (it still held it in the 1960s, the present chief being Arisi Kpole), and was at the time his lineage's *abusua kpanyinli* (lineage head). A central plot was thus found at some distance from Bɔsɔ's own compound, not just carved out of it or added at the town outskirts, as often happens nowadays, there being a land shortage.

Bebu grew to be a rich farmer mainly thanks to the hard work he did as a young man, early in the century, on a coconut plantation near the Bulazo stream, two or three miles inland from Ɛlonyi. The plantation had been started by a close relative of his on his father's side (father's sister's son) called Danoma, a Twea from Beyin. According to the Akan kinship system, any male member of a person's father's lineage and clan is regarded as that person's "father," irrespective of the generation to which he belongs; therefore, Bebu correctly called Danoma "father." Indeed, the latter—in western terms, a cousin—could theoretically one day become a substitute father to Bebu, if called to succeed his maternal uncle Bɔsɔ, thus becoming a potential husband to Bebu's mother. Bebu did not merely respect Danoma; he admired him for his farsighted agricultural initiatives, collaborated with him at first, and then began on his own to imitate him. He worked hard, enlarged the plantation on new plots, and made it one of the finest in Western Nzema, so that by the time Danoma died, Bebu was a comparatively rich man, the object of envy by many of his Nvavile clanspeople, who would have liked to share the benefits of the plantation with him.

But these people were soon disappointed. Bebu was firmly determined not to allow any lazy kinsman to take advantage of the wealth he had created with his own toil. He discouraged petitioners and secretly entrusted all his coconut groves to the stream *bozonle* called Bulazo, after the locality, asking him to punish whoever interfered with the coconuts, stranger or kinsman alike.

Bebu had two wives in his lifetime. By the first one, Ɛku, he had several children, all of whom died young except the first-born, whom he named Bɔsɔ after his own father. He later married Ahɔba, who also bore him many children; some died, but five survived, four girls (who in the course of time became mothers and grandmothers)—Aya, Ɛku, Ahwia, and Nyamekɛ—and one male named Arisi Kakula.

The fact that he had many children of his own whom he liked to bring up himself, allowing none of them to be handed over to relatives or friends in the *adanelilɛ* way, did not prevent Bebu from taking a just interest in his matrikin. He only had one full sister, Adwo Bia, by his own mother; but he had several sisters by his other mothers within the lineage, through whom he was provided with a large number of nephews and nieces, and his nieces in turn had plenty of children. Many of these he helped most generously, inviting them for long periods to his Ɛlonyi compound, feeding and dressing them and paying for their studies. To avoid overcrowding and jealousies, he selected his young guests carefully, one from each descent matriline.

Our informant and friend Mɔkɛ Mieza, the youngest son of Bebu's niece Bomo Bonya, was one of these. He was fatherless, his father having died when he was a small boy, and his mother could not possibly have paid for his studies had not Bebu volunteered to do so. Mieza thus spent ten years in Ɛlonyi, supported by Bebu, through his school days. Also during the same period there were some classificatory brothers of his living in the compound of the rich "grandfather," as had their uncles before them.

Bebu's generosity would never be forgotten by those who benefited by it. Yet in sharp contrast to this he was remembered by many as a cruel man because of the harshness with which he defended his coconut plantation, causing—it is said—many people to die.

To what extent this was true is difficult to say, as Bebu owned the plantation for about half a century and placed the curse on it with the *bozonle* a long time ago. So just how many copra thieves and casual trespassers the fetish god actually did punish and possibly kill over the decades is anybody's guess. Some of these may have been struck without even knowing who or what was killing them. But a few cases are undeniable, because they affected Bebu's kinsfolk.

The most obvious case is that of young Nyanzu. This boy, a son of Ɛba (Bebu's sister's daughter) and hence a brother to Mieza and a grandson to Bebu, had earlier been studying at Sekondi, where he reached form 3, but interrupted his studies because he suffered from *avinliwule*, sometimes called tuberculosis, and was under treatment at the Eikwe Catholic Hospital for more than one year. In 1962 his condition appeared to be improving, and his mother Ɛba sent him to her uncle Bebu, with the understanding that Nyanzu, without exerting himself too much, would work with him on the coconut farm. This the boy did for a few months, assisting his elderly grandfather in the weeding under the palms and the tidy heaping of the crops. But in 1963 he became sick again and died, and a *kɔmenle* revealed to Ɛba that this happened because during a short absence of Bebu the boy had secretly taken and sold for his own profit some of the dry coconuts. A god had noticed this dishonest action and killed Nyanzu for it.

Several times, while the boy was sick with a high fever and spitting blood, and later at the time of his burial and funeral, his mother went to Ɛlonyi to assist him, and on those occasions she naturally met Bebu and talked to him. But Bebu never said a single word about the *amonle* he had set on the plantation. The identity of the fetish god not being revealed, the god could not be properly pacified and continued to threaten all those that were considered

Coconut palms near the beach, Ngelekazo

directly or indirectly responsible for any attempt against the plantation's integrity.

The next victim in the lineage was Ɛba herself, bitten by a poisonous snake in the Menzezɔ bush, as elsewhere related (see chapter 10, "The Vindictive Ghost"). Still, at that time, in 1965, Mieza emphasized, the lineage people knew nothing about the old curse and the Bulazo god. Bebu kept his secret. He was an old man by now, his hair all white, living with his two equally old wives in the same old compound, his children all grown up and gone. Yet the deaths in his *abusua*, and those who were to follow, were in some way connected with Bebu's own impending fate.

Bebu was taken ill toward the end of 1965. He suffered from pains in his legs and strange heat in his body. Then a large boil appeared on his groin. Mieza himself, a modern-minded man, took him to the Eikwe Catholic Hospital, where he was visited by Dr. Alfonso del Val, the Spanish physician attached to the hospital in those years. But neither he nor the expert German sisters could really explain the reason for Bebu's sickness. As they are wont to do, these white people just gave the sick old man tablets and injections without any sensible explanation, and the cure did not help him at all. So the family took Bebu to a male *ɛsɔfo* of the *awa* (or Twelve Apostles) sect, a man called Mgbali, who collected herbs in the forest for Bebu and did a lot of talking and praying. But even this was of little use. By this time, one of Bebu's wives had died, but the junior one, Ahɔba, was assisting him. Some of his nieces also came on and off to Ɛlonyi to help Ahɔba, including Mɔkɛ Mieza's real mother, Bomo Bonya, and one of her sisters, Bomo Ekyi, as well as Bebu's own children Ahwia and Arisi Kakula. All these people were present when Bɔsɔ Bebu died on 6 March 1966.

According to Mɔkɛ Mieza and his full sister Nyima, who were both deeply grieved by the event, the causes of their grandfather's death were threefold.

First and foremost was the wrath of his niece Ɛba's ghost. As soon as the news of Ɛba's death following the snake bite reached Ngelekazo, a few members of the local Nvavile lineage segment were dispatched to Anyinaseɛ to fetch the body, as it was rightly presumed (and authoritatively confirmed later) that Ɛba would have wished to be buried in Ngelekazo. But Bebu, the dead woman's senior and most influential uncle, did not bother to join them. Bile Kaku, head of the Anyinaseɛ branch of the family, did not agree to the request,[2] and Ɛba was consequently buried in the Anyinaseɛ cemetery against her will. Her *nwomenle* was offended and logically put the blame on Bebu. Had he gone with the others to Anyinaseɛ and used his personal prestige and authority as *abusua kpanyinli*, Bile Kaku would no doubt have bowed to his will. So the niece's ghost was justified in considering Bebu responsible, and it rightly made him sick and caused him to die.

Second, the Nvavile ancestors in Hades, on their part, thought Bebu had been too harsh in his determination to protect his beloved coconuts, thus causing two lineage members to die within a short period. They wanted him to join them in *ɛbolɔ* to justify himself. This is not an idle supposition; in several previous cases, ancestors have demonstrably been known to act in a similar way.

Third, Bulazo, the fetish god who had been asked to guard the coconut groves, was also annoyed with Bebu. He was supposed to have told him, "I have been looking after thy coconuts as thou wished me to do, and I have even killed two of thy matrikin for thee, but thou never didst offer me even a fowl to thank me." It was incredible, my informants remarked, how a man could be generous and even profligate and extravagant at times, yet a miser in other regards.

These three causes must indeed have been the real ones because they were revealed quite independently by two experts: Mgbali, the Twelve Apostles priest; and Azira, the wise Ɛlonyi fetish priestess.

Azira, with whom I discussed the matter after having collected the above information, confirmed to me the exactness of these conclusions. She made no mystery of her opinion that Bebu, for all his showy extravagance, was at heart a cruel, avaricious old man. Having lived in the same town for years, she knew him well. When Nyanzu was mortally ill in Bebu's compound, Azira told me, Nyanzu's mother, Ɛba, went to Bebu and challenged him: "I have heard that my son's illness has something to do with thy coconuts. What hast thou to say?" Bebu flatly denied the allegation and did nothing about it, thus allowing his poor grandson to die. Even after his death, Bebu continued to wreak vengeance on his own lineage people. As related elsewhere in these pages (see chapter 10, "The Vindictive Ghost"), the death of Bomo Bonya in 1968, if not directly attributed to the action of the Bulazo god, was indirectly connected to the fates of Nyanzu, her sister Ɛba, and her uncle Bebu himself.

But Azira only saw and considered one side of the picture. She did not know that the younger members of the dead man's matrilineage who had been converted to Christianity, even those who had inherited no part of his coconut plantation, sometimes prayed for old Bebu's soul, because he was a generous man.

8 / *The Man Who Fell from the Roof*

Mokyia was the only son born from his mother's marriage to a Ngelekazo farmer of the Mafole clan, Eduku Kolɔra. But as his Nvavile mother, Alumua, had remarried twice after her first divorce, Mokyia had two half-brothers and two half-sisters by different fathers, apart from the classificatory brothers and sisters he had from his other Nvavile "mothers." It was mainly from two of these siblings, who had dutifully assisted him in the last dramatic hours of his life, that I learned of the unusual and much-discussed circumstances that led to Mokyia's death on 1 September 1969. One of these siblings was Mɔkɛ Mieza, Mokyia's mother's senior sister's son; the other was Bile, Alumua's son by another husband.

Mokyia made his home in his father's compound in Ngelekazo, near Beyin, the capital of Western Nzema. He had two wives in succession. At the time of these events, he was aged fifty-four and living with his second wife, Kua, an Azanwule from Alawule, and his little son, Kolɔra (named after Mokyia's father). When he decided to go west to the lagoon area for a fishing season, he took neither with him. They would join him, he said, as soon as he had built a proper house for the three of them.

The Nzema friends who had preceded him had chosen as their base a very isolated spot on the lagoon banks, in Ivory Coast territory, some twenty miles from Ekpu and with no village in the immediate vicinity. Here they had set up a tiny cluster of houses on piles above the water, something like a diminutive Nzulezo.[1] In the ten days of his stay there, which he did not know were to be the last of his life, Mokyia slept in the house of one of his colleagues. During the daytime he joined the other fishermen in their work, but devoted part of his time to the completion of a house that had been left uninhabited and unfinished by its previous occupants. He had made arrangements with the latter to turn it into his own dwelling.

It so happened that on that fatal day, August 30, his colleagues had decided not to go out fishing and were sitting together in their lagoon compound mending their nets. According to their common agreements, Mokyia, too, should have joined them in this part of their work. But being eager to complete the roofing of his new house, he asked them to excuse him and satisfied them with the gift of a bottle of *nza* (palm wine). Having done this, he set about to tie the *ezumule* to the rafters.[2]

All of a sudden, while the other fishermen were stitching the nets and chatting, they heard a shout and a loud splash from outside. Mokyia had lost his balance from the top of his hut next door and fallen right down into the lagoon. Before he sank into the water, he hit a canoe that was moored at the edge of the platform. They all rushed out, dragged him out of the water, and carried him up into their compound.

He was unconscious for a short while but soon came to. Though he moaned, complaining of great pain in his neck and shoulders, he was able to speak to his friends, and even helped them to rub some medicine on to his body. In a while, he was taken by repeated fits of vomiting, and he lapsed in and out of consciousness again. Realizing his condition was serious, they laid him on the bottom of a canoe and paddled to Ekpu as fast as they could. It is a long trip, and Mokyia was moaning and groaning the entire time. There was a dispensary at Ekpu, but the man in charge had no more than a few white tablets to give them, supposed to be effective against malaria, but of no use whatsoever for injuries caused by a fall from the roof. So they hired a truck in Ekpu and drove the sick man all the way to Eikwe in Ghana, which they reached the next day, where they took him straight to the local Catholic hospital, the best in the whole area. There was no available bed because the place was crammed with patients, but the kind German sisters at once found a nice stretcher for Mokyia and laid him down gently on it. But the Lithuanian-born American doctor, who was attached to the hospital at the time, shook his head and said it was too late to do anything; the case was absolutely hopeless.

So the fishermen—Kodwo Ekyi from Ngelekazo, Ɛlea from Miegyina, and Mɛnla from Ɛkɛbaku—drove the dying man back to his hometown, Ngelekazo, and at once alerted all of Mokyia's relatives and friends, who rushed out to assist him. These included his wife, Kua, his already-mentioned brothers Bile and Mɔkɛ Mieza, and his sister Alua, Mokyia's mother's sister's daughter. His

Beyin children with their miniature fishing net

other sister, Bɛneɛ, who was married and living at Kpɔkazo, could not be reached in time; and his brother Aka Bedu, a leper who usually lived in Samenye, was far away from Nzemaland in those days, at Cape Coast.

By the time he was driven back home, and an hour later brought to the compound of James Kodwo, the distinguished Ngelekazo medicine man, Mokyia was unconscious once more and unable to speak. At rare intervals he seemed to wake up, trying to explain, by mumbling and mute gestures, that he felt great pain in his left shoulder and in his chest. Kodwo did his best to cure him with his herbs, potions, and plasters, but to no avail. By 5 P.M. on September 1 Mokyia died.

The unusual circumstances of his accident, leading to a typical *ɔtɔfoɔ* death, naturally prompted the shocked lineage kin to seek at once an explanation by turning to an oracle. Mieza and Bile themselves, accompanied by their sister Alua and other townspeople, went for this purpose to the famous diviner Ɛzonle Kanra, both before and after Mokyia's funeral.

A response of the *adunyi* oracle, announced by Kanra, pointed to a death by magic poisoning at the hands of some unnamed "friend" associated with Mokyia in the fishing business. At first this was accepted by Mieza as being the final and correct response, and it was reported as such in the initial account. But even at the time (summer 1969) people were aware that this was not the only explanation emerging from the divining séances. Bile, for one, was not entirely convinced by it. There was no apparent reason, he told me, for any of Mokyia's associates to poison him, as Mokyia had barely begun fishing with them in the lagoon. There was no evidence of any dispute or jealousy among them. Indeed, there would hardly have been the time or the occasion for hostility to arise. And when the fatal accident occurred, all the fishermen concerned had proved their sincere goodwill, assisting their injured colleague and going out of their way, at their personal cost, to take Mokyia first to the hospital and then home.

From our repeated conversations on the subject in 1971, it soon became clear that two years earlier, in 1969, Ɛzonle Kanra's divining strings had tentatively pointed out a variety of alternative explanations for that fatal fall.

First, the strings had suggested a connection with the curse placed by Mokyia's grandfather Bebu on intruders in his coconut plantation (see chapter 7, "The Rich Uncle's Coconuts"). At the time the curse was already known to have caused two or three deaths within that particular Nvavile lineage, possibly including old Bebu himself. When this rich old man died in 1966, and before any of his three legal successors took over, it was Bile—the nearest of kin living in Ɛlonyi—who looked after the famous plantation. In spite of Bile's undoubted good will and honesty, some of his actions as a temporary manager may have displeased the heirs, or Bebu's ghost, or the Bulazo fetish god who had taken the coconuts under his protection, or all of these together. But it was a fact that Bile never suffered any noxious consequences. As for Mokyia, Bile's "brother," he never had anything to do with Bebu's succession. Therefore, Mɔkɛ Mieza had been very surprised in the first place when the oracle brought up this suggestion and discounted it as being utterly improbable.

A second suggestion put forward by Ɛzonle Kanra's divining strings was the following. When Mokyia's "mother" (mother's junior sister) Ɛba died of a snake bite in Anyinaseɛ and her soul remained imprisoned in the bush near Menzezɔ (see chapter 10, "The Vindictive Ghost"), Mokyia happened to be the eldest of her surviving sons, and it would thus have been his duty to take the initiative of liberating her *ɛkɛla*. But he had failed to do so, causing the dead woman's wrath. Quite possibly, as ghosts are the most unpredictable of beings, the ghost of this mother of his had suddenly appeared to him while he was roofing his house, frightening him and causing his fall. As Ɛba's ghost had already proved its revengeful disposition by bringing about Bomo's death, this hypothesis seemed to Bile and Mieza more credible than the previous one.

A third possible cause was quite different in nature. Some unnamed person in town had approached Mokyia, asking him for a loan, and Mokyia had refused, declaring that he did not have enough money to go around lending it to anybody. This was probably quite true. But the person had not believed it and had taken the refusal as an offense, remarking that Mokyia was rich enough to provide his own house in Ngelekazo with a corrugated iron roof—which was also true. So the offended party had put a curse on him with Bula, the *bozonle* at the pool where the

Ngelekazo women go to fetch water. It might well have been this god that pushed Mokyia off the roof.

Now, these three alternative explanations, added to the fourth one credited by Mieza in his first report, could not possibly be all true. But it would be unfair to blame Ɛzonle Kanra for this inconsistency, because all he did was reveal and explain what the *adunyi* strings were telling him, without adding anything of his own. Mokyia's case really just proves the difficulty of establishing one single cause for any accident or death. So often—as Kanra sensibly remarked—several causes concur.

Mokyia was not considered to be a Christian, though as a boy he had attended meetings at the Catholic church. Like so many Nzema, he was regarded as *ɔngɔ asɔne biala*, "one who attends no church." He was buried on 2 September 1969, in the Ngelekazo cemetery, where pagans rest side by side with Christians, just as there are no separate sections for individual clans.

He did not leave much property, except his clothes, a gold chain, and some coconut palms he had planted on a Nvavile-owned farm. The first of the three "brothers" (by the same great-great-grandmother, Alekyi) nominated to succeed him was Nyanzu, from the Ezinlibo branch of the lineage. He came dutifully to attend Mokyia's funeral, but after this he showed no interest in taking up the succession and did not even make an appearance when the box of the deceased was formally opened at the end of one year.[3] Bile, who was fond of his sister-in-law Kua and did not want her to leave the family, then approached the second successor, the one "sitting on Nyanzu's knees."[4] This man, Awua, who was married and lived in Eholaka, a small town in the interior of Agyeza, agreed to the suggestion. He came to Ngelekazo to have a careful look at Kua and a practical talk with her, then took her back with him to Eholaka as a wife, along with the gold chain and one of poor Mokyia's cloths. He left Bile to take care of the coconut palms.

9 / *The Ghost, the God, and the Goblins*

The story of Nda Dwukwa deserves being told because it is an eloquent example of cases, alas too numerous, in which the origin of a serious misfortune is tentatively interpreted by relatives and even by experts in several conflicting ways, thus thwarting the painstaking efforts of those, such as historians and anthropologists, who try to reconstruct the true course of events.

Nda Dwukwa was an Alɔnwɔba matron from Ɛlonyi, aged about seventy-six, who died after a long illness in her own house, attended by her sons and daughters, on 7 May 1971. No general agreement was ever reached as to the cause of her death.

Despite her first name, usually used for twins either as a personal birth name or as a patronym (from *ndalɛ*, "twins"), she was neither a twin herself nor the daughter of a twin parent. She was named thus by her father in remembrance of her father's mother. Her soul name was Yaba, "Thursday born."

She had been married twice in her lifetime, and had nine children, four by her first husband and five by the second. These children, six of whom were still living, were: (1) Bozoma (female), married and living in Ɛlonyi; (2) Ɛtwɛ (male), also living in Ɛlonyi; (3) an unnamed male child who died shortly after birth; (4) Yaba (female), who also died as a baby before she was properly named; (5) Aka Bile (male), staying at Asɛmpɛyɛ, near Etikɔbɔ no. 1; (6) Boa (male), also living at Asɛmpɛyɛ but who frequent visited Beyin and Ngelekazo; (7) Tɛna (female), who was first married and lived at Asɛmpɛyɛ but was now divorced and remarried at and living Egbazo; (8) Nyɔnra (female), married and living at Egbazo; and (9) Agyalua (female), who died before the age of puberty. It was our original intention to elicit separate accounts of the matron's death from each of her surviving children, but transport difficulties at the time made the journeys to Asɛmpɛyɛ and Egbazo impossible.

A first account, presenting no problems or doubts in its simplicity, was given verbally by Boa to Mɔkɛ Mieza of Ngelekazo a few days after the old woman's funeral. Well aware of the fragility of human memory, Mieza wisely summarized Boa's words and handed me the following written report:

"Dwukwa fell sick a first time and was cured by the German sisters at Eikwe. The same sickness came again and was cured by the doctor at Axim. The third time her sons consulted *adunyi* and saw that the sickness came from a *nwomenle* (ghost). The reason was that Dwukwa had an old brother in the Ivory Coast who had many properties. Before dying, this man divided the properties in two parts. One for Dwukwa's family at Ɛlonyi and the other for the family of the same *suakunlu abusua* at Kabenlasuazo. But after the funeral obsequies in Ivory Coast, the family brought the properties to Nzemaland and there came a dispute about their division. The ghost, seeing that Dwukwa was the oldest person in the family, and also the right person to settle the case, but never settled it, caused her death. This death is called *nwomenle ewule* (ghost death)."

The report was substantially correct, as I was able to check personally when, a few months after these events, in September 1971, I returned to Ghana and met Boa in Beyin. But things began to appear less clear when, in that same month, I had the opportunity to talk at length with another son of Nda Dwukwa's, Ɛtwɛ of Ɛlonyi, an intelligent farmer in his early fifties. He confirmed that his late mother had an elder brother (mother's mother's daughter's son) called Nyanzu, who had long ago migrated to Ayeboso in the French Ivory Coast.[1] He met with considerable success with his fishing and farming there, causing his nephews in Ghana to consider him a rich uncle from whom a pleasant inheritance might one day be expected. Several years earlier, Nda Dwukwa decided to visit him; from Ayeboso, she then went to another Ivory Coast town, Grand Bassam, where her own real mother, Nyamua was then living. This took place, Ɛtwɛ thought, more than fifteen years earlier (that is, before 1956). Nyamua was a very old and sick woman at the time, and she died a few months after her daughter had come from Ghana to visit her. While staying with her mother, Nda Dwukwa naturally wished to help her, and therefore joined the local people in their farm work. In connection with this, she was apparently attacked by the *asonwu*, the unpredictable little goblins who are very powerful in the southern provinces of the Ivory Coast.[2] It is a fact that Nda Dwukwa fell seriously sick for the first time while she was attending

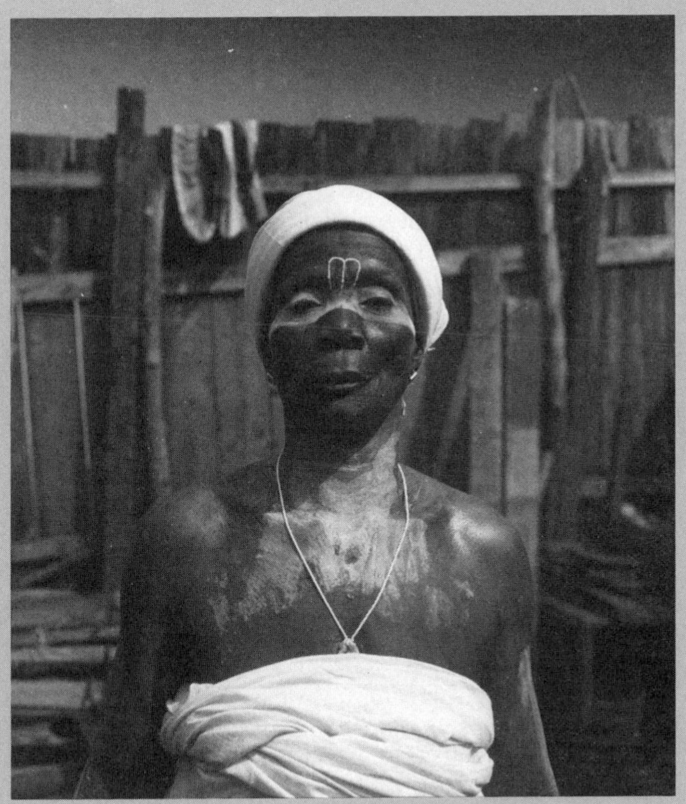

Facial painting on a fetish priestess

her mother's funeral at Grand Bassam and had to be brought home in a hurry. The reason for her sickness, Ɛtwɛ added, was plainly confirmed by Ɛzonle Kanra, the Ngelekazo doctor and soothsayer.

When we pointed out to Ɛtwɛ that his brother Boa attributed that same sickness to the attack by their common uncle's ghost, Ɛtwɛ did not deny that there may have been some truth also in this explanation. Nyanzu, the rich uncle in the Ivory Coast, died several years earlier, not long after his sister Nyamua. Ɛtwɛ himself knew him very well, having once lived with him for a few months in Ayeboso and worked on his farms there. It was true that there was a dispute about Nyanzu's succession, as Boa said. The dispute was complicated by the fact that, during his lifetime, Nyanzu had occasionally returned to Ghana, where he had allegedly donated part of his riches to his relatives of the Kabenlasuazo branch. But what was worse, he had handed over another part of his property (cloths, gold ornaments, and money) to yet another nephew, a classificatory brother to the informant, Mɔkɛ of Kyapum in the lagoon area.[3] In Ɛtwɛ's opinion, Mɔkɛ did not stand in a position of legitimate priority within the lineage succession line. After Nyanzu's death, Ɛtwɛ himself and other members of the Ɛlonyi branch of the family went thrice to Kyapum in the attempt to recover at least part of this property, which they considered should be returned to them, but with no success. Mɔkɛ did not altogether deny having received the goods. But he declared they had been donated to him as a personal present, and gave nothing back. Nyanzu's ghost was annoyed by this refusal, and was actually making Mɔkɛ sick, but Mɔkɛ had so far taken no notice of this warning.

Nda Dwukwa's senior daughter, Bozoma, whom I interviewed in Ɛlonyi a few days later, did not seem to give much credit to the influence of Nyanzu's ghost in causing her mother's last illness. The reason, she said, is a quite different one. A few years ago, Nda Dwukwa started work on a new farm near Asɛmpɛyɛ with other Alɔnwɔba women, and a litigation arose on a question of boundaries between the different portions of the farm. One of the litigants "gave" Dwukwa to a *bozonle*. Not content with this, the same woman (of whose identity Bozoma was certain, though she would not disclose it) buried one or two *asonwu* terra-cotta figurines in her rival's plot. The little goblin figures, so wickedly and deceitfully hidden, caught Dwukwa unawares and made her sick. She had to return to Ɛlonyi, where she was brought for treatment to Azira the priestess.

Bozoma would say no more than this. She politely but clearly made me understand that, since her mother was completely dead, she was not really interested in discussing the whys and wherefores of her sickness.[4] She had work to do. If I wanted to know more, I had only to ask Azira.

The next step in our inquiry was a visit to this priestess. Though she had a constantly large clientele, both in Ɛlonyi and from other towns, Azira remembered Dwukwa's case quite well. But she had little of importance to add, except that she was able to tell me the name of the *bozonle* to whom her former patient had been "given" by her enemy. It was Kyiribenli, a stream god in the Asɛmpɛyɛ area. The detail about the *asonwu* was also correct; it had been revealed not only by her own spirits but by Ɛzonle Kanra in Ngelekazo by means of his oracular strings. She agreed with Bozoma that the *asonwu* had attacked Nda Dwukwa on the Asɛmpɛyɛ farm, not in the Ivory Coast, as Ɛtwɛ maintained. Of course, it could not be excluded that some other group of these goblins might have made her sick once before, when she was staying with her mother. But that had happened several years earlier, and that time Dwukwa had recovered.

Azira put much of the blame on Nda Dwukwa herself. The plot of land in Asɛmpɛyɛ, over which the litigation arose, "was not for her." When Dwukwa had come to her a first time for treatment, Azira had strongly advised her not to go back to Asɛmpɛyɛ at all. But the old woman had disregarded the advice. When she had returned to Ɛlonyi for good, her health had deteriorated so much that nothing more could be done to help her.

It would have been easy for Azira to emphasize the fact that, if her treatments had failed to save Nda Dwukwa, the same could be said of the German sisters at the Eikwe hospital, as well as of the Ghanaian doctor in Axim (who had studied medicine in Europe), who had cured the patient before her. Or Azira could have emphasized that sheer old age had at least had a part in determining her death. But she did not do so. Only the almightly God, she concluded, could have saved Dwukwa. But He decided otherwise.

10 / The Vindictive Ghost

Bomo Bonya and Ɛba were middle-aged sisters of the Nvavile clan, born by the same mother, Sɛnzaba. Both were widows living in the same town, Ngelekazo, though in different compounds. Bomo Bonya was the senior, being the first-born child of her mother, whereas Ɛba was the fourth and last born. They understandably saw very much of one another, often worked and ate together, and, having been brought up together in their youth and never having quarrelled in later years, were on the most intimate and affectionate terms. Therefore, it is all the more sad that the tragic end of both their lives, as described to me by their daughter Nyima and their son Mɔkɛ Mieza should have been marked by mutual misunderstandings and hostility.[1]

In the late autumn of 1965, Ɛba received a message from her first-born daughter, Avola, married and living at Menzezɔ in Eastern Nzema, saying that her time of delivery had come. This was important news for Ɛba, because Avola, her only surviving daughter, represented her sole chance of continuing her own descent line within the *abusua*, and so far Avola had only had a single and sickly little girl, Manye. Therefore Ɛba dutifully left for Menzezɔ to assist her daughter, who a few days later brought forth another baby girl, Avola Ekyi. Ɛba, who had taken over most of the housework and cooking in her daughter's house, occasionally also did some farm work for her, and this proved fatal. One day, as she was walking through the forest on the way to Avola's farm to collect some cassava, she inadvertently trod on a big poisonous snake, *ɛkyelebenle*, which was wriggling across the path among the dry leaves. The snake, a splendid specimen of the kind that white people call green mamba, sprang up and bit her before it darted away into the bush. Ɛba cried out in pain and terror. The woman who was following her rushed to the rescue and did her best under the circumstances. She tied Ɛba's leg tightly above the wound with *beleko nyɛma* (strips of oil palm leaves), called for help, and with the assistance of other people managed to take her unfortunate neighbor back to the Menzezɔ compound.[2] From there, they drove her by the first available truck to the nearest dispensary, in Anyinaseɛ. But all this was useless, because the poor woman died in agony shortly after her arrival.

The body was at once taken from the dispensary to the compound of Bile Kaku, the eldest representative of the dead woman's lineage in Anyinaseɛ, and incidentally one of her brothers (mother's mother's sister's daughter's son). At the same time, two messengers were dispatched by bus to Ngelekazo to inform Ɛba's near of kin of the tragic accident and to fetch her best clothes and jewels, which were urgently needed to dress and adorn the body properly before it was laid in state for the whole public to see.

The messengers were naturally directed to the senior sister of the deceased. Perhaps the announcement was conveyed to her too bluntly; perhaps Bomo Bonya, who was rather deaf, did not grasp fully at first what she was being asked; perhaps the messengers, in their haste to return immediately to Anyinaseɛ in time for the obsequies, did not leave her the time to consider the matter more calmly. Be this as it may, Bomo Bonya was surely distracted and dismayed at the sudden tragic news when she gave her unfortunate reply—that her late sister's box was empty. The consequences of this reply, which implied that in her lifetime Ɛba had possessed no clothes or ornaments worth wearing, Bomo Bonya could not possibly foresee.

Though this was surely a tactless thing to say aloud in the presence of strangers, no one gave the incident much importance at the time. All of Ɛba's relatives and friends in Ngelekazo were too aghast at the news of her painful and inexplicable death. But Bomo Bonya's words created surprise and embarrassment when they were reported to the group of mourners assembled around her sister's lifeless body in Anyinaseɛ. The body was, of course, laid in state all the same, fine clothes or no fine clothes. As related elsewhere in these pages (see chapter 7, "The Rich Uncle's Coconuts"), Ɛba was eventually buried—though against her will—in the Anyinaseɛ cemetery.

Death by snake bite is a rare occurrence in Nzemaland nowadays. Like any other *ɔtɔfoɔ* death, it calls for prompt investigation into its causes.[3] The family resorted to Azira, the distinguished Ɛlonyi priestess. She revealed that the fatal accident had been caused by the fetish god Bulazo, who had temporarily transformed himself into a serpent; it is well known that gods can easily achieve these metamorphoses. Bulazo was vexed because no one had pacified him after he killed Nyanzu, Ɛba's son, for secretly selling in 1963 some of her uncle Bebu's coconuts, which had been entrusted to the god's protection. So Bulazo had understandably punished another member of the same Nvavile line.

Azira's pronouncement, made at the inspiration of her main goddess, Ayisa, clearly explained the cause not only of Ɛba's death but also of that of her son two years earlier, showing the logical link between the two events. It should also have sounded a warning to old Bebu, who at the time did not imagine that he himself would soon be third in the chain of connected deaths within his lineage segment. But Bebu was apparently already too old and ill to take notice. When the *abusua* people, advised and led by Azira, went to the bush in the Bulazo area to appease the god with the necessary offerings, he declined to join them. Old people are often lazy like that, and they inevitably pay a high price for their laziness. Bomo Bonya did not go either, leaving the rather tiresome performance to the *abusua* people of the younger generation, such as her "daughters" Elua and Avola, her "son" Bile, and Mɔkɛ Mieza himself.

The same thing happened when the other essential rite was performed—what was thought to be the final pacification of Ɛba's ghost, the dragging of her imprisoned *ɛkɛla* from the bush near Menzezɔ to her grave in the Anyinaseɛ cemetery.[4] It was once more the younger lineage members who went from Ngelekazo to join Avola and the relatives of the Anyinaseɛ branch.

But apparently, possibly because of the unusual circumstances of her death, or because the lineage members against whom she bore a grudge had not taken the trouble of personally taking part in the rites, or because the rites were not correctly performed, Ɛba's ghost was not at all satisfied. It watched, took note of every detail, and showed its displeasure. In March 1966, Bebu went to his grave; and almost exactly two years later, in February 1968, Bomo Bonya was taken ill.

Her sickness manifested itself suddenly at night, with a feeling

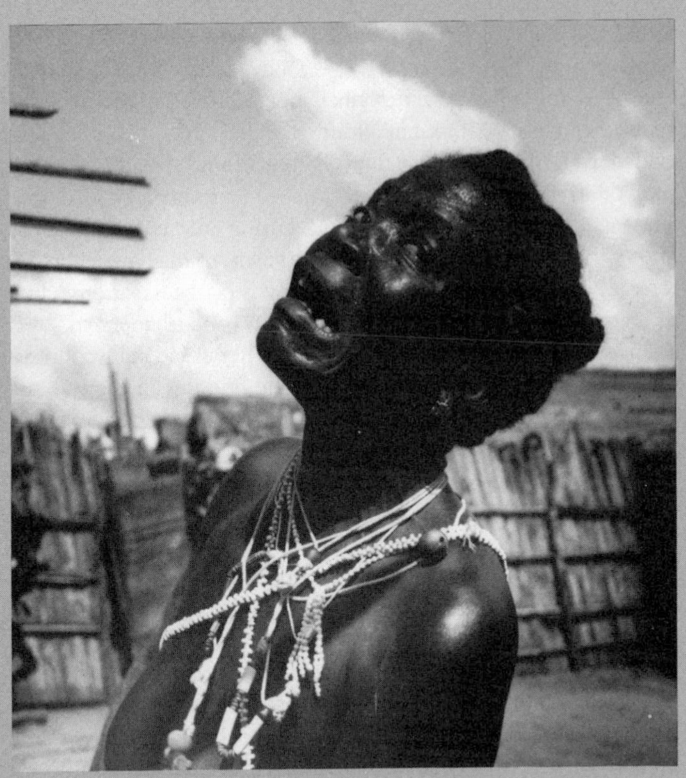

Fetish priestess on the verge of a trance during an ahɔne dance, Atuabo, 1954

of intense cold in her whole body and violent shivers. These symptoms by themselves, as everybody knows and as Nyima reminded me when she described her mother's illness, suggest attack by a ghost, though admittedly they are not conclusive evidence. In the very first days of that illness, Nyima took her mother all the way to Anyinaseɛ to consult a *kɔmenle* named Aya, who specialized in detecting and curing ailments caused by ghosts. But the woman was away from town, so they made the trip for nothing. Soon afterward, a swelling described as a large boil developed in Bomo Bonya's groin—just as had happened, by a strange coincidence, in the final stages of her uncle Bebu's illness. Her children then took her to Azira, the priestess in Ɛlonyi, and left her there for two weeks of treatment.

Azira, as usual, did things very seriously. She danced *ahɔne*, the fetish dance, to enter in contact with her guiding spirits. One of these, the ghost of the famous old priestess Kɔkɔ, descended on her almost at once and spoke through Azira's mouth, revealing that it was Ɛba's ghost that was causing her sister's illness. Two *awozonle*, who followed Kɔkɔ during Azira's trance, confirmed this explanation. The ghost was seriously offended and grieved because Bomo Bonya had humiliated her dead sister and put her to shame in public by her unwise statement about the empty box. Regaining her full human consciousness after the dance, Azira prepared the herb decoctions to protect her patient—some for drinking, some to smear on the patient's body, and some to be syringed in enema form; unlike many of her colleagues, Azira also had a fair knowledge of practical medicine. She poured a libation to the incensed ghost in the attempt to appease it. She offered it several hens. But all was in vain; Bomo Bonya's conditions deteriorated. At the very end, when the case became plainly hopeless, Bonya's children took her back to her Ngelekazo home, where she died almost immediately.

After the funeral, the lineage relatives contributed to buy a sheep, some rice, eggs, and drinks, including two bottles of Coca-Cola that in modern times appear to be greatly appreciated by ghosts. A Thursday was chosen, suggested as being the most favorable day of the week to invoke ghosts.[5] The food was cooked at the Ngelekazo compound; *afɔtɔ* was prepared.[6] A large group of kinsfolk and friends, including Azira, who had come for the occasion, walked to the cemetery. Azira poured the libation, this time using expensive French wine imported from the Ivory Coast, to all the deceased widow's *abusua* ancestors in general, but mentioning explicitly the names of Ɛba and Bomo Bonya. She informed them that food was being offered to them, asked them to allow the surviving family members to live in peace and good health, and sprinkled some *afɔtɔ* around the last freshly covered grave.

The following day, at Azira's suggestion, the same lineage people drove to Ɛlonyi, where the priestess danced *ahɔne* once more. Her main goddess, Ayisa, came on her, and spoke, informing them that the ghosts had benevolently accepted the food and drink offered to them at the Ngelekazo cemetery; there would be no more harm in the family. The prediction turned out to be true. From the spring of 1968 until my last encounter with Bomo Bonya's children, in 1975, there were no more deaths or other grave calamities in their lineage segment.

When discussing with them, in 1971, the sequence of sad events I have just reported, I once took the liberty of putting to them a question typical of the white man's mentality: Did they not consider that the reaction of Ɛba's ghost, which caused the death of her full sister, was out of proportion with the offense she had suffered—that is, the remark about her box being empty?

Nyima, like her late mother formally a Catholic, reflected for a moment and then explained. Living human beings, she said, should not, and in fact usually do not, take serious offense for such trivial reasons. But things are different in the afterworld. The spirits of the deceased have little to do. They devote all their attention to what goes on in this world, and above all to the actions and words of their living relatives that have direct or indirect reference to them, the ghosts. In the bustle of everyday existence, living men and women are apt to overlook details, to forget and forgive; but ghosts, who live in such a quiet and silent world, overlook nothing. Their punishment may be slow to come, but it will be ruthless.

11 / An Unlucky Husband

At the end of the rainy season of 1970, Kodwo Nda, a young Adahonle farmer from Kɛngɛne, moved to a small village called Azenganezo in the lagoon area near the Ivory Coast border. He naturally took with him his wife, nineteen-year-old Manu, from the Nvavile clan, and their only son, Adwoka, aged four.

Soon Manu was pregnant once more. Nda, being a modern-minded man, decided that the delivery should take place in a white man's hospital. There is just one such hospital in Nzemaland, at Eikwe on the eastern coast, run by German sisters. So when her time approached, Manu undertook the long truck journey to Eikwe, accompanied by her real mother, Azane Akuba. Little Adwoka was entrusted to Asɔ, Manu's junior full sister, aged eighteen, married and living in Kɛngɛne and the mother of a child herself. Nda remained at Azenganezo to do his farming.

It was here that a few days later the sad news reached him: on 22 February 1971, Manu had died at the Eikwe hospital after having delivered still born twins.

At the time, there happened to be no doctor at the hospital, and the German sisters with whom I spoke later merely registered the event as a case of death following a difficult twin delivery. The sisters themselves, who assist hundreds of patients, did not remember anything particular about this one. They knew the two babies had been buried without ceremony at the Eikwe cemetery, while the body of the mother was claimed by her kin, who took it away for burial at the Kɛngɛne cemetery.

If, in accordance with their superficial mentality, Europeans show little or no interest in ascertaining the real causes of deaths and other dramatic events, this is not so among the Nzema. In Kɛngɛne and in the neighboring villages, public opinion was shocked and intrigued by the young woman's sudden death, and people discussed at length the fact and its precedents, trying to discover what had caused it.

The better-informed people soon agreed in assigning the

original cause to a dispute that had arisen a few months earlier among Nda, Manu, and her mother, creating a state of *sipe* (inner grudge, psychic tension). As everybody knows, *sipe* itself is such a strong feeling that it often causes the illness or even the death of the person against whom it is secretly directed. But in the present case, Azane Akuba spread the rumor that the person holding the evil grudge in his heart—poor Manu's husband—had gone further, approaching a *bozonle* (fetish god) and asking him to kill his wife. Akuba had suspected as much from the start, but she had been confirmed in her opinion after consulting a renowned fetish priest in town.

The nature of the original dispute at the base of the whole trouble was well known. In 1970, Nda had prepared a farm near Kɛngɛne for his mother-in-law so that she could cultivate cassava on it. When the cassava grew, Akuba sold it to her daughter every time that Nda needed it for his food. When the fact became known, it caused a quarrel between Nda and his wife, because Nda insisted that it was absurd to have him pay for the cassava considering he was the one who had prepared the farm in the first place. Manu disagreed with him, taking her mother's side. Akuba joined in the quarrel and abused him, and went as far as taking him to the district court.

The case was far from clear, because nobody knew for sure what the original arrangements had been. Some people took sides with the two women, others with Nda. The latter came to the conclusion, contrary to Akuba's version, that the *bozonle* from the area where the farm was had understood that Nda was being cheated, and of his own initiative had killed the girl during her delivery. The fact that he should have punished Manu rather than her more responsible mother was, of course, quite irrelevant, as they belonged to the same matrilineage, Akuba, Manu, and Manu's children were interchangeable. All of them were Nvavile.

When the sad case was reported to me in Western Nzema in 1971, it seemed difficult to assess where the truth lay without having personally interviewed the people concerned. They were difficult to find. Nda was allegedly still busy at his farm work in the remote lagoon area. Akuba, who had assisted her daughter at the hospital and had been present at her death, had subsequently left for some unknown place in the Ivory Coast. It was possible, however, to contact one of Manu's two surviving full sisters, called Nyaku, who was living with her husband and child at Kɛngɛne.

Nyaku, a pleasant-looking girl of about twenty-one, substantially confirmed her mother's version of the events leading to Manu's death. The cassava farm, at a place in the bush inland from Kɛngɛne called Bokabo, from the name of the small local stream, had actually been prepared by Azane Akuba and Manu, though Nda had admittedly helped in clearing the land. When the cassava was ready, Akuba went and uprooted the tubers, as she was legitimately entitled to do. A male neighbor, called Bilewe, saw her doing this and reported the fact to her son-in-law. Nda was very angry. He rushed to the farm and verified that some of the tubers had actually been taken out and that another part of the crop was marked for sale. He cut some of the cassava sticks for evidence, brought them to the court in Beyin, and made summons against Akuba and Manu. People said it was wrong to bring up the case at this level; he should rather have tried to settle it in Kɛngɛne, in front of the local elders. As it was, news of the quarrel reached the fetish god who had his abode in the bush where the farm had been made, named Bokabo after the local stream, and the god killed poor Manu at the moment of her delivery.

Though Nyaku did not actually accuse Nda of having asked the *bozonle* to kill his wife, it was clear that she sided with her kinswomen against her brother-in-law. Nda, she said, was an utterly despicable man. Had the family known him better in the first place, they would no doubt have objected to Manu marrying him. But they knew little about him at the time, as he was not originally a Kɛngɛne man, having been born and brought up in Eholaka, a distant town. The main asset that had made him acceptable to the family was that he was a junior brother to Adwoka, a highly respectable store owner in Kɛngɛne. As for Manu herself, she was barely thirteen when she married him, and naturally quite unexperienced. Even at the current time, Nyaku said, Nda was giving nothing to her sister Asɔ for his child's upkeeping, contrary to his duties as a father. This confirmed Nyaku's opinion of her former brother-in-law as a miser and a good-for-nothing.

From the very beginning, she had felt sure that he was entirely responsible for her late sister's troubles. In fact, Manu had been

Priestess dancing ahɔne

sick most of the time during her last pregnancy. But the exact causes of her sickness and death became known to them with certainty only some time after the funeral, when she and her mother went to consult Kofi, the renowned Kpɔkazo fetish priest. His verdict was authoritatively confirmed two weeks later by the esteemed herbalist and diviner, Ɛzonle Kanra of Ngelekazo. Both added that, as often happens in such cases, Manu's *ɛkɛla* (soul) was being held in captivity in the bush by the Bokabo god. Since then, the lineage people had been setting money aside to buy the sheep and fowls that would have to be offered to Bokabo in order to pacify him and to release the captive soul. They were planning to perform the rite shortly after the end of the 1971 New Year festival, in October.

Having thus obtained from Nyaku the version of the facts accepted by Manu's family, we took leave from her. It was she who a few days later sent us a message informing us that Nda had returned from the lagoon area in a poor state of health. He could now be found in Kɛngɛne once more, in the compound of Ekue, a priestess of the Water Carriers (Twelve Apostles) sect.

This meant an opportunity to hear the accused husband's own version of the facts, so on 8 October 1971, Mr. Mieza and I again undertook the journey from Beyin to Kɛngɛne. Ekue's compound on the northern side of the main Kɛngɛne street was not difficult to locate. The priestess was in and amiably received us as soon as she had finished praying for one of her female visitors, for whom she had just administered an enema. She confirmed that Nda was actually one of her in-patients. He had come to her some three weeks earlier, with an ugly swelling in his abdomen and complaining of severe pains. She had accepted him as an in-patient and was still treating him with medicines and prayers. He was, in fact, on the way to recovery, and at the moment was not in the compound, having walked to the beach to buy some fish from the local fishermen, who had just come ashore with their nets.

Nda's present sickness, Ekue told us, had nothing to do with his wife's and children's deaths eight months earlier, about which we were inquiring. But if we were prepared to wait for his return, she would gladly tell us about it in the meanwhile. As we thought that this might shed light, however indirectly, on the young man's character, we agreed to listen to Ekue's story.

A few months earlier, she said, Nda, during one of his periodical visits to Kɛngɛne, had stolen the valuable velvet cloth of a respected townsman called Nwia Aka. This man was very annoyed by the theft he had suffered, anxiously looked for his cloth all over town, and one day eventually saw Nda wearing it. So he went straight to Nda's senior brother, Adwoka, demanding that the cloth be returned to him. Nda brazenly denied his guilt, alleging that he had received the cloth from his own brother, who in fact kept a variety of fabrics for sale in his Kɛngɛne store. A meeting of town elders was called to settle the case, and Nda was summoned in the presence of Nwia Aka and Adwoka. The latter addressed him: "Nda, thou art my brother, but nonetheless I must say that what thou didst is shameful. The cloth in question thou never didst get from me, because I never kept any of this type in my store, as thou well knowest, and none are to be found for sale in town, and we know that thou hast not traveled to places where they can be bought. So I regret to say, thou must return the velvet cloth at once to its owner, Nwia Aka."

The palaver was in fact a long one, but in the end Nda had no choice but to obey the order given him by his brother in front of the elders, and he gave the cloth back. Nwia Aka was satisfied and willing to take the matter no further, but the dispute was not closed. Nda was furious with his brother, and said, "Thou hast disgraced me in public." The next day, he took an egg, walked to the Ɛlɛmɛnza stream just outside town, where it flows into the sea, and addressed the local fetish god, offering him the egg and asking him in return to kill Adwoka. As chance would have it, a man who was on the beach casting his small net from the shore saw Nda from a distance, became suspicious, and followed him without being seen. So this man overheard what Nda was saying to the god and rushed straight back to town to report the fact to Adwoka. Once more, a small meeting of elders was hastily convened, Nda was summoned in their presence, and questioned as to what he had done. As he heard his own words repeated by a witness, he could not deny them, and he was forced to admit his new guilt.

However, Adwoka was afraid of his brother's wicked curse, and to be on the safe side he hastened to pacify the Ɛlɛmɛnza god. He went to the trouble of securing, not without difficulty, a *komu* monkey (this god's favorite food) from a hunter, sacrificed it to the *bozonle* near the stream, asking him to disregard anything Nda had said. The god appreciated Adwoka's sacrifice, all the more so as in the meantime he had not received from Nda the further offerings the latter had promised him in order that he should kill Adwoka. So the god took a dislike to Nda and returned the egg he had been given to start with; he placed it into Nda's stomach and caused it to swell.

This time, it was Nda's turn to be scared. He hurried to pacify his brother with some gin, and also to appease the incensed *bozonle* with the sacrifice of another monkey. But the swelling and the pains were still not retreating. In the end, he applied to Ekue for help and settled in her compound. Now, Ekue said, her treatments and prayers were beginning to prove effective, and in her opinion Nda was out of danger, even if not completely cured.

Ekue, of course, was at the same time well acquainted with the story of Manu's death in childbirth, because everybody in town had been gossiping about this case for months. She was well aware of the fact that Manu's family were frequently pouring libations to Manu's ghost and asking it to come and kill Nda. She did not disclose what she personally thought about this story; but as Nda was now her client, she felt she must professionally protect him. She assured him (and us) that, as long as he resided in her compound protected by the Holy Cross, no ghost would be able to come and attack him.

In fact, as she told us, she did something more in favor of her patient. In a vision at night, she saw the souls of the two dead babies coming to her and asking her to bring them back to their father. Through their father, they had been on the point of coming to life, but something had stopped them. Now they demanded to be brought back to him, so that some day they might succeed in really coming into this world, entering the womb of some woman of their father's choice, if this woman was agreeable to them. They bore no *sipe* against Nda at all. So Ekue took a truck to Eikwe, where she knew the twins had been buried, walked to the cemetery with a townswoman who showed her the actual place of interment, and called out their souls. To do this, she took a thin strip of white calico, placed it on the grave, and dragged it away for a few yards while calling out their names. She could not use their personal names, because, being stillborn, they never had them; she just addressed them as *ndalɛ*, "twins." Their souls came out of the grave, and she tied them up into the calico by making a knot in it. Then she brought the calico strip back to Kɛngɛne and gave it to Nda. Nda could tie the strip around his forehead, or his knee, as he pleased, in order to keep the two souls with him. (In fact, as Nda later told us himself, he put the strip under the pillow on the mat he slept on.) The two souls were held by the calico, and would not escape, Ekue concluded, so that Nda would be sure to beget twins when he remarried.

By the time Ekue was recounting the last part of her story, Nda returned from the beach. He greeted us and sat down beside us. Though he declared he was feeling much better, a greyish poultice smeared on his alarmingly bulging stomach, which he showed us after untying the mottled cloth that covered it and the palm fibers that kept it in place, testified to the persistence of his ailment.

When we tactfully brought up the sad subject of Manu's case, Nda's reactions were very bitter. Of course he was grieved by the sudden death of his wife and his two children, but what upset him most was the shocking behavior of Manu's kinsfolk toward him after the tragedy. When poor Manu's body was laid in state in Kɛngɛne, with all the townsfolk present and many who had come from other towns near and far, Akuba and her sisters and daughters, supported by their Nvavile male kin, tried to stop him from sitting near her death bed, as the custom compels a husband to do. Later, on the eighth-day funeral celebrations, they would not even let him enter the compound. Nda felt insulted; the outrage was worse than the grief. "Why should they all hate me so much," Nda asked. "I know they go around saying I killed my wife, but why should a loving man in his right senses do such a thing? Ever since the funeral, Manu's *abusua* have time and time again been pouring libation on her grave, praying that her ghost may come out and kill me, but why should they do this? I am innocent," said Nda. "I suffered enough through my wife's death. And as for seeking the causes, it is a problem for her lineage and not for me."

Indeed, as Nda himself admitted, this was not his first unfortunate experience with marriage. As a very young man, some fifteen years earlier, when he was still living in Eholaka Nda had married a girl called Asua Anlima, with whom he had lived for eight years. Yes, he had children with her—two of them. But both died in the first months of life. Why? Everybody knew about that, unfortunately. Asua Anlima turned out to be notoriously promiscuous. She reached the point of having intercourse with six different men in the same period, and behavior of this sort, which is called *huhunli nyɛleɛ*, is bound to make the babies die. There was little that Nda could do about it. Of course, he beat his wife, but that was of no use. In the beginning, he would go and complain to Anlima's parents, and they reprimanded the girl. But as his complaints became more frequent, they became bored and told him bluntly that they were giving up their daughter, because she was hopeless. In the end, they refused to listen to him altogether; indeed, they became so annoyed with his grievances that he feared they would end up by poisoning him. So Nda decided to put the matter into the hands of his senior brother, Adwoka, who discreetly managed to collect the adultery fees from most of Anlima's lovers—all but one, who bolted from town for good and has not been heard from since. As for the others, it was such a public affair that they could not deny the adultery charges, and one after another they were forced to pay. That was all the satisfaction Nda was able to get. Then he preferred to divorce Asua Anlima quietly.

When he later decided to remarry, he took care to choose a very young and inexperienced girl for a change. Manu had not yet passed her first menses when he married her, and though they lived and sometimes slept together, for several months Nda had no intercourse with her at all. In due time, the situation became normal. By the time she was fourteen, Manu was pregnant with her first child, who was born without difficulty and is alive to this day. Nda named him Adwoka, after his respected senior brother. But Manu, being so young, was completely under the influence of that dreadful mother of hers, Azane Akuba. The two women soon began taking advantage of him, exploiting his work, and squeezing every penny out of him. The question of the cassava farm was only the last straw.

How did this affair really go, I asked. "Well," Nda said, "I decided to make a small farm at Bokabo. I set fire to the bush, cut down the trees and stumps, and cleared the plot nicely; it was a hard job. I intended Manu to work on the farm after this. But her *abusua* women said no; Manu was still too young for such heavy work. The tilling should be done by Akuba. I could not oppose them. As soon as the cassava grew, however, Manu discovered she was quite strong enough to go out to the farm with her mother and collect it. She did this without telling me, brought home some cassava, told me she had bought it, and made me pay for it. Not knowing how things stood, I went on for quite a while paying for my own cassava. Then one day a friend came along and told me, 'Look here, thy wife and her mother have already sold all the cassava on thy farm to so-and-so, and they are beginning to collect the money.' I was astonished. They had not said a word to me about it. So I rushed to the farm, and, true enough, there were signs of sale (reeds tied onto the cassava sticks) all over the place. Taking advantage of a period when I had been away to do some fishing, those two women had sold all my cassava without telling me. I quickly put an *amonle* (charm) on the farm to protect it, but it was too late. I also took out four of the knotted sticks, brought them back with me to town, went to my mother-in-law, and showed them to her. '*Me zebɛla,*' I said. 'Here is the evidence. Thou canst not deny that during my absence thou hast sold out all the cassava that belonged to me.'

"Instead of apologizing and trying to pacify me with some *nza* or some native gin, which indeed was the least a decent person should have done under the circumstances, Azane Akuba abused me and had the cheek to go herself to the district court and make summons against me. She said the farm was hers, that I had threatened her for exploiting it, and that I was on the point of poisoning her. The police believed her lies; they came around and handcuffed me and threw me into prison. The case was eventually settled here in Kɛngɛne, in Ndede's [the town *tufuhene*'s] compound. But to get out of prison I was forced to pay a fine of ¢28.

"I realized too late," concluded Nda, "that my brother had been right when he advised me to avoid Manu, because she was the daughter of a wicked woman. I see now I was wrong to have patience with her for so long, but the trouble was that I loved her, and besides I thought that if I divorced her this would lead me into still greater trouble. Did I have *sipe* against Manu and her kinswomen? Well, there would have been reasons enough, but it was not my *sipe* who caused Manu and the twin babies to die. Maybe it was Bokabo, the god, who punished her because of her duplicity. Or maybe the *amonle* I placed on the farm in the end stirred Bokabo into action. But as I repeat, it is not for me to find out how things really went. The matter is the concern of Manu's *abusua*."

Nda's report cannot be completely reconciled with Nyaku's. But perhaps this was to be expected. Perhaps Nda would recover from his present ailment. Perhaps the fetish god in the bush would sooner or later release young Manu's soul and allow her to join her clan ancestors in Hades. Perhaps some day the baby twins could be conceived and happily brought forth by some other woman, with Nda their proud father. But before we left him Nda said he was not sure that he would marry a third time.

12 / *The Little Boy Whose Soul Flew Away*

Eduku was the seventh child of a Catholic couple living in Elibo (or, as Aowin people pronounce it, Elubo), an inland village on the left bank of the great Tano River, at the northern border of the Nzemaland. His father, Ahoa Akatia, was a farmer of the Adahonle clan; his mother, Nda Ahɔba (Adwoba—that is, Monday-born—by her "soul name," hence familiarly called Ndadwoba by most people) was a Twea housewife in her early forties, who, judging by her present appearance, must have been an unusually attractive girl in her day.

Ahoa Akatia and Ndadwoba were what by Nzema standards may be called a happy couple. They met when both were very young and had been united in lawful wedlock (though not by church matrimony) ever since, giving birth to eight children, all of whom except Eduku were still alive. Their two eldest daughters were married with children, and they too lived in Elibo, so that Ndadwoba often had grandchildren of her own playing in her yard.

Eduku, a Thursday-born (Kwao), also lived and played with his siblings and his senior sisters' small children in his father's compound until the age of three. Then, some time in 1968, Ndadwoba brought forth her eighth and last child, a girl who was later named Aya. A few days later, after the end of the 1968 *kundum*, or New Year festival—that is, in mid-November—Ndadwoba received the visit of her "brother" Atobila Nyanzu from Ɛlonyi. He took a liking to little Eduku, and before leaving he asked his sister and her husband to let him take the child back with him to his own town.

Ahoa Akatia and Ndadwoba agreed. The request was a quite natural one, coming as it did from the child's maternal uncle; of all the forms of *adanelilɛ*, or child fostering, this is the most logical and approved one throughout Nzemaland. Nyanzu was Ndadwoba's brother not by the same mother but by the same great-grandmother. His branch of the lineage and Ndadwoba's were in a mutual succession relationship. Indeed, when Ndadwoba's real mother, Bɛbɛnwo Tanoɛ, had died several years earlier, she had actually been succeeded by Nyanzu's mother, Ɛzoma. Naturally, in due course of time, little Eduku could in turn be one of Nyanzu's potential successors and heirs.

So Eduku, sitting on his uncle's lap, left his parents' compound near the banks of the Tano and made the long truck ride to Ɛlonyi on the Atlantic coast.

Nyanzu lived in a pleasant, well-kept compound with his wife Avola and his younger children.[1] Four of these children were still at home when little Eduku came to stay: Ɛzoma (thus named after her paternal grandmother), then about thirteen, and later married and living in Abidjan; the two twins, Ahwia (female) and Kabenla (male), aged eight; and Anlima, a boy just a few months older than Eduku.

Eduku spent almost three years in this new environment, without ever returning to his native home. He was never to see his father again; the journey from Elibo is an expensive one, and Ahoa Akatia, busy with his farming, had no particular reason to come to the coast. But after three years, the boy's mother did come once. Even in the past, she sometimes used to travel to the coast in order to visit her relatives and to ask for medicines at the white man's hospital in Eikwe. On these occasions, she would stop in Ɛlonyi and stay with her brother Nyanzu for three or four days. Now she had one more reason to do so. When, in the first days of August 1971, she undertook the journey once more, she was eagerly looking forward to embracing at last her little son again. Surely he must have grown and changed a great deal, and she wondered a little anxiously whether he would recognize her; at that age, three years is a very long time. In this, her fears proved unjustified. Her child, though of course greatly changed and now a sturdy little boy of six, did appear to recognize her and was happy to be with her during all her stay. As usual, she remained three or four days at Nyanzu's place, then she left for home. Three days after her departure, Eduku died.

At the time, Nyanzu was temporarily away from home; as soon as his sister had left for Elibo, he had gone to Abidjan on business and to visit his young daughter now living in that city. So, although the general outline of the present case was provided by him, in conversations first with our common friend Mɔkɛ Mieza and then

The Rolling Game, or Round Is Happy

with me, the details about the events leading to the boy's death and following it immediately were supplied by Nyanzu's wife, Avola, and by the boy's mother. When the sad event occurred, I was in Nzemaland, not many miles away from Ɛlonyi; but a little boy's death is considered there such a minor occurrence that it was not reported to me at the time. When Mɔkɛ Mieza gave me a first summary account of the facts, I hastened to contact personally all the people connected with it that I could reach, as the case was one that moved me deeply.

Nyanzu himself, who had grown as fond of his little nephew as of his own children, was grieved and upset. On an earlier occasion, he told me, he had warned Ndadwoba against her coming to Ɛlonyi again. "The boy," he had explained to her, "is now used to living with us, considers us as his only true family, and is quite happy. If he sees you again, and realizes that you—and not Avola—are his real mother, he will suffer a severe shock, and will want to go away with you." But Ndadwoba disregarded her brother's advice.

Nyanzu's guess, alas, proved to be only too correct. Little Eduku was no doubt at first intrigued, and then delighted, by his mother's arrival, and he enjoyed her loving company as long as she stayed. When he understood she was about to leave, he did ask her to take him away with her, as Nyanzu had foreseen; perhaps he implored. When Ndadwoba said this was impossible, we can only guess what tumult of feelings her refusal roused in the child's mind and heart. But his yearning to follow his long-lost mother must have been very great, because we were told by Avola that, on the third night after Ndadwoba's departure, Eduku "flew" to her in an *ayɛne* way, thus unwittingly causing his own destruction. Being such a small boy, he could not possibly know that at the outskirts of most towns and villages the herbalist doctors are wont to place magic traps to catch the witches flying at night on their evil errands, or to cause their downfall. One of these traps, it is impossible to know exactly where, must have caught Eduku's little soul on its flight northward.

This, of course, was understood only later. We have a precise account by Avola, who at the time was the only adult person in the compound. After Ndadwoba's departure, Eduku had behaved quite normally, perhaps a little morose; he had asked her a few questions about his mother, but that was natural. On the third day, August 8, he had eaten, played, and talked in his usual way, went to sleep with the other children. Then during the night she suddenly heard him cry and shout. As she got up to see what was the matter, he complained of an acute stomach ache and started to vomit and defecate; the smell, Avola explained, was awful. First thing the next morning, as his condition worsened, she took him to the Eikwe hospital. When they stepped out of the truck there, she said, the boy was able to walk; he even carried his bucket into the hospital compound. He continued to be sick for a few hours, and the Dutch doctor visited him. The doctor shook his head. but made him lie down. At noon, Eduku died. The white doctor rushed again to his bedside and gave him two injections, but to no avail; Eduku, as the Nzema say, was completely dead.[2]

It was the white doctor, Avola told me, who said that the boy died because his soul tried to fly to his mother and was somehow knocked down.

They took the body back to Ɛlonyi and buried it unceremonially at once in the local cemetery, using a box rather than a real coffin, because he was such a small boy. The very next day Avola and Nyanzu, who had just returned from Abidjan, sent their second-born son, Nyanzu Ekyi to Elibo to inform Eduku's parents.[3] The young messenger was instructed not to give the bad news straight away or too bluntly, and he abided by his instructions. But when the two parents were on the way to Ɛlonyi, and before anyone had a chance to speak to them, Ndadwoba cried out, "No, it's not true that Eduku is sick. I know he is dead, because I saw it in a dream." This detail was reported to me later by Nyanzu, but there was, as I shall presently describe, further and direct confirmation of the dream.

The explanation offered for Eduku's death confronts the unbiased investigator with some problems. The faculty of magic flying at night is admittedly attributed to witches, but to no other class of human beings except possibly some very powerful herbalist-diviners who are known to "have an eye"—that is, suspected to be potential witches themselves. Could it be that little Eduku belonged to this dreaded category of beings? Had he given any previous sign of his ability to fly in spirit if not in body, or to perform other magical feats? Questioned on this point, both

Nyanzu and Avola said he had not. He was, as they described him, quite a normal little boy—boisterous, keen on playing with other children, occasionally mischievous. He had been too small to attend school yet, but Nyanzu was considering sending him there as soon as the schools opened in September—had the boy not died before. Did they ever find Eduku in a deep slumber, unable to wake up in the morning, as is known to happen to witches when their *sunsum* (spirit) is flying far away after having left the body during sleep? No, they said, never. Occasionally the child was fast asleep in the morning, and it took him some time to wake up; but then this is normal in children, and they had thought nothing of it. So, had the revelation of the sudden flight on that last fatal occasion come to them as a complete surprise? It had. Had they inquired further into this strange death, through the intermediary of a fetish priest or by consulting the *adunyi* oracle? No, they had not. Both being Christians—Nyanzu a Catholic and Avola a Methodist—they had no inclination for this sort of things. Besides, Avola argued, the white doctor himself had clearly understood and revealed the real cause of Eduku's death. Why not believe him, since he is a learned white man as well as a Christian? Also, considering that Eduku was just a child, there was no reason to inquire any further.

The doctor, of course, had never dreamed of giving such an explanation, nor had he said at the time in Avola's presence anything that might have been erroneously interpreted, and translated to her, in a similar sense. It was easy to check this point when I met him in Eikwe a few days later; it having been only one month earlier, in spite of the hundreds of cases to which he had to attend, the little boy's death at the hospital had made a deep impression on him. The doctor, a Dutchman with a fair knowledge of English, as is common to so many Dutch, was a newcomer to Ghana and to Africa in general, and knew little if anything at all about Akan beliefs in flying souls and witches. All he remembered having said on that occasion was that the relatives should not have waited to take the child to the hospital when he was on the point of death. His personal impression, as he told me in confidence, was that the case looked very much like one of poisoning. But he had naturally kept this to himself. A reliable diagnosis would have been possible only after an accurate postmortem, which under the circumstances he had neither the medical and technical means nor the legal permission to perform.

An interview with Ndadwoba in Elibo (15 September 1971) proved hardly worth the long journey on jerky dirt roads, as it provided scarcely any additional information; and Ahoa Akatia was out of town that day. Ndadwoba wished to make it clear she had no doubts that her brother Nyanzu had taken good care of Eduku all along and that no one was to blame for the boy's death. It was an act of God. She regretted she only had a single chance to see her little son in three years. But then she had heavy farm- and housework to do all the time, and she had her husband and the other children to look after. Parting with her own child in the first place had been painful, but it was the proper thing to do. It would have been absurd and wrong to interfere with an uncle's legitimate claim to take care of his nephew and to bring him up in his own home. Indeed, another of her children, Ebahua, a boy of about eight, was happily staying with another brother of hers, Bilaka, the Twea *abusua kpanyinli* (lineage head) in Ngalekyi.

When she heard that Eduku had suffered from acute stomach trouble before he died, she remembered he had been subject to similar crises during his early childhood—only, of course, he had then recovered. Had any empirical remedy been possible on that last fatal occasion, her brother's wife, Avola, would no doubt have known it and resorted to it. Though not formally a *ninsinli*, she had in her environment a well-earned renown as an expert in medicine and herbs of all sorts.

Ndadwoba also confirmed the detail of her prophetic dream, but in a somewhat different and surely more accurate version than that provided a few days earlier by Nyanzu. During her long return journey from Ɛlonyi to Elibo (6 August 1971), she had stopped overnight in Etikɔbɔ no. 1. While she was asleep, she had seen a creature like an *anwuma bɔvolɛ* (a winged angel) flying toward her; but it had vanished suddenly or changed into something else, as happens in dreams, without speaking a single word, so it had not occurred to her that it could be Eduku. At any rate, as she had just left her child in perfect health a few hours earlier, at the time she had not attributed any special meaning to this dream.

Asked the direct question, whether she really believed that Eduku's illness and death had been brought about in the way suggested by Avola and Nyanzu, Ndadwoba hesitated and appeared to be embarrassed. More precisely, she said no at first, yes later. It is quite possible, as was afterward pointed out to me by one of my Nzema friends acquainted with the case, that Ndadwoba was nervous or even afraid throughout our talk. The visit of a white man to a small out-of-the-way place like Elibo is no doubt a most unusual event. Though I had taken pains to explain the totally harmless and friendly nature of my call, she may have entertained the fear of being in some obscure way involved or held responsible for the sad event that the unknown stranger had come a long way to discuss. She surely also regretted that her husband was away from Elibo on that day, leaving her to answer all the questions.

"It may be," Ndadwoba said, "that the child missed me very much at first, when he was first taken to Ɛlonyi. That was to be expected. But when I saw him again last month, he appeared to be quite happy with the other children in his uncle's compound. He recognized me even after such a long time, and did ask me to take him away with me when he realized I was leaving. But he did not insist much and did not cry when I bid him farewell. How could I have guessed that his secret yearning to follow me was so great? It is a fact of common knowledge, of course, that children's souls can occasionally fly away in an *ayɛne* way just as those of adults. But what happened in Eduku's case," she concluded, "I just cannot tell."

Ndadwoba, however, was very firm on one point. Neither she nor Ahoa Akatia had ever considered asking a fetish priest, or a professional diviner, to give them the true version of their child's death, as most other people would naturally have done. They were Christians and did not have much faith in such things.

Like her brother Nyanzu, Ndadwoba courageously accepted her bereavement. At this stage, it would have been pointless to tell her that the accepted explanation of little Eduku's death was based on what was, on Avola's part, at the same time a deliberate lie and (to European eyes) a naive miscalculation—that is, attributing to the white doctor the story of Edulu's soul's fatal flight.

Taking leave from Ndadwoba, I casually quoted to her the words written some years ago by one of our European poets: "There are more things in heaven and earth. . . ." She frowned slightly.

She had not heard this sentence before, but judging from what she was taught as a Christian, she didn't think it was true. "Anyhow," she added as my foot was already on her threshold, "What is the meaning of that quaint word you have just used, 'a poet'?"

13 / The Unremitting Goddess

Alua was born in her father's compound at Ezinlibo, on the coast of Western Nzema, not far from Half Assini. She traveled and worked during her lifetime in different parts of Nzemaland, but the place she really felt she belonged to, and where she returned as a widow when her second husband died, was Alenrenzule, also along the same coast. Here was the compound of the *abusua kpanyinli* of her own lineage within the great Twea clan, the lineage head who also happened to be her uncle. The compound had been founded ages ago by one of her Twea grandfathers called Kwame Agyiba. It was here she wished to end her days, a proud old Twea woman on pure Twea soil.

But God Almighty had in his inscrutable wisdom decided otherwise. Alua's fate was to die, at the age of sixty-seven, in somebody else's house, in a place with which she was never familiar and did not like, the victim of two different fetish gods and some ghosts she had offended. The place was Mbem in the interior of the country, far from the sea; the date was 2 April 1971.

While she was alive, she had two husbands.[1] The first one, to whom she was married by her parents before she reached puberty (a typical *beyia ye*, or promissory pact case), was a Nvavile man from Ezinlibo named Amihyia. The second, called Nyamekɛ, was an Alɔnwɔba from Alawule. She had four children by her first husband: Awua (male), Mɔkɛ Ɛmenla (female), Aboagye (male), and Adɛla (female), all of whom but the last died during her lifetime. She also had one son by her second husband, named Amonle Kaku after his father's father Amonle, who also died before her. Her full siblings of both sexes were also dead, as well as her two husbands, so that during the illness that was to take her to the grave the only relative to assist her was her one surviving daughter, Adɛla. This was doubly right, because the mother's illness happened to be closely connected with events concerning her daughter.

It should be stated at the outset that Alua was a church-attending Catholic.[2] She had even wanted to marry her second husband, also a Catholic, by holy matrimony after their child was born. But they met with some minor difficulties in the arrangements for the ceremony, they waited too long, and then Nyamekɛ died. Her daughter Adɛla was also baptized as a Catholic, but admitted she was not nearly as pious as her late mother. In order to understand Alua's case properly, it is necessary to get acquainted with a few facts concerning this daughter of hers. When we met her in 1971, Adɛla was a woman in her forties; but her constant influence on her mother's destiny long antedates these times.

Way back in the mid-1940s, when Alua was still a young woman, living with her first husband, Amihyia, in Ezinlibo, she and Amihyia arranged to marry their last-born daughter to a young Mafole man of the same town called Bile. At the time, Adɛla was little more than a child; her breasts had not yet developed, and she had not passed her first menses, so she was still looking to her mother for support and advice, and obeying her father's orders. At the same time she respected the husband her parents had given her, and she tried to serve him as dutifully as her young age allowed.

Now, it happened that Bile's mother Tayiba took a strong dislike to her daughter-in-law. She thought and said that Adɛla was a badly brought up and stupid girl, still unable to do any proper housework and hopeless in the kitchen, where she spoiled all the food she cooked—by no means a suitable wife for her son. The truth was that Bile was very much in love with his child wife and spent on her most of the money he had been giving to his mother as long as he had been a bachelor. Tayiba, who shared the young couple's living quarters, thus found herself stranded with more housework to do and less money to spend, and she became envious. Whatever the causes of her grudge and hatred, which we shall never know for certain because she is now dead, Tayiba "took" her daughter-in-law to a *bozonle* to be killed. Indeed, if we are to believe Adɛla's suspicions, Tayiba went as far as to take even her own son to the same god, because in the early days of their marriage Bile was often sick without any apparent reason.

Surely because of this wicked curse, during her first pregnancy Adɛla felt very ill and almost died during her delivery. Her mother, who had naturally assisted her, took her as soon as possible to a *kɛnlamo* (Muslim medicine man), who found out very clearly what was happening to her. He revealed that the *bozonle* causing the trouble was Edena Adwoba (a female) located in the stream where the Ezinlibo women fetch their water, and he succeeded in saving the lives of both Adɛla and the baby. The baby was a little girl, later named Nda after one of Bile's many mothers, who was still alive and well. Indeed, the clever *kɛnlamo* appeased the goddess so thoroughly at the time that, when three years later Adɛla brought forth her second child (another girl, named Bɔsa), the delivery was easy and almost painless.

Some time after Bɔsa's birth, however, Adɛla was very sick once more. But the *kɛnlamo* had left in the meanwhile for a distant place. So this time Alua took her daughter to a diviner called Adwo, a Nzema woman from Alenrenzule who had learned her profession among the Anyi of the Ivory Coast and had made quite a good name for herself in a large area of Western Nzema. But popular fame is not always matched by efficiency and success in every venture. Adwo performed her *adunyi* operations twice without discovering the cause of this illness, and Adɛla continued to suffer. So they tried an Ezinlibo priestess, Manye, a quiet woman who asked for incredibly modest fees. Not only was she more successful but she provided a surprising revelation. It was still the same goddess, Edena Adwoba, who was causing the sickness, but not at all with the intention of punishing Adɛla, even less of killing her. The goddess was merely trying to make the young woman understand that she wished Adɛla to become her mouthpiece and priestess.

At the time, feeling sick as she did and thinking only of the quickest way to put an end to her suffering, Adɛla let the goddess know that she accepted, whereupon she promptly recovered. But her assent had been given half-heartedly. Being a Christian she never really considered becoming a fetish priestess, and her mother opposed the project even more strongly. So, though having pledged herself to the *bozonle,* she put off indefinitely the day when she would actually begin to operate as her priestess. And without ever showing herself, the goddess watched, noticed, and kept record of everything in her superhuman memory.

Years passed, and the time came when Adɛla's first-born daughter, Nda, approached puberty and married. Like her

Fetish priestess during her ritual dance on a pile-supported platform in Nzulezo

grandmother and her mother before her, Nda also married when she was barely thirteen. At her first delivery, she brought forth a girl, and the goddess killed the baby almost at once. Nda's second child was a boy, who had reached the age of beginning to walk when the *bozonle* killed him, too. Within the same segment of that particular Twea lineage, this was the fourth generation that the forest deity Edena Adwoba was punishing, and the Ezinlibo people began to wonder at her relentless perseverance.

Then it was the turn of Adɛla's second daughter, Bɔsa, to marry and have a child. Her child, too, fell sick. This was in 1969.

Bɔsa's husband, an Alenrenzule man called Kwasi Bendɔbenli, was naturally very worried and took his young wife and child to an Eikwe *kɔmenle* called Kanwa Badwo, whom he knew and trusted. This woman interrogated her gods and learned from them that it was once again Edena Adwoba who was causing the baby to be sick, just as she had brought about the death of Nda's two children. Measures were taken, and thanks to Kanra Badwo's farsightedness this time the baby's life was spared. But the goddess was not satisfied, and a couple of months later she attacked Alua once more.

Since her second husband had died, as already mentioned, Alua had in the meanwhile been living for a few years in the old family compound at Alenrenzule. But some time in 1967, owing to a farmland shortage in the coastal area, she had moved by herself to a small inland village called Asɛmpɛyɛ, between Bɔnyɛle Junction and Takinta, where free land was still plentiful. It was here that her sickness began. Adɛla and Bile Bozoma (one of Alua's classificatory sisters, now living with Adɛla) remembered the details very well. It started with pains all over her body. Shortly afterward, an ugly boil appeared on her waist, her stomach began to swell, and the swelling gradually spread to all of her right leg, so that during the last few weeks of her life she was nearly paralyzed. At first, she had tried hospital treatment with the German sisters in Eikwe. But Kanra Badwo had once more been consulted, and since she had ascertained that the cause of Alua's ailments was the same one that had caused the death of her great-grandchildren years before, it was obvious that the white man's medicine could be of little use.

Soon it became evident that the disease was becoming more and more serious and that Alua had few chances, if any, of ever being able to do farm work any more. Her daughter decided there was no point either in letting her return to Asɛmpɛyɛ or in allowing her to remain at the Catholic hospital. The limited number of beds and the long waiting list of other patients were already making the white sisters nervous. So Adɛla took the sick old woman to her own new compound at Mbem, on the main inland highway; Adɛla had been living there for the past two years, after having divorced her first husband Bile and marrying her second husband, an Adahonle farmer by the name of Francis E. Anwonzo, who was ten years her junior. It was in Mbem, as said at the outset, that a few weeks later Alua died.

Most of the information hitherto related was given to me directly by Adɛla in the course of two long conversations I had with her in Mbem in September of that same year, 1971; Bile Bozoma, one of Adɛla's mothers, who was also present, supplied some minor details. In Adɛla's mind there seemed to be no doubt that the last fatal illness of her late mother had been inflicted by that same goddess, Adena Adwoba, who had already caused so much misery in their lineage and who had never forgiven Alua for preventing Adɛla from serving as her priestess. Gods do not like their invitations to be refused; in other words, a god's invitation is really an order that cannot be disobeyed. So Adɛla's explanation sounded logical.

There were, however, other alternative and conflicting hypotheses about the causes of Alua's demise. One, which my Mbem informants had not mentioned, had originated in Alenrenzule. It had been accepted and repeated by the inhabitants of that town, among them Ɛba—daughter of one of Alua's deceased full brothers—who had reported it to our friend Mɔkɛ Mieza before she left Ghana to live in the Ivory Coast with her husband. It concerned Alua's ancestral compound in Alenrenzule. It is well known that ghosts of deceased clan members retain a lasting interest not only in their living descendants but in the family compound they founded or simply inhabited while living. This is why they are always remembered and, if possible, called aloud by their personal names whenever a libation is poured within the compound. Though they are reputed to dwell in Hades, far away, they are still informed of what goes on among the living, and they are hurt when they see that the ancestral home—the *mgbanyinli sua*—is decaying or abandoned. In the present case, Alua was closely linked, as said at the beginning, with the compound of her Twea forefathers. She had come to live there as a young woman with her full brother, many years ago, when their father had died, but when her uncle, the lineage head, was still alive. She had returned there as a widow. When her brother died in turn, leaving children, all of whom had migrated to the Ivory Coast, Alua had been left alone in charge of the old compound. She may have neglected the repairs to the roofs and the fences because she was getting old and had little money. If in the end she had definitely forsaken the place, it had admittedly been out of necessity; an aged and lonely widow sometimes has to forgo her sentiments if she has to work to make a living. But it may well be that the ghosts were offended all the same by the state of disrepair and decay of their old home and contributed to make Alua sick. Even Adɛla, with whom I later discussed this hypothesis, admits that this is possible. (After Alua's death, incidentally, the old compound was inhabited once more and properly looked after. Kwasi, a classificatory Twea son of Alua's by her late junior sister, Nyamekɛ, came to settle there with his wife and children.)

A third and last possible cause of Alua's sad fate is related to the last phase of her life at Asɛmpɛyɛ. Unfortunately we have no direct information on what actually happened there, because none of her kinsfolk lived with her during that period. What follows is drawn from incomplete bits of news casually given to her sister Bile Bozoma by Alua herself in Mbem during the last days of her life.

At Asɛmpɛyɛ, Alua had reached an arrangement with another unnamed woman of the Twea clan (but belonging to a different lineage) for working on a small portion of a farm. In spite of her age, Alua was still strong and clever at farming. When she was temporarily given this bit of farm in the bush, she set fire to the plot to clear it for cultivation, but it did not burn well, and the local people said, "Alua will never be able to get anything out of this land." But Alua tried hard, she set fire to the bush a second time, tilled the land, planted her cassava and plantain, weeded with untiring energy, and eventually—much to the neighbors' surprise and envy—she was able to give a handsome part to the other Twea woman who had lent her the land and to make a good profit herself.

So the neighbors, out of envy, were "speaking badly" of her as they walked through the bush on the way to their farms.

When Alua fell sick and consulted a local Asɛmpɛyɛ fetish priestess, this woman told her that some god had overheard these criticisms and taken action against her. But she was unable to reveal the god's name; all she could say was that it was a fetish deity of the area where Alua had been farming. At any rate, Bile Bozoma and Adɛla commented, the action of this Asɛmpɛyɛ *bozonle* may have been only subsidiary. When he came to attack Alua, he met Edena Adwoba, the goddess who was already contriving to destroy the old woman. Edena must have said to her divine colleague, "Aha, I know this woman well. I have had a grudge against her for many years. Now I will gladly assist thee in killing her for good." So anyone can see that the action of the second *bozonle*, whatever its name, was only the last straw in finishing an already condemned victim. The uncertain reports concerning this third hypothetical explanation leave another doubt: Was it the neighbors' gossip, or the grudge of the Twea landowner who had leased the plot to Alua, that set the unnamed Asɛmpɛyɛ fetish god on to Alua?[3]

At the end of Alua's funerals, the Twea matrons assembled and according to custom nominated her two successors, Adwo from Ɛlɛna and Ama Ɛba from Ezinlibo.[4] Never having been a rich woman in her lifetime, Alua surely had not left anything of great value, except a few old clothes and trinkets—no gold jewels, it seemed. Not being directly interested, Adɛla pretended she did not know what her late mother's box contained.[5] It was the correct answer for her to give. The box had been packed and locked, quite possibly in Adɛla's presence, but the key remained with the local Twea lineage head until the day of the official reopening, which would take place in the presence of the successors some time in April 1972. It would be a gross lack of civility to mention or discuss its contents before that date.

As for Adɛla, she by then realized that she could not escape the fate of becoming Edena Adwoba's priestess. It would plainly be dangerous at this stage to continue to refuse. Asked whether she already considered herself a real *kɔmenle*, she shook her head and laughed shyly. She did not yet dance or lead *ahɔne*, she said after a moment, but she admitted she did join the fetish dances and on such occasions was sometimes possessed by her goddess. Her outward attire, her special beads, and above all her striking face painting in sinuous stripes were at any rate worthy of an accomplished priestess.

Though already a grandmother, Adɛla was at that time still young enough to bring forth children, and Anwonzo was a strong and healthy young man. Yet they had no offspring. Perhaps this was once more because of Edena Adwoba, this unremitting goddess, who claimed for herself all of her favorite servant's time and attention. It is quite true that children interfere with a full priestess's profession, Adɛla remarked, so she had not asked the goddess to give her any. But there would be another favor she would ask her, as soon as she became a fully fledged *kɔmenle*: to assist her in retrieving her mother's soul from the bush where it was still held in captivity by the gods.

14 / The Promiscuous Bride

Misfortunes, diseases, and accidents may have manifold causes, as experience has taught us. The first and main one, as Christians assure us, is the will of God Almighty, which nobody dares to question or modify. But, of course, there are others, more easily checked and detected, that may often be controlled and even neutralized by appropriate human action, such as punishment by a fetish god, an offended ghost's wrath, a goblin's mischievousness, and so on. Among the causes directly depending on human behavior is one that is seldom mentioned in the course of diviners' inquiries but that surely represents a potential source of danger in several cases. This is *munzule*, which Europeans translate as "scandal," "abomination," or more simply but less correctly "mishap." Yaba's case is an eloquent, if unfortunately incomplete, illustration of the dangerous forces it can unleash.

Yaba was a fifteen-year-old Twea girl from Etikɔbɔ no. 1, belonging to the matrilineage segment of Adukyi, the local Twea lineage head. Like many other Nzema couples, Yaba's parents migrated a few years earlier to the frontier area in the Tano Valley, where good farmland was still abundant. They took their daughter with them, and settled in a small village called Kwabile; they quarreled; they divorced. Soon after, when Yaba was fourteen, she married a young man from the Mafole clan called Nyɔnra, a palm-wine tapper whom she met in the village. She decided she and her bridegroom would go and live with her mother, who had remarried in the meanwhile. Her mother had settled in the comfortable compound of her second husband, Menlivolɛ Awie, an Ezohile farmer, one of the many Nzemas from Ghana who had made their home in Kwabile and other villages of the great Tano basin. As there was plenty of room and life was cheap in the area, Menlivolɛ's elderly father Akatia, a widower also belonging to the Ezohile clan, had joined his son.[1] Young Nyɔnra took a second wife, Nyamekɛ. They all happily shared the same compound.

Now, Nyɔnra the palm-wine tapper for professional reasons

spent most of his time far out in the forest, and also Yaba's mother was often far away from home cultivating her farm. So the young girl often remained in the compound alone with her stepfather and started having a love affair with him. Then, when Menlivolɛ also left the house for his errands, she began another love affair with old Akatia. In a matter of a few hours, it was murmured, while waiting for her young husband to return from the forest, she would have intercourse with both in quick succession.

In a tiny village such as Kwabile these things cannot be kept secret for long, and soon people were gossiping. The situation was naturally much worse than ordinary adultery (*awuvolɛvalɛ*); being lawfully married to her mother, Menlivolɛ Awie was *egya* (father) to Yaba, even though not related to her by consanguinity. Consequently, Akatia was *nenya* (grandfather) to her. But apart from the girl's formal (albeit nonblood) kinship closeness to both men, the fact of having simultaneous sexual affairs with a father and his son is in itself abominable. This is because the two men share the same blood, not counting the fact that in this particular case they were also members of the same lineage. So this was plainly a case of incest—scandal and abomination on a double count.

My old friend and informant from Etikɔbɔ no. 1, James E. Quarm, knew all these people very well. At the time he, too, was working on his Kwabile farms and lived in a compound practically next door to theirs. So he naturally heard all the gossip and all the neighbors' comments, and he wondered what this incredible situation would lead to.

He did not have to wait long. One afternoon, when Quarm was sleeping in his house, he woke up at the sound of women shouting and running. Yaba's co-wife, Nyamekɛ, rushed into his bedroom, asking him to go out at once to the bush and look for Nyɔnra, because Yaba had suddenly been taken ill and was dying. Quarm promptly complied, ran to the forest area where he knew Nyɔnra would be tapping his palm wine, found him, and quickly returned with him to the village. Here they found Yaba stretched on her mat, unable to stand up or even sit upright. She complained of feeling cold in the waist, but at any rate she was still alive. Surrounded by excited and chattering female neighbors, they carried her down to the river bank, laid her in the bottom of a

Young priestess-apprentice with figurine of her tutelary deity

canoe, and paddled as rapidly as they could to a nearby village on the right (Ivory Coast) bank of the Tano. There lived a famous fetish priestess called Ɛkɔla.[2]

When Yaba was carried almost lifeless into Ɛkɔla's compound, Ɛkɔla poured a libation to her gods, calling them loudly by their personal names and even absurdly threatening them with death if they did not come at once, practically swearing at them. (It was a naive way, Quarm remarked to me, of impressing the public.) She soon showed signs of entering a state of trance, started shaking all over and mumbling "mm-mm-mm." Presently her voice changed altogether, and the gods spoke through her. They revealed with surprising accuracy the true causes of Yaba's sudden sickness, which we have already mentioned. The actual names of the men involved in the scandal were, of course, not openly mentioned. But all the people present knew only too well to whom the gods were referring.

The priestess's gods also revealed that purification rites had already been performed by kinsfolk of Yaba's lineage "at home" (by which they surely meant Etikɔbɔ no. 1, though they did not mention the name of the town), but this was not enough.[3] They would have to repeat afresh in Kwabile, where the scandal had actually happened. Therefore Yaba, or somebody for her, would have to provide one fowl, two eggs, a fee of ¢0.80, one large leaf of tobacco, and one bottle of schnapps, in addition to the one that the consultants had already presented to Ɛkɔla. She would then offer all these to the local gods, who would in turn reveal the required forms of purification. For the time being, Ɛkɔla could only suggest some simple first-aid remedy that would bring temporary relief to Yaba, but surely it would not cure her. However, the worst part of Yaba's crisis seemed to be over when, the consultation being concluded, the men carried the ailing girl back to the canoe and returned to Kwabile.

Almost immediately after this visit to the priestess, James E. Quarm had to leave the banks of the Tano to join me and my assistants in Beyin, according to our previous arrangements. So, apart from the general assurance that Yaba had not actually died, he could not provide direct information on the further developments of her case. Some of the formalities, however, can be guessed. According to custom, some of the herbs used in purification rites of this type were likely to be *ezuvinli*, *tadeɛ*, and *nyinanyina*. First, these herbs are pounded together in a mortar or ground on a stone. They are then mixed with water, some *ewuole* (white clay), and blood of a sheep required as an offering to the gods. (For a serious case such as this one, two sheep would probably have to be sacrificed, paid for by the girl's lecherous stepfather and grandfather.) The sinful girl would be anointed with the mixture, and some of it will be placed on her tongue to swallow. The rest would be sprinkled around the village by the priestess herself, pronouncing the appropriate formulas. *Ahɔne* would then be danced, to summon the gods again and to inquire from them whether they are satisfied and consider the scandal finally removed.

15 / The Wrong Sacrifice

It is normal that gods—the severe guardians of social order, morals, and justice—should punish mortals for their faults, sins, and mistakes, or for transgressing the divine orders and rules. But that they should chastise in a similar way—by accidents, diseases, and death—their own priests and priestesses, as a rule initially chosen and inspired by the gods themselves as their own faithful servants, their trusted interpreters and mouthpieces over the years and sometimes for a whole lifetime, is indeed a rare and almost unexplainable occurrence. It leaves even the unbiased observer bewildered and incredulous.

Nevertheless, the case of Kanra Amonle provides us with the well-documented evidence of such an exceptional event, obtained not by indirect hearsay as often happens but thanks to the circumstantial testimony of reliable informants. For reasons both of close kinship and residence, these informants were intimately connected with the woman in question, her real daughter Afo, and Afo's husband, Mɔkɛ Mieza.

Kanra Amonle was born in Beyin circa 1920. Her parents had several children, but all the ones born before her died very young. This is why her father named her Kanra ("slave"), in order to mislead the evil agencies that had destroyed her infant siblings before her. They would spare her when they learned from her personal given name that she was no more than a humble, worthless little thing. The second name, Amonle, was added not merely to distinguish her from the many other children named Kanra (for the same reasons) in Beyin and in the whole country but in thankfulness to the god Amonle, who had given her to her parents and protected her during the first two years of life.

She was married twice in her lifetime and brought forth nine children. But the data of her family life, dutifully recorded and elsewhere published,[1] can here be overlooked, because both her husbands died before her and of her children only Afo—her first born—is relevant in the present context, having lived next door to her mother until the day of Kanra's death in Ngelekazo, on 23 July 1970.

Kanra's experiences with the fetish gods marked her entire life. Her very birth and survival as a baby, at least in her parents' conviction, were because of one of these gods, Amonle.[2] At the time of her first pregnancy, some unnamed female enemy "gave" her to a *bozonle* to be killed. In the attempt to save her life, her family sent her to a Twelve Apostles priestess at Adoabo Ahonlezo (inland of Adoabo or Atuabo, the capital of Eastern Nzema). This priestess cured her so well that, by the time little Afo was born, Kanra was again in perfect health and a devout follower of the Twelve Apostles sect—also called the "Water Carriers," or *awa*, church.

But when her first husband died and she remarried in Ngelekazo, another envious person "gave" her once more to a fetish god. This time, the god—who happened to be Ngeleka-Ngeleka, the stream *bozonle* after whom the town was named—instead of killing her, as he had been asked to do, took a liking for her. He spoke through her mouth when she was ill and delirious, thus making it clear that he would like her to become his priestess. So, with her second husband Ayeba's consent, Kanra eventually became the god's *kɔmenle*, and she held this position for the rest of her life—that is to say, for almost thirty years. The Twelve Apostles people were disappointed, but recognized that such a strong vocation could not be resisted.

Apart from the main god who had chosen her, Kanra also served (and spoke for) other gods in his retinue, especially Nyanya, the wife of Ngeleka-Ngeleka, and Amɛnla, the goddess of the area in the bush north of Ngelekazo, where her husband, Ayeba, made his *pɛlɛ* or rice farm. Each of these deities has his or her *kyibadeɛ*, or food taboo, from which Kanra was obliged to abstain.[3] Ngeleka-Ngeleka has *komu* (monkey—good food but difficult to find nowadays in the coastal zone of Ghana) and *ɛbɔ*, a long fish with many bones that luckily is not very good to eat. Nyanya has *tomandese* (tomatoes, as the name shows, a foreign food introduced by the white man), so Kanra could not use these vegetables in her sauces. And Amɛnla has *bote*, the rat—a pity, because in her youth Kanra was very fond of rats, the meat of which is so tasty.

To counterbalance, as it were, these alimentary interdicts, each deity has a favorite food. This preference must obviously be memorized by worshippers when offering sacrifices. For the correct understanding of Kanra's fate, it is important to remember that Ngeleka-Ngeleka's favorite food is dog.[4]

The health troubles that in the end were to bring Kanra to her grave originated, oddly enough, from political causes. For many years an influential member of the Twea clan in Awiabo, called Ogonlo, had been competing and intriguing for the Ngelekazo stool. This stool was already occupied by another Twea man in the face of stubborn, if intermittent, opposition by the Ezohile people who claimed priority in the foundation of that township. As an additional precaution in view of the fulfilment of his ambitions, Ogonlo deemed it wise to promise a generous offering to the leading Ngelekazo deity in case he eventually obtained the desired stool. The cow being by far the most expensive animal in the market, he decided he would present the god with a cow. More than once, when pouring a libation to the gods in public, he allegedly pledged himself to do so.

In the course of time, Ogonlo was in fact elected to the Ngelekazo stool, on which he sat for many years, having taken the name of Nana Andualu Kwagya II.[5] In his new lordly position, he naturally went on pouring libations to the gods on all official occasions, but the allegedly promised cow was never sacrificed. As years passed and the chief grew to be old, he became seriously ill. In her capacity as the main local god's priestess, Kanra Amonle was summoned to the palace. She invoked Ngeleka-Ngeleka, and the god came upon her. Through her mouth he addressed the ailing chief: "When thou wert competing for the stool, thou promised me a cow. Now that thou hast won the litigation, why dost thou not give it to me?" The chief denied ever having made such a promise, but Kanra insisted, and in the end Nana Andualu gave in.[6] For one thing, he was suffering and afraid that disregarding the *kɔmenle*'s words might cause the sickness to grow more serious. Besides, rumors were being reported to him; the townspeople were murmuring that his refusal to offer the cow could only mean that the chief was either poverty-stricken or a miser—not flattering alternatives for a proud chief of the noble Twea clan.

The king of western Nzema near the *Nyangonle* shrine in the courtyard of his Beyin palace, 1954

So Nana Andualu Kwagya II provided the cow. When the proper time came for honoring the gods (their "purification," as the vernacular has it), after the end of the 1968 *kundum* festival, the animal was finally sacrificed. It was Kanra Amonle, in her role of Ngeleka-Ngeleka's main priestess, who offered it to the god.

The local people gasped at the sight of the cow. It was surely a sign of the chief's wealth and generosity, but also an entirely new feature in the customary ceremony, which takes place every year near the god's shrine—a hut at the edge of the coconut groves near the beach, at the eastern end of the town. Usually, the sacrifices are one dog and two fowls. Also, of course, these are the occasional offerings brought by individuals who have recently benefited by the god's favors or protection. But even farsighted people could not foresee the consequences of this novelty.

About two months after the public sacrifice, Kanra fell ill. At first she suffered from an eye disease and gradually became blind. This limited her professional activities, as she was obliged to spend most of her time in her compound. She could no longer dance *ahɔne*, and she now seldom visited the god's shrine near the beach, though once in a while she would ask some children to lead her there. But she continued to make occasional indoor offerings of fowl to Ngeleka-Ngeleka if asked by the faithful. And for the rest she was still able to do some simple cooking and housework. But soon other ailments set in. She felt pains in her stomach and in her whole body and was obliged to stay in bed for long weeks. Three of her daughters took turns in looking after her—Afo, Buluma, and Asamoa, who for this purpose left for a while her husband and children in the Ivory Coast. Treatment was supervised by the reputed Ngelekazo herbalist doctor Ɛzonle Kanra, as well as by several priests and priestesses. These were Kanra's colleagues, who used to visit her frequently, occasionally presenting her with medicines. In spite of all these attentions, after two years of intermittent sickness she died, on 23 July 1970, and was buried in the Ngelekazo cemetery. By that time, everybody in town was convinced that her misfortunes and her death had been directly caused by Ngeleka-Ngeleka, incensed by the wrong sacrifice she had offered him.

However, the circumstances were not altogether clear, and some people were left perplexed. Kanra should have known—

indeed, she doubtless knew—that a cow was not agreeable as a sacrifice to the god she had served for so many years; why she should have accepted such an offering, or even worse solicited it, remains a mystery. Even more strange is that the request should have been made by the god himself, if one supposes—as Afo's report would lead us to believe—that the priestess had really spoken inspired by him in a state of trance. If, on the other hand, Kanra had spoken on that occasion in a state of normal full consciousness, the responsibility for the blunder would be entirely hers. Perhaps the chief's sincerity in denying that he had ever pledged himself to offer a cow would be vindicated. Now that both Kanra Amonle and Nana Andualu II are no longer in this world, the truth will never be known.[7]

In any case, Ɛzonle Kanra, who as medicine man and diviner was an expert on these matters, thought that Kanra Amonle's blunder was a very serious one; the misfortunes that afflicted her afterward were no more than a just retribution. Had he been in town at the time, he told me, he would have used all his influence to prevent such a sacrifice from ever being offered. Unfortunately, when these events happened, he was traveling. The same judgment, he added, was also given by Kaku, the Ewe herbalist who lived in the interior, when he was consulted by Mɔkɛ Mieza and other relatives of the deceased.

For the sake of completeness, it should be added that the accepted explanation of Kanra's death, as just given, was not the only one. A different, or at least subsidiary, one was offered by Kyɛkyɛ, the Twelve Apostles priestess of Canaan Garden in Kelisane (Krisan). She was another of the expert healers consulted by Kanra's relatives at some stage of her long illness. Kyɛkyɛ disclosed that several years earlier, when Kanra was working on a groundnut farm near an inland stream called Ekyia Ɛkɛra, she had had a quarrel with a woman working on an adjoining plot.[8] The local god, also known by the name Ekyia Ɛkɛra, who had overheard the dispute, took the side of this unnamed woman and strove to punish Kanra. Such an explanation is surely neither original nor easily disprovable. Women farming together almost inevitably start some quarrel, which is regularly overheard by some local *bozonle*; one hears of dozens of such cases. Kanra's relatives and friends didn't deny that this version might contain some truth.

But they still hold that the main cause of her death lay in the episode of the wrong sacrifice.

Kanra Amonle's first successor, a classificatory sister of hers called Adwoba Ekyi, who came to live in Ngelekazo in her father's compound, did not inherit the office of the local god's cult, because he is the god for the whole town, not just for their *abusua*. It was entirely up to Ngeleka-Ngeleka himself to show his preference for the man or woman who he wanted to succeed Kanra as his caretaker. He had not yet done so when I last heard.

16 / *The Widow Who Asked to Die*

Ahwia Akuba, one of James E. Quarm's mothers, was married as a young girl to an Azanwule farmer from her own town, Etikɔbɔ no. 1, which is an important junction center on the main inland road crossing the whole Nzema country from east to west. Akuba's husband was called Nyamekɛ Nenyane. They lived happily together for many years, but after a miscarriage Akuba suffered the first year, they never had any children. The ablest herbalist doctors and the most renowned fetish priests were consulted, but to no avail. When Nyamekɛ Nenyane died, around thirty years before the time of this story, Akuba did not remarry. Whether her husband's three successors and other men failed to ask her, considering she had proved to be sterile, or whether she herself discouraged the potential suitors, is difficult to assess after such a long time. In any case, she remained single ever since, accepting once and for all the lonely fate of a *mota*, a person with no progeny.

Of course, Akuba did have several children in a different sense. Among the Nzema, all the sons and daughters of a woman's brothers and sisters are called and considered that woman's children, *mralɛ*; she refers to them all as *memra*, "my children." It is a wise convention, which conversely allows a person to have several mothers. Thus James E. Quarm, the son of one of Akuba's sisters, referred to Akuba as "my aunt" when speaking to me in English, but as "my mother" when speaking in Nzema.

In the last week of August 1971, one of these "children" died at Menzezɔ. This man, called Ezane and aged about forty, was the son of Akuba's full brother Ebukɛle and of a Mafole woman by the name of Bomo, hence technically a son to Akuba. He had been a cripple for most of his life, since he fell from a tall raffia palm as a lad while tapping palm wine. Indeed, he had been lucky to live as long as he did. He was badly injured by that fall, and had it not been for a little boy who had accompanied him and who ran for help at once, Ezane would have died then and there all alone in the bush miles away from any living person. But Ezane recovered, and, though lame ever since, he lived long enough to marry, have three children, and become at one time the Menzezɔ *tufuhene*, chief of the local gunners, as the Europeans would say. In the last phase of his life he had divorced his wife and was living with his own widowed mother, Bomo.

As soon as the news of her nephew's death reached her, Akuba naturally left at once for Menzezɔ to attend the funeral. As she was looking at her relative laid in state on his deathbed, she started wailing. In an outburst of grief, she called out the dead man's name loudly, urging him to speed to Hades and tell her dead siblings and the other lineage ghosts there to come and take her, too, because she had had enough of this cruel life.

It is disrespectful and definitely contrary to custom to speak loudly and rudely to a deceased person, especially during funeral obsequies and in the presence of all lineage members and townsfolk. Akuba knew this well. But she did it deliberately, to make sure that the message, just for being so harshly conveyed, would be remembered by the deceased and delivered to her dead kinsfolk.

In this she proved right, for scarcely had she returned to her compound in Etikɔbɔ no. 1 when she was taken ill. The next day her state became serious, and kindly neighbors flocked in to assist her. Feverish and almost unconscious, she was seen to make odd gestures with her arms, as if shooing invisible beings away. She was also heard to mumble such phrases as "I am not ready," "My time has not yet come," and "Go away." It was clear she was addressing her two dead brothers, Ebukɛle and Akyɛ, and her three dead sisters, Nyɔnra Ama, Etima, and Hɔma, who had promptly come from Hades in answer to her call.

Presently, Akuba died—or at least the onlookers thought so and began to wail. But she was not completely dead, because an hour later she moved a little, opened her eyes, and regained consciousness.[1] By the time she was able to speak, she had apparently changed her mind about life altogether, because she begged the people assisting her to help her recover.

Her bewildered relatives called in a clever herbalist doctor and diviner of the Twea clan called Moni, and duly informed him of the episode at Ezane's funeral, which some of them had witnessed. Akuba herself, as soon as she was able to answer questions, confirmed the facts to the doctor and told him the names of the

Adunyi diviner

dead siblings she had seen crowding around her in her fever. Moni poured a libation to their ghosts and promised a sheep to pacify them, to be slaughtered at the end of the New Year festival. The ghosts were apparently satisfied and did not return to harass Akuba, who soon recovered. When Mr. Quarm returned to Etikɔbɔ no. 1 after reporting these events to me, he found his aunt in quite good health once more. All was well—up to a point. During her recent illness, Akuba had naturally to be looked after. As she is living all alone in her late husband's compound, and there is a limit to the generosity and kindness of neighbors, some of Akuba's classificatory daughters had to come from other villages to assist her and cook for her. This cost money to the lineage as a body, and as a dutiful "son" Mr. Quarm had to contribute his share, ¢4—at the time officially equivalent to U.S. $4—a substantial sum.

Mr. Quarm's reaction to his aunt's behavior was decidedly censorious. Her self-pity, he thought, was unjustified. True, she was very old, possibly sixty-five. But she lived in a comfortable compound, she was still strong enough to do some farm work, and she was not really short of money. Indeed, it was said that she lent some to neighbors at a high interest. She was renowned as an able potter, and her cash income came from selling pots. True, she now complained of being too old to fetch the clay herself from the quarry, but we all knew that clay was conveyed by canoe to Elɛna Wharf, and from there by truck to all towns and villages along the road. People went to her all the time to buy earthenware pots for raffia wine, and paid her ¢1 for each pot, and even ¢1.50 for the bigger ones. "My own mother, the one who brought me forth," said Mr. Quarm, "also made and sold pots for a living, and with her gain she kept and fed all her children, though in those days a pot only sold for 2/6d. Yet she never complained."

But money, I ventured to suggest to my Nzema friend, is not all. In Europe, and possibly even in America, every now and then one hears of millionaires who commit suicide out of sheer loneliness. Mr. Quarm obviously thought it would not be polite to contradict me, but he was patently skeptical as to the possibility that anyone in Nzemaland could be lonely without wanting to be. At any rate, he said a Christian should bear her unhappiness with fortitude.

In 1971, time limitations and transport difficulties had not allowed me to devote a day to the Etikɔbɔ no. 1 trip in order to get, as I wished to do, Akuba's personal version of her experience. The opportunity came two years later. In September 1973, Mr. Quarm, busy with his farms near the Tano River, was no longer working with our group. But the old lady had heard about the odd white man staying at Fort Apollonia on the ocean coast, knew of our old friendship with her "son," and even in Mr. Quarm's absence gave us the politest welcome when we knocked at her Etikɔbɔ no. 1 compound.

As good manners command, after the inevitable *amaneɛ* (formal presentation preliminaries), the conversation dwelt for a certain time on such neutral, formal topics as the rains, the price of fish, and the increasing cost of thatch repairs, before I dared introduce the subject discussed in these pages. Akuba was not embarrassed in the least. Yes, she said, a barren woman's life is never a happy one and may lead to moments of crisis and utter discouragement. But she had not really been as lonely as her son Quarm supposed. Through her siblings, and thanks to the wise old custom of *adanelilɛ* (family fostering), she had plenty of children. In particular, when she was still young she decided to adopt all of her sister Hɔma's eight children, one after the other, rearing each one of them in turn in her house and teaching them a number of things. Although Hɔma was now dead, the arrangement between the two sisters was reached long ago. Hɔma loved her children, but she understood Akuba's situation and gladly allowed one or two of them to stay with her even during their infancy. The boys stayed for a year or so and then left for good, but the girls often returned and took turns staying with her from the time she fell sick in 1971 onward. Tɛna, her sister's fifth-born, was the one who stayed longest and cured her during her illness. Then one of the twins, Ndakyia, came from Menzezɔ and helped for a few months, until she strained her ankle badly and had to return home. Then Ndakyia's place was taken by Agyeba, another sister, who was also married with children in Menzezɔ; but, of course, her husband gave her permission. When she planned to leave, Tɛna would take over again; it was easier for her, because her husband, Stephen Akolati, was an Etikɔbɔ no. 1 man.

When at last I asked Ahwia Akuba about her interrupted journey to Hades, she laughed nervously, but seemed to be flattered by my question. "One does not choose the moment of one's death," she said sententiously. On the subject of her meeting with her dead siblings she was very vague. I was left with the doubt that some details may have been overemphasized in Mr. Quarm's first report. But, she added, one thing she remembered most distinctly was her encounter with her late uncle Nwiaa Mɔne on the way to Hades. The dead man looked at her, did not speak a single word, but slapped her on her back, pointing his finger to the direction she was coming from. She understood the gesture as an order to return to the world she was about to leave. Though she had already died, she reopened her eyes and saw all the people around her wailing and weeping. In that moment, she knew she had come back to life. She told me she now wanted to live on as long as possible.

17 / The Contended Acolyte

In any country or on any continent, a virtuous widow left alone in poor health, with a young son to bring up and no money, is faced with serious problems. Courageous attempts to solve these problems sometimes entail a risk of life, as Azɛmɛla's case proves.

Azɛmɛla was a woman from Sanzule in Eastern Nzema, aged about forty-five, belonging to the Alɔnwɔba clan. She married thrice. Her first marriage was of the *mgbɔnlahwenle* type (recognized concubinage).[1] It ended in divorce after several years, no children having been born of the union. By her second husband, Alu, she had a male child named Enuampa, after Alu's father, who was by this time a young man of twenty-one. When Enuampa was a little boy, Azɛmɛla began to suffer from leprosy. A few years later, following Alu's death, she married another man, called Ayimu.[2] By him she had another male child, who was named Ayimu Ekyi after his own father, as well as two more children who died before they could walk or talk. Then, for reasons that were not disclosed, Ayimu divorced her, taking his son away with him; the boy was being reared by one of his father's brothers.

This left Azɛmɛla a lonely woman, with no means of subsistence and her fatherless son Enuampa to look after. Her leprosy continued to trouble her. By and by her fingers and toes were slowly eaten away, which caused her increasing difficulty in her farming and household work. It was plain that she would soon have to look to her son for their joint maintenance.

So when Enuampa was about seventeen, his mother thought of preparing a lucrative career for him by having him trained as an *awa ɛsɔfo*, or priest of the Twelve Apostles sect, the so-called "Water Carriers." She took him to an established Sanzule *ɛsɔfo* called Namua, with whom she was well acquainted. The arrangements were made on friendly terms. She brought the man two packages of candles as a gift and promised him ¢40 when the training period was concluded. In the meanwhile, as they were living in the same town, she would take care of the boy's food and clothing. This agreement was reached more than three years earlier, and worked out to the satisfaction of both parties. The boy had been staying with Namua as an apprentice for two years when Namua died. By that time Enuampa's training was well under way, but he had not yet obtained from his master the *meanubaka*, or tall cross-shaped staff, which is the emblem of the fully licensed Twelve Apostles priests.

At this point, Azɛmɛla approached her senior brother, Ɛlea, whose advice she always sought on important matters. She asked him whether he would agree that Enuampa be sent to Alenrenzule to complete his apprenticeship with another *ɛsɔfo* called Nda. Ɛlea said no, it would not be fair at this stage to take the boy away from his deceased master's garden, where he was treating a number of sick people, and leave all these patients with their cures unfinished. So Azɛmɛla and her brother agreed that Enuampa should stay on at the *awa* garden in Sanzule for another six months.

A few weeks later, Ɛlea had to travel to a distant area outside Nzemaland, Nkawkaw beyond Koforidua, in the Eastern Region of Ghana. While he was away, Azɛmɛla continued to worry over her son's future. She found out that Nda, the *ɛsɔfo* she had thought of at first, belonged to a slightly different *awa* sect, which practiced other healing methods. However, there was an *awa* priest at Adoabo Ahonlezo, by the name of Mieza Kodwo, who belonged to the same school as the late Namua. So she made up her mind, and of her own initiative, without bothering to consult any other member of her *abusua*, she took her son to Mieza Kodwo.

This was no doubt a rash decision to take without normal consultation with lineage members. Even in Ɛlea's absence, several Alɔnwɔba relatives were in town with whom Azɛmɛla could and should have taken counsel: Kofi, her mother's brother; Adwo Ekyi, her "mother" (mother's sister); the lineage head, Kabenla Enoku, who was at the same time her "grandfather" (mother's mother's brother); her two full sisters, Kyɛkyɛkɔ and Hɔma; Eduku Aka, also a "brother"; and young Boadi, the son of one of her sisters.

When Ɛlea returned from his long journey, not finding Enuampa in town, he asked Azɛmɛla about his nephew and learned that he had been sent off to Adoabo Ahonlezo. Why had she done this, contrary to their agreements? "Well," Azɛmɛla replied, "no

Kɔmenle in ceremonial attire with images of his tutelary gods

one was training the boy since Namua's death, and how can we expect him to become a successful *awa* priest without proper guidance?" Ɛlea saw her point, but all the same he blamed her, because no woman should take such a decision against her brother's advice and without even informing the lineage people in town. Furthermore, Ɛlea now feared that Namua's ghost would attack him, as the boy (for whom as an uncle he was responsible) had abandoned the Sanzule *awa* garden and his former patients. So Ɛlea angrily told his sister that from now on he refused to take any interest in the boy—a serious decision on the part of a maternal uncle. He stuck to this decision, and even eight months later, when he learned that Mieza Kodwo was about to present Enuampa with the holy staff, thus officially concluding the period of apprenticeship, Ɛlea declared that he would not attend the ceremony.

But the most serious development was yet to come. He heard about it one day from some friends of his and could hardly believe his ears. According to insistent rumors, Azɛmɛla had gone to Mieza Kodwo to tell him that, her kinsfolk and her own brother having deserted her and her son, Enuampa now belonged to no clan whatsoever, so that Mieza Kodwo could, if he wished, adopt him into his own *abusua*.

This absurd suggestion was untenable on two counts. On the practical side, if such a situation ever materialized, it meant that whatever money the boy earned in the future would be for the benefit of the clan that had adopted him. But the question of principle was even more incongruous. No matter what happens, one always belongs to the clan and lineage into which one was born. There is no such thing as the change of clan, or the expulsion from it.[3] As the popular saying goes, *abusua nyɛma bɛmpɛ nu*, "the clan's rope is never severed." So Ɛlea was deeply shocked and at once convened a *suakunlu abusua* meeting at the lineage head's compound, where the new issue was discussed.

The lineage head appointed a committee of four to investigate the matter: Ɛlea, Eduku Aka, Boadi, and Kyɛkyɛkɔ. They were to go to Adoabo Ahonlezo, witness the final ceremony that was shortly scheduled to take place, discuss the situation with the *ɛsɔfo*, and in any case take the boy back home with them.

On the appointed day, the four kinspeople made the long trip, partly by truck and partly on foot, but when they reached the *awa* garden only Ɛlea entered the priest's room. As they went through the customary *amaneɛ* formalities (exchange of news), he gave the reason for his visit. He explained that he was Enuampa's maternal uncle and that he naturally would have called on the *ɛsɔfo* before, but he had been away from the land when his nephew had been placed in Mieza Kodwo's care. The *ɛsɔfo* asked, "What did thy sister tell thee?" "She said thou promised thou wouldst complete the boy's training." "Then go back to Sanzule," said the *ɛsɔfo*, "and ask Azɛmɛla about the arrangements we reached." "The arrangements," answered Ɛlea, "were already made with Namua that we should pay ¢40 at the end of the apprenticeship." "Not at all," retorted Mieza Kodwo. "Thy sister brought the boy to me as a gift, so that I may adopt him into my *abusua*." Ɛlea felt his temper rising, but he tried to keep calm and to stick to practical details. "What difference is there between thy work and that of the late Namua?" "Our work was and is the same, but in this case the arrangements were different." So Ɛlea asked, "When my sister came to thee, didst thou inquire as to what the lineage people thought of such an arrangement?" Mieza Kodwo replied that Azɛmɛla had informed the Alɔnwɔba women of Adoabo Ahonlezo. "But these women," Ɛlea remarked, "are not part of our *suakunlu abusua*, so their assent has no value whatsoever." Finally, to end the debate, Ɛlea produced his trump card; he asked the priest to show him the papers proving the arrangement. At this, Mieza Kodwo flew into a temper, got up from his stool, and walked out of the room without answering.

Ɛlea's account of his verbal struggle with the *awa* priest was long and passionate, and it must be stripped of some of its details. After the stalemate in the first round, Ɛlea summoned the Alɔnwɔba townswomen whom his sister had contacted on the occasion of her visit. For his part, Mieza Kodwo convened a meeting of Twelve Apostles church elders, who (if we are to believe Ɛlea) were all afraid of him and never dared contradict him. These two groups held a joint meeting in the *ɛsɔfo*'s compound. As the rumor of the dispute had by this time spread throughout the town, many more people who had nothing to do with the matter flocked in just out of curiosity. So when Ɛlea stood up first to speak, he found himself addressing a considerable audience.

Would Mieza Kodwo, he began, kindly explain to the

Alɔnwɔba women under which terms he had accepted Enuampa as an apprentice? "I have nothing to explain," was the *ɛsɔfo*'s rude reply. "It is thy business to ask thy own clanswomen how things were settled." Then one of the Alɔnwɔba women, a certain Sena, the local *abusua raalɛ kpanyinli*, or lineage female elder, explained that the main reason adduced by Azɛmɛla was that at the time she just did not have the ¢40 to redeem her son, because her brother was away and there was nobody else she could turn to. Although the original agreement had been made with Namua, the credit was vested in the *awa* church as a body; now that Namua was dead the sum was due to Mieza Kodwo as a representative of the same sect. But as she did not have the money, Sena added, Azɛmɛla had offered her son instead.

Sena's admission was obviously a point in favor of Mieza Kodwo, and Ɛlea resented it, though he knew perfectly well that such a deal was altogether illegal. Therefore, he insisted once more that the *ɛsɔfo* should produce the papers proving the agreement. "There are no such papers," Mieza Kodwo shouted. "But thou hast just heard the testimony of thy own clanswomen." At this, Ɛlea said, "Well, all right, I shall pay the ¢40 and take my nephew back to Sanzule." "I will not even listen to such nonsense," Mieza Kodwo answered.

Some of the neutral town elders present, fearing that the two men would come to blows, interposed their offices as arbitrators. Let Ɛlea first refund the cost of the boy's maintenance, they said, according to the bill that Mieza Kodwo will prepare. Then he will be entitled to take the boy back to Sanzule. This bill, which the priest had obviously prepared in advance, as he produced it at once, ran up to ¢300 for a year's food and lodging. The town elders, though favoring Mieza Kodwo, found this sum excessive, and they asked him to reduce his request. So the *ɛsɔfo* cut it down by one-third, leaving ¢200 to be paid. Ɛlea only had ¢40 on him, which he gave, solemnly pledging himself to pay the remaining ¢160 in installments. This agreement was ratified in a written document with two signed copies, one of which Ɛlea later showed me.

Having thus assumed the obligation to pay the *ɛsɔfo* what was for him a huge sum, Ɛlea boarded the next truck back to Sanzule with his kinsfolk. He took Enuampa with him, now a fully accomplished Twelve Apostles priest.

As a dutiful uncle, Ɛlea went even further. He built for his nephew a nice new compound in Kelisane (spelled Krisan on the maps, a village less than a mile west of Sanzule) that was named Jerusalem Garden. Here Enuampa settled down, having just married a young girl from Aloa Bokazo called Nyamekɛ Hɔma, and started his career as an independent *ɛsɔfo*. His mother went to stay with him. Truly, Ɛlea had done for him far more than most uncles do for their nephews nowadays. Being a quiet and reserved man, he did not boast of his generosity, but surely he was entitled to some gratitude.

Now, one day, some time after these events, Ɛlea happened to be walking past the Jerusalem Garden on his way to Eikwe, when the echo of a loud hubbub reached his ears. So he entered the compound to see what was happening. Azɛmɛla was standing in the yard, gesticulating and shouting at the top of her voice as she abused Enuampa, who was obviously at pains to counter her fury. Far from stopping the quarrel, Ɛlea's appearance only seemed to add zest to the woman's passion. Enuampa was a good-for-nothing, she went on crying, and Ɛlea and the other kinspeople were just as bad; they had ruined her. Had the boy been allowed to stay on with Mieza Kodwo, as she had arranged, he would now be making lots of money and be able to give her a full-length cloth every month. But since he had stupidly left Adoabo Ahonlezo and settled down on his own in this miserable little garden, he had not even given her a single scarf.

Flustered and apparently frightened by his irate mother, Enuampa did not react. But Ɛlea was deeply offended; as there was no way of reasoning with his enraged sister, he made a dignified exit. After all he had done and was still doing for Enuampa, this was really too much. As soon as he returned to Sanzule, he reported the facts to the lineage people in town, who shared his indignation and sided with him completely. So when Azɛmɛla came to Sanzule, they all acted as if she were dead and did not even return her greeting. From that day, no Alɔnwɔba in town would speak to the woman.

A week later, Azɛmɛla fell sick, with unbearable pains all over her body. None of the treatments attempted, first by her son according to Twelve Apostles methods, and then by a local herbalist doctor, had any effect. She was brought to the nearby

Catholic hospital at Eikwe, but even the American doctor there could do nothing for her. Indeed, as the rumor went, the white man was utterly unable to find out what was wrong with the woman. In the end, when it seemed that Azɛmɛla was about to die, Enuampa gave up his professional pride as an *awa* healer and had his mother taken to a rival but more experienced *ɛsɔfo* of his same sect in Kelisane, old Asua Akuba. This priestess at once detected the nature and cause of the sickness: Azɛmɛla had been struck by the joint resentment (*sipe*) of her lineage relatives. Unless she pacified them at once, she would surely die.

So, following Asua Akuba's instructions, Enuampa set out to buy a sheep, a bottle of palm wine, one of *akpetekyi* (illicit gin), and two Coca-Colas. In the meanwhile, Ɛlea informed all his lineage relatives in Sanzule of the diagnosis. His sister had made a mistake. But she had already been severely punished for it; she was dying. Would they withdraw their *sipe*, as he, for one, was prepared to do?

The relatives said no; they would not do so until they saw the announced offerings with their own eyes. Before this, they refused even to approach Azɛmɛla.

When all was ready, however, they agreed to go to Kelisane, where they congregated at the Jerusalem Garden. It was Asua Akuba who directed the ceremony, assisted by Enuampa, in the presence of the ailing Azɛmɛla. Several Kelisane townspeople of other clans also attended. First, the sheep was produced, and Asua Akuba told the Alɔnwɔba people they must "bring out" their feelings, because Azɛmɛla had repented and was ready to pacify them. Each *abusua* member in turn then "embraced" the sheep thrice as a sign of forgiveness.[4] Then each took a mouthful of one of the drinks and spat it out on Azɛmɛla's body as a blessing. Then Azɛmɛla, who until that moment was lying down on a mat, was made to kneel on the ground and bow, touching the earth with her mouth thrice, which is the ritual gesture for expiating serious offenses, called *kyikyi ɛnloa aze*. After this, all the lineage members present, one by one, expressed their past grievances against her.

Finally, a formal libation was poured by Ɛlea himself, who on behalf of the whole lineage pronounced loudly the following prayer and announcement (here translated word by word from the tape-recorded Nzema text):

Ah, protector Azɛlɛ Yaba (Thursday-born Earth), come and drink this wine. This matter we have come about; any one who says he is not sorry, he is lying. I am happy that the priestess has been able to find out this scandal, and has summoned us to a meeting, to vomit out all the *sipe* that is in our stomachs. Now that I have been asked to stand up in your midst, I stand for all *abusua* people and I am taking out this *sipe*. Whatever I shall say will be in the clan's interest, no one dare to stand up and speak against it. What Azɛmɛla has done, the suffering we endured, she never appreciated it. She stood somewhere and talked foolishly about us, and the matter came to our face, made us sorry, and its *sipe* attacked her, and she was about to die. Now that we have been called to a meeting, she has gone for a sheep and placed it in our face; she has prostrated herself on the ground [promising] that she will not continue to do that again, so we must forgive her. Now that we have taken away the *sipe* in our stomach, we have seen that God is satisfied, Earth is satisfied. Scandal may go to the bush, may good come to town, may prosperity come to town, may glory come; we bless her. This small case and the sorrow-sorrow we have taken out of our stomachs, may protector Azɛlɛ Yaba bless it to let Azɛmɛla recover.[5]

When the ceremony was over and the drinks finished, the Alɔnwɔba people expressed one by one their wishes for Azɛmɛla's recovery and for Enuampa's success as an *ɛsɔfo*. Then they returned to Sanzule. Barely one week later, they heard news that the woman had recovered, which confirmed that her illness had indeed been caused by their *sipe*.

By the time I was told this story, several months later, Enuampa had moved to Dunkwa far north of Nzemaland, to a bigger center to improve his preparation as a Twelve Apostles priest. Azɛmɛla was still staying at the Jerusalem Garden, and I was eager to go to Kelisane in order to get *her* version of the events narrated by her brother. But the territorial chief of Sanzule, Nana Afful III, in whose palace the conversation was taking place, and who knew Azɛmɛla very well, advised me against this plan. The outward signs of the woman's leprosy, he explained, were becoming increasingly conspicuous, so that she would probably not welcome visits by strangers, especially a foreigner. But, as her brother confirmed, she was not suffering much. Her sister Kyɛkyɛkɔ, who was also a leper, has moved to the Garden to live with her and keep her company, and they are happy together. Kyɛkyɛkɔ had an only child, a boy named Mieza, who also lived in Kelisane in a nearby compound and ran errands for his two mothers.

The only one really left to suffer was Ɛlea. He still has a long series of installments to pay before his debt to Mieza Kodwo would be repaid. The Alɔnwɔba lineage head, Kabenla Enoku, could provide no more than ¢40 toward the total sum, and it was for Ɛlea as Enuampa's uncle to pay the rest—with God's and Azɛlɛ Yaba's help.

18 / *The Woman Who Was Punished For Being Too Kind*

Some misfortunes, accidents, diseases, and deaths are caused by the sheer wickedness of certain neighbors of ours, sorcerers, and witches—a sad truth that cannot be denied. But experience assures us that in most other cases such mishaps are the consequence of our own faults, sins, mistakes, bad behavior, or sheer foolishness—whether our own personally or of any other member of our own lineage, of course, it makes no difference. The acceptance of this perennial reality satisfies our inborn sense of righteousness and confirms our faith in the justice of God Almighty and of the minor gods who act as His ministers on earth. But there are exceptions. One hears of people who meet with disaster, or have to bear the severest trials, at the end of honest, faultless lives. Such is the case of Ɛnnɔ Nwoza, an elderly divorced woman of the Mafole clan from Twinɛne, who suffered from a serious and most painful illness in the summer of 1973. As she told me herself, and as reliable witnesses confirmed at my request, this illness was shown to be the consequence of several actions of hers dictated by her virtuous principles and kindness of heart. As a well-documented example of such situations, so difficult to explain by logical reasoning, Nwoza's case deserves careful examination and meditation.

When Ɛnnɔ Nwoza fell sick in early June 1973, with high fever, pains all over her body that did not allow her to sleep at night, and a complete loss of appetite, she was practically all alone in her large Twinɛne compound. This was not only a sad predicament but also an ironical one. Nwoza—once a good-looking woman who was now in her early sixties—had several brothers and sisters still living; she had married twice, and six of her children were still alive. But for one reason or another, they were all away from Twinɛne.

Her first husband, a Twinɛne man of the Nvavile clan called Ɛnwi Ekyi, had been the son of one of her father's sisters. It had been a successful *suanu agyalɛ* ("home marriage") at first, from which her two senior sons were born, Takpole Kanra and Boadi.

But it had ended in divorce over some minor misunderstanding. Then, as years passed, Ɛnwi Ekyi had died.

In the meanwhile, Nwoza had married her second husband, a Twea farmer from Ɛlonyi named Bile Aka. By him she had twins (*ɛntelema*, of different sex), Ndabia and Ndabela, and two more daughters, Sɛnza Ɛba and Bozoma. But this marriage also did not last long; in 1960, Nwoza divorced once more. By this time, she had had enough of married life, and it is difficult for a woman of fifty to find another suitor. So she went back to her late father's compound in Twinɛne, which also happened to be her first husband's house, as Ɛnwi Ekyi had been brought up as a foster child by his maternal uncle Ɛnnɔ, Nwoza's father.

Her children were scattered in various distant places. Takpole Kanra had for years been fishing in the Ivory Coast lagoons; Boadi was a private soldier in Takoradi; the three girls had followed their husbands to their respective native towns, two of them outside Nzemaland; Ndabia was a policeman in the Tarkwa area. Nwoza would thus have had no kinsperson to assist her and keep her company in her big compound had her eldest son not allowed one of his daughters to stay with her. Not by sheer coincidence Takpole Kanra had named this little girl, now about ten years old, after his own mother. To distinguish her from her grandmother and namesake, people called her Nwoza Ekyi, "little Nwoza." "She is a good, obedient girl," Nwoza said, "who used to fetch water and firewood for me whenever I asked her, swept the yard, and was even beginning to do some simple cooking and pounding cassava or plantain for a few minutes if helped by someone. But when I began to feel so sick, she could not really look after me. She is much too young."

So Nwoza sent for Adayi Kwame and asked him to help her. Adayi, a married man of forty living only a few blocks away on the same Twinɛne street, belonged to the Azanwule clan and was in no way related to Nwoza. But there was a long tradition of friendship between their families. Adayi's mother, Anlima Boni, was such a close friend of Nwoza's that they considered each other as *mediema*, sisters. Surely she would have helped Nwoza in this predicament. But at the time she was in Alawule looking after her sick brother Mozu. In his lifetime, Nwoza's husband Ɛnwi Ekyi had been an *agɔnwolɛ kpalɛ* or intimate friend of Adayi's father.[1]

Keeping mother's house clean

And Adayi himself was a close friend of Boadi, whom he considered as a brother. So on more than one count, Adayi looked on Nwoza as one of his mothers.

Adayi, who was luckily in town that day, lost no time and by the first available truck took the sick woman to the Etikɔbɔ no. 1 dispensary. There the Ghanaian male nurse on duty examined her a little and gave her some white people's medicines. For a couple of days after her return home, Nwoza's condition seemed to improve. But the remedies proved to have no lasting effect. Soon her illness returned in an even more virulent form.

This time Nwoza told Adayi that she wished to be taken to a really good doctor, and she suggested the name of Ɛzonle Kanra of Ngelekazo. There were two reasons for this choice. First, Kanra was an esteemed herbalist and diviner; his merits are discussed elsewhere in these pages. Second, he also happened to be the junior half-brother (by the same father) of Amo Kanra, who was a classificatory brother of Nwoza's on the mother's side; the two brothers lived in the same compound. But Adayi had another suggestion in mind. He wanted Nwoza to consult a classificatory sister of his, called Mary, who was a well-known priestess of the Twelve Apostles sect (often called "Water Carriers") in Twinɛne itself. There was no harm, he told the woman, in consulting his sister first. Nwoza was far too ill to object, so after Adayi had sent from the nearest post office a telegram to his friend Boadi, informing him of his mother's serious conditions, they approached the priestess.

Mary received them with great kindness and set to her task almost immediately. She began by praying very fervently, invoking Nyamenle (God) and Jesus Christ. Then she took her cup of holy water, twirling it in her hands until the liquid was full of miniature whirlpools and bubbles. Still reciting her prayers, she gazed intently at the water until she was able to read the divine message in it. It was the god Tanoɛ, the message read, who was disturbing Nwoza. He had been the main god for her lineage since the day when he possessed one of her maternal grandmothers, choosing her as his priestess. After this woman's death he had continued to receive a yearly sacrifice from the *abusua*. But for the last two or three years these offerings had been discontinued, as Nwoza herself had to admit. Hence the god's anger. The present illness was a warning to Nwoza, now the eldest *ɛrɛladane* (matron with offspring) in the lineage and therefore personally responsible for the collective worship. Furthermore—as Mary read in the cup, with Nwoza filling in the missing details—when her son Ndabia had been gravely ill in his early childhood, Nwoza had promised Tanoɛ a sheep if the child recovered; but she had failed to fulfill the promise. So the god had a double reason to attack her. It was imperative, the priestess concluded, that Nwoza contact the main *kɔmenle* of Tanoɛ at Ezinlibo to find out the proper way of appeasing the irate god; she, Mary, a Christian priestess, could surely not meddle with the worship of fetish gods, of which since the days of prophet Harris her religion strongly disapproved.

So Adayi, physically supporting the increasingly sick woman, took her by the next truck all the way to Ezinlibo, only to find out that the local priest was himself seriously ill, having for some reason been punished in turn by his own god, Tanoɛ.

At this point, the only solution appeared to be the one previously suggested by Nwoza; the two directed themselves to Ngelekazo. By the time they finally reached Amo Kanra's compound, Nwoza's pains were so great and her fever so high that she almost collapsed in her old brother's arms. They had to wait until she recovered a little before she could be submitted to a new examination of her health problems.

Ɛzonle Kanra's oracular performance a couple of days later was, as usual, exhaustive and accurate. He succeeded in identifying three independent causes for the widow's ailment, quite different from those read by Mary in her holy water. The oracle strings revealed them in Nwoza's presence little by little, interwoven with each other, as it were. For clarity's sake, however, we shall here deal with each one of them separately.

The first cause.

There was a petty storekeeper and part-time fisherman in Twinɛne, by the name of Tayi, who was a grandson (sister's daughter's son) to Ɛnnɔ, Nwoza's father. Technically, Tayi was classified in the group of Nwoza's "fathers." But as he was at least twenty years her junior, though she correctly called him *egya* (father), she really considered him as a sort of son. They used to visit each other from time to time, and on a few occasions Tayi gave his "daughter" a little money, which she accepted in good faith as presents in view of their relationship. But one day when he called on her and found her alone at home as she always was when her granddaughter was playing with the other children in town, he unexpectedly proposed having sexual intercourse with her. Nwoza could hardly believe her ears; she indignantly refused. An angry quarrel followed, in the course of which they abused each other. Tayi shouted that he had paid her in advance; she retorted that a father's normal gift to his daughter has nothing to do with the payment of a whore and that she would no longer have anything to do with such a lecherous relative.[2] Tayi left in a rage, called the ghost of his late grandfather Ɛnnɔ from Hades and perhaps also a *bozonle* from the bush, and put a curse with them on Nwoza. He also addressed to the same effect a private juju, or charm, which he secretly kept in his bedroom for his own protection. It was three days after these curses, as it was later proved, that Nwoza began to feel the symptoms of her ailment.

The second cause.

A classificatory son of Nwoza's by the name of Ndakyia (a "given" name from some ancestor, the man not being a twin himself), at the time engaged in fishing at Givo, far to the west of Abidjan in the Ivory Coast, decided in 1972 that he wanted to marry. Naturally, he did not wish to marry a woman of a foreign, unreliable race. So he sent a verbal message to Twinɛne in Ghana to the effect that his kinsfolk should find and send him a suitable Nzema wife. As Ndakyia's real parents were away from town at the time, it was his mother Nwoza who undertook this task. She found a nice Twinɛne girl who met all the necessary requirements, first of all those of lineage exogamy. She had long and satisfactory talks with this girl, approached her parents, obtained their consent, and informed Ndakyia accordingly. No reply came from the Ivory Coast. Embarrassed, but still inflamed with goodwill, she decided she would advance the bridewealth herself. Possessing no money of her own, she used some that her other sons (the ones she had brought forth, her *real* children as Europeans would say) had left in her custody, paid the head money and all the rest, and again sent a message to Ndakyia to say the matter was settled, and would he come home to collect the bride she had found him and refund the expenses? Again there was no answer. The promised bride became nervous, and Nwoza even more so, whereupon she decided she would wait no longer. Taking the girl with her, she undertook the long and tiresome journey to Givo, a foreign place where she had never been before. But when they eventually succeeded in locating Ndakyia, he hardly looked at his bride, who admittedly is not reported to have been a pretty girl. What is worse, he bluntly said he had no money for the whole matter.

Taken aback, Nwoza hoped she could at least settle the affair with her sister, Ndakyia's mother, who she knew had followed her son in the Ivory Coast and was living not far from Givo. But when at last she met her, even this woman did not appear at all grateful for all the trouble Nwoza had taken. In fact, she looked rather annoyed, and declared that not even she, nor her husband, had the necessary sum at the moment. She could at most put together one third of the sum. Would Nwoza be content with that? Nwoza would surely not, and coldly took leave of her sister.

She now realized that not only had she undertaken an expensive and uncomfortable journey for nothing but that she was being disapproved and blamed for her generous deed. Above all, she dreaded her sons' reproaches when she would have to tell them that their money was gone. She had betrayed her children's trust in her. She had never felt so miserable in her life before, and as she returned empty-handed to Ghana, accompanied by the rejected and sadly disappointed bride, she openly said so to anybody who would listen to her. Her wails and laments during that unfortunate period, Ɛzonle Kanra's oracle now explained, had surely been a cause of her present predicament; they were overheard by the fetish gods on her way, and in particular by a god from Avoleɛnu (Newtown), who said, "Why, if thou art really so unhappy among humans in this world, I will take thee with me." So this was a second reason for her illness.

The third cause.

During the 1972 rainy season, a young man called Nwiaa Mieza was looking for a lodging in Twinɛne, as none of his own lineage people had suitable accommodation to offer in that town. His eyes fell on Nwoza's large and almost uninhabited compound, and he asked her for permission to settle down with her. Now, Nwiaa Mieza was no relative of Nwoza's and even belonged to a different clan, so she was under no obligation whatsoever to offer him hospitality. But on account of her usual kindheartedness, she agreed to his request. Perhaps she also thought that, with somebody else staying in the empty compound, she might feel less lonely. So Nwiaa Mieza moved in, taking with him his senior full sister Sɔba and her four children. Sɔba incidentally happened to be a *nwɔmenle*, having a fetish god with her by the name of Abekpo. Things went well for a while, but soon Nwoza began to regret her generosity. Sɔba's children turned out to be noisy, untidy, and unbearable, as most children are; one of the daughters in particular, a little girl called Ama, was incredibly rude and insolent to Nwoza. Frequent brawls arose, and one day, when Ama shamelessly insulted her in the presence of visitors, Kindhearted Nwoza lost her temper and shouted back to her, "Get thee out of my sight once and for all, and go and stay in thy father's house, as any decent girl should!" After this, not only did Ama leave the compound but her mother and all the rest of the family sided with her and, having taken offense, indignantly moved out along with the girl. The god Abekpo, realizing that he was in a way being turned out, too, took a strong dislike to Nwoza and made her sick.

Such then were the revelations made by the *adunyi* strings. Nwoza had half forgotten these past occurrences, or thought them irrelevant. But the oracle made her remember and drew them out of her. So she found herself faced with three new plausible causes for her predicament, in addition to the two previously pointed out by Mary, the Twelve Apostles priestess. There were ample reasons for dismay, but luckily she was now in good hands. With all the promptness permitted by Ɛzonle Kanra's many other engagements, action was taken.

As Tanoɛ happened to be Ɛzonle Kanra's main god, the easiest threats to counteract were those indicated by Mary. In his own compound, in Nwoza's presence, the wily diviner poured a libation to Tanoɛ and showed him a live sheep brought in for the occasion, promising to sacrifice him the animal as soon as the patient recovered. He likewise pacified the god from Avoleɛnu (mentioned above in the second cause) with the promise of another sheep.

Then Tayi had to be contacted. There was no question of Nwoza herself leaving Ngelekazo in her state of health. So Adayi rode a truck to Twinɛne accompanied by the woman's real son, Takpole Kanra, who had joined them in the meanwhile, by her half-brother Amo Kanra, and by the doctor-diviner himself. Tayi admitted that the story of his dispute with the widow was accurate, and he said he regretted the consequences, which he had in no way foreseen. Leaving the small deputation in the *asalo*, or sitting room, he retired briefly to his bedroom next door, where they heard him ringing a bell to call his juju (on the subject of which he was understandably reticent) and speaking to it for a minute or two. Though the exact words could not be heard through the closed door, it was understood that he was withdrawing his curse. In the presence of the four visitors, he then poured a libation to Nyamenle and Azɛlɛ Yaba, as well as to all the gods and ancestors, mentioning by name in particular his own grandfather Ɛnnɔ (Nwoza's father), asking them to forget his previous angry words and to lead Nwoza to a steady recovery. The four delegates left Twinɛne feeling that another dangerous threat had been removed. More than that, they were taking back with them a special medicine from Tayi's secret juju, with accurate instructions regarding its use, which Ɛzonle Kanra had duly memorized.

Finally, there remained the quarrel with Sɔba and her group. This proved more difficult to settle because the offended fetish priestess was still very incensed. The same four people drove once more to Twinɛne, made an appointment with Sɔba and her brother at the new compound in which they had settled, supplied themselves with palm wine and *akpetekyi* (illicit gin), and offered them to Sɔba along with Nwoza's apologies. After a long palaver, the priestess accepted them, and poured a libation to show her forgiveness. A chicken was bought by Takpole Kanra, and the whole party walked to Sɔba's shrine out in the bush, at the outskirts of town. Here the priestess once more poured libations, first to Awozinli, the township's main god, then to her own *bozonle*, Abakpo, as well as to Bulazo and several other gods. After a short while, all these came at her bidding. They descended on her and spoke through her voice, accepting the chicken that was slaughtered in their honor. The last obstacle to Nwoza's recovery was thereby removed—as far as oracles can be relied on and the shifting favor of the gods trusted.

But doubts and skepticism are perhaps unjustified in this case.

The circumstances related to this strange illness—accurately related by Adayi Kwame and Ɛzonle Kanra, who took such a direct interest in the whole true story—were personally confirmed to me and enriched in detail by Nwoza herself when I visited her in Twinɛne in October of that same year, 1973. Three months after the severe crisis that almost led her to the grave, she had completely recovered her health and good spirits, which it was hoped she would retain for years to come, along with her proverbial kindness of character.

19 / The Two Priestesses' Husband

Most men with whom one discusses the everyday problems of married life say they would not like to take a fetish priestess for a wife. Though such a woman is socially respected and useful to the general public, they argue, she tends to be too absorbed by her religious duties also to be at the same time an efficient housewife. Perhaps this is an unjustified prejudice; I have known quite a few women of this vocation who have been excellent cooks, wives, mothers, and providers and made their husbands happy. Be this as it may, the situation of a man being simultaneously married to *two* priestesses is surely exceptional, and judging by the only example of this kind known to me, it is also a dangerous one.

The case I am referring to, and which deserves to be reported on account of its rarity, is that of Adayi Ɛzonle, a fisherman and palm wine tapper of the Alɔnwɔba clan, from Nzulezo in Western Nzema, who died in Beyin in November 1970 at the age of approximately forty. His death was allegedly caused by jealousy—not of the co-wives but of the two different fetish gods they served.

But let us start from the beginning. Ɛzonle was the seventh of twelve children born to the same parents in Beyin, the capital of Western Nzema. His father was an Adahonle named Nyamekɛ Adayi (hence Adayi Ɛzonle's patronymic); his mother was an Alɔnwɔba, Mɛlɛ Ɛya. Both were nominal Methodists, and both were dead. Ɛzonlɛ and his full brother Akpɔ were brought up as Methodists in Beyin and never changed their religion, not even when in their late teens they left their father's compound and moved north to Nzulezo in order to be independant and to make their living in that very fertile area. There is, in fact, a tiny Methodist chapel, as well as a Catholic one, on one of the quaint and very lovely platforms built on piles above the lagoon, which forms the village of Nzulezo. Though I did not know Ɛzonle personally, I obtained the most detailed information on his life from his devoted niece Afo, my friend Mɔkɛ Mieza's wife, and later also from Apkɔ, his brother, and from Sɔma, his full sister, who lives in Beyin but ran a bar in Ɛkɛbaku.

Ɛzonle married three times during his lifetime, but he only had two wives, because on the third occasion he remarried the woman who had been his first wife and whom he had previously divorced. It is the unusual form called *ɛkpɔdalɛ agyalɛ* ("marriage with apologies"), because the husband must declare he is sorry for having erroneously divorced his wife a first time and promise he will not divorce her again.

This woman was Hɔma, also from Nzulezo, of the Ezohile clan. According to Afo, Hɔma was not a Christian, though Akpɔ thought she was a Methodist, like her husband. When still a very young girl, she had been "given" by some unnamed enemy to a *bozonle* called Kogyakɛ. As sometimes happens, the god who was expected to kill her took a liking for her, reconsidered his plans, and thought he would like to choose her as his priestess. When Ɛzonle met her and asked her to marry him, Hɔma was already a *kɔmenle* apprentice, and Ɛzonle had nothing to do with her vocation. They lived together only two or three years, had a child who died within a few months, and then divorced. Shortly afterward, Hɔma married a man from Nvelenu called Ɛkyɔloboa, with whom she remained for about ten years. She had four children by him, all of them still alive. Then she divorced him, too, left her children with him in Nvelenu, and returned to her people in Nzulezo.

By this time, Ɛzonle had remarried. Almost directly after he had divorced Hɔma, he had started a love affair with a local girl called Afiba, aged about fourteen. A few months later Afiba was expecting a child. It was her first pregnancy, and a difficult one, because during the period she fell sick. Ɛzonle took full responsibility and took her to a priestess, who invoked her god, asking him to show her how she should cure the girl. The god not only revealed the appropriate remedies but also took a benevolent interest in Afiba, spoke through her mouth while she was ill, and showed clearly that he wished her to become his priestess. By a significant coincidence, this fetish god called Bɔsɔndole, from the Miegyina area near Beyin, happened to be the same god who many years before had possessed and called to his service Afiba's maternal grandmother. It is well known that gods prefer to choose their caretakers, whenever possible, within the same matrilineage.

Street in Nzulezo

Considering that they had approached the *bozonle* together and that this god had granted not only Afiba's recovery but also the happy birth and survival of their child, Ɛzonle accepted Bɔsɔndole as his own tutelary god as well as the girl's. In no way did he discourage her from becoming the god's priestess. True, he was a Methodist, and the Methodist church disapproves of fetish cults, but there was no denying that Bɔsɔndole had shown him mercy and favor by saving the lives of his new child and the woman who was shortly afterward to become his second wife.

Years later, when Hɔma returned to Nzulezo after her divorce, Ɛzonle remarried her, with Afiba's full consent and approval. But to understand correctly the facts that follow, it is important to bear in mind that from the very beginning Ɛzonle's attitude toward Hɔma's god, Kogyakɛ, was one of indifference; on the other hand, he owed Afiba's god, Bɔsɔndole, personal gratitude and respect. This may explain the man's different behavior toward his two wives in the performance of their respective cult duties, as we shall presently see. For the rest, witnesses assure us that he showed no preference to either of them. The two women had separate farms, and he did the same amount of work on Hɔma's as on Afiba's. He cohabited normally with both his wives, respecting the established turns. If he begot eight children by Afiba, and only three from Hɔma (not counting the one born at the time of their first marriage, who died), that was surely not his fault.

Akpɔ, who lived in the same village, saw the three of them constantly for many years. He assured us that the two co-wives were on normal and even friendly terms with each other. Afo did not altogether agree with this opinion, but her judgment was less germane on this point, because she never really lived in Nzulezo with her uncle and his wives.

The first serious trouble, which was indirectly to lead to Ɛzonle's ruin, began with a dramatic and unprecedented accident in 1967, during the time of *kundum*, the so-called New Year festival. One night, a violent fire broke out in Nzulezo and destroyed half the village. Such a catastrophe could hardly happen in any normal town or village on the mainland. But Nzulezo was built on piles above the lagoon water and formed entirely of thatched huts of raffia sticks perched on wooden poles. It is an easy prey to flames, especially during the dry season. Luckily, most of the inhabitants were away on that particular night, having gone to nearby Beyin on the ocean coast to take part in the *kundum* festivities; only a few old people and children had been left behind, none of whom were casualties.

Afiba's house suffered only light damage, which could be repaired within the next few days. But Hɔma's house and the shrine of Kogyakɛ that it contained were in the part of the village that was reduced to ashes. They had to be rebuilt, and naturally enough Hɔma asked her husband to see to this. Ɛzonle, who was not a rich man, worried at the prospect of the considerable expenditure, and suggested that Hɔma should ask for financial assistance from her own lineage relatives at Mpataba.[1] It was obvious, he argued, that Kogyakɛ's cult was entirely the responsibility of her clansfolk. Was it not true that even before this god had chosen Hɔma as his *kɔmenle*, Hɔma's own senior "sister" Bɛya had been for years his acknowledged priestess?

The Ezohile clansfolk at Mpataba, Hɔma's relatives, could not deny this fact, meaning that Kogyakɛ preferred their clan to all others. But this did not mean that they intended to accept Ɛzonle's request. Rebuilding a house for his wife, they retorted, was indisputably his business. Besides, had he not rebuilt his other wife's house and shrine? "Repaired, not rebuilt," Ɛzonle corrected them; the case was quite different. If they implied that he favored one wife at the expense of the other, they were liars. The discussion went on for months, and the shrine was never rebuilt. So the god became annoyed, made Hɔma sick, and quickly killed her. They buried her in the Nzulezo cemetery.

Six months later, it was Ɛzonle's turn to be attacked by the *bozonle*. First, he suffered from *babaso*, a disease that some interpreters translate as syphilis, but that in this case was probably gonorrhea, and was cured of this by Ɛzonle Kanra, the distinguished Ngelekazo medicine man. A second time, he had *ewule mɔɔ maa bɛ sa woso la*, which caused his body to swell. This was possibly a form of palsy, for which he consulted a Beyin specialist called Kasi, who kept him in his compound for two weeks and succeeded in curing him a little. But he had not completely recovered when a third ailment intervened, this time affecting his eyesight. Hɔma's relatives in Mpataba insisted that he should consult a medicine man and diviner from Ɛbonloa named Ama, in whom they had great faith.

Ama revealed that some time before, when Ɛzonle was working on a farm he had near Nuba, a fetish god from that area had for reasons unknown hit him in the eye and was set on killing him. The god was called Amɛnlabo and had to be at once be appeased with a sheep. So the stricken Ɛzonle, who by this time was almost blind, bought the sheep in Mpataba (there were none worth mentioning in the Nzulezo lagoon area) and made the long journey to Nuba to pacify the *bozonle*. Three people accompanied him: his good friend Ata; a male herbalist, Kwa Mensa; and a priestess, Nyamekɛ Sua. But even this sacrifice did not help.

His devoted niece Afo, who visited the sick man several times, could bear direct witness to the fact that two or more gods were struggling over his fate—one endeavoring to kill him and another trying to save him. This caused the sick man to shake all over. Occasionally one of the competing gods possessed him and spoke through his mouth, announcing, "I shall allow him to recover," and this encouraged the hopes of his relatives. Afo assumed this benevolent god to be Bɔsɔndole, to whom Afiba was frequently appealing; she also assumed that the hostile god was Kogyakɛ, not Amɛnlabo, but the two could naturally have entered an alliance. Be this as it may, the fetish god who had promised Ɛzonle's recovery was either powerless to counteract the destructive action of his colleagues or simply untruthful, because Ɛzonle grew worse and worse.

When he felt his end approaching, he asked to be taken to a Twelve Apostles *ɛsɔfo* in Beyin, and he spent the last few days of his life in her compound. He belonged to that sort of people who wish to die in the same town where they were born. At this stage, as all witnesses confirm, he behaved like a madman. People had to hold him down to prevent him from rushing out into the street, half blind as he was. He felt a hostile crowd tearing at his throat and limbs, moaned and shouted "Keep them away from me," and made wild gestures with his arms as if to push the invisible beings back.

On the last day of his agony, they carried him back to the same Beyin compound where his late parents had lived and where he was born. It was here, to use the Nzema expression, that he died completely. They buried him next to his *abusua* ancestors in the Beyin cemetery.

After the funeral, his full brother Akpɔ and other Alɔnwɔba kinsfolk returned to the Nuba bush, near his former farm, to pacify Amɛnlabo with another sheep and to perform the prescribed rite in order to release the dead man's *ɛkɛla* from the bush. No similar sacrifice, as far as I was told, was offered to the other offended god, Kogyakɛ, allegedly because (in Akpɔ's opinion, not shared by Afo) it was Amɛnlabo who delivered the final blow. Besides, it is well known that when a chop is presented to one fetish god, many others flock in for their share.

In this case, the offering was apparently well accepted, because there were no further threats to the health and welfare of either Ɛzonle's lineage or Hɔma's. Not only Akpɔ and Sɔma, Ɛzonle's full siblings, but also Afo and her sisters and children, all belonging to the same Alɔnwɔba lineage, were exempt from trouble. On the Ezohile clan's side, Hɔma's children as well as her surviving full sisters, Ndede and Ekpantema, and their children, also all remained in good health.[2] One can therefore hopefully assume that Kogyakɛ is by now pacified; at any rate those women's classificatory sister Bɛya competently kept the situation under control.

As for Afiba, who under Bɔsɔndole's benevolent protection never ran any comparable risks, she continued to live in her late husband's restored compound in Nzulezo. When we revisited this picturesque lagoon village in 1971, she let us know that much to her regret she was unable to receive us. This was partly because of her impurity, her year of widowhood not yet being completed, and partly on account of the absorbing duties of her profession. None of Ɛzonle's three successors, her neighbors told us in strict confidence, had so far made even an informal proposal to keep her as a wife. As remarked at the beginning, the enviable situation of a fetish priestess has its drawbacks.

20 / *The Sick Child and the Participant Observer*

(*Editor's Note:* The author's role in this story differs from his role in the previous nineteen; that is, he is an active player, not a passive observer. Therefore, he presents the narrative in the third person, so that readers will see all players on an equal footing.)

Little Kofi was an eighteen-month-old child of the Nvavile clan who lived with his four-year-old brother, Kwasi, his mother, Awiane, aged seventeen and probably the prettiest girl in Ngelekazo, and his maternal grandmother, Nyima. They lived in a nice compound on the southern side of the main coastal road, near the wide sandy beach of the Atlantic Ocean. The head of the compound was also a Nvavile, Nyima's junior full brother, Mɔkɛ Mieza, who was therefore technically Kofi's grandfather (mother's mother's brother); but the compound was originally founded by a Twea man, Mɔkɛ Mieza's real father, Ɛhɔlade Mɔkɛ.

As his mother was not married, Kofi had no legal father. As everybody knew, however, his biological father was Anaman, a bachelor of the Ezohile clan from Awiabo, son of the late Ngelekazo chief Nana Andualu Kwagya II. Anaman was an educated young man, a schoolteacher. He formerly taught at the Akponu school, and for the past few years had been attached to the Anokyi school, which was only about ten miles from Anokyi to Ngelekazo along the main road. So, whenever he was free from his teaching duties, Anaman used to come and stay with his father at the Ngelekazo palace.

At the time—in 1966, five years before the main events of this story—Awiane was still a schoolgirl. She attended school not in her own town but in Takinta, a village in the interior. The reason was simple: The headmaster of the Takinta school was one of her fathers, Boa Nwia (father's brother), in whose house she could have her meals and sleep. She used to come back to her mother in Ngelekazo during the holidays, which of course coincided with those of Anaman; all primary schools in Western Nzema as in most of Ghana, opened and closed on the same dates. During one of these common vacation periods, the young man took a fancy to Awiane, whose breasts were then just beginning to swell, and seduced her.

So it happened that before she reached the age of thirteen Awiane was pregnant. The fact naturally did not escape her mother's attentive eye, and Nyima at once asked who was the man? As many inexperienced young girls do out of shyness, at first Awiane denied everything and refused to give explanations. It took all of Nyima's stubbornness and patience to get the truth out of her. When at last she confessed to her mother, admitting her affair with Anaman, the family approached the young man. But he in turn denied the whole thing.

Nyima and her brother Mieza then approached Anaman's father, Nana Andualu Kwagya II, and explained the matter. The chief summoned his son to Ngelekazo, but even in his presence Anaman persisted in his denial. Nyima was puzzled, frustrated, and, in a word, furious. A few months later, Awiane brought forth her child, a male Sunday-born (Kwasi), the splendid little boy who was now almost four years old. At this point, Nyima decided that the matter must be cleared once and for all, and she asked for the support of her daughter's fathers—Boa Nwia, who was still generously paying for Awiane's maintenance, and Munda Aka, his brother, who though paying nothing was Nyima's former husband and the man who had begotten Awiane. (Munda Aka and Nyima had divorced a few years earlier, and Munda Aka had remarried and was living with his second wife in his father's compound in Ɛlonyi.)

The two brothers came from their respective villages to Ngelekazo. A new formal palaver was arranged at the chief's palace. Among the people present were Nyima and Mieza for the girl's *abusua*, Awiane's two fathers mentioned above, and two influential townsmen and family friends, Amo Kanra and his half-brother Ɛzonle Kanra. The chief had naturally wanted an authoritative representative of his son's lineage and clan to be present, and had asked the local Ezohile lineage head to attend the meeting. Anaman was once more summoned in the presence of his father and these other people, and formally requested to make a truthful statement. This time, the young teacher at last confessed what everybody already knew or strongly suspected—that he had seduced Awiane and that the baby was his. He had denied it at first, he explained, because he was afraid of Nyima, who was continually shouting at him, cursing and threatening. Anaman's responsibility thus being established in front of witnesses, he was legally bound to pay the girl's family ¢100 as the customary seduction fee, plus a monthly sum (to be established by mutual agreement) for his child's maintenance. But months passed, and Anaman never paid a single penny.

The matter might have been brought to court, and there is no doubt that in the end Anaman would have been forced to pay. But considerations of political expediency prevented the controversy from going so far. Just at this time, Awiane's "father" Boa Nwia, the former headmaster at Takinta, had been elected to the Twea stool of a neighboring town, Kɛngɛne. And Anaman's father, as we have seen, was at the same time sitting on the Ngelekazo stool, again held by the Twea clan. It would surely have looked very bad if the chiefs to two neighboring towns, both belonging to the same *abusua*, were seen litigating at the king's court in Beyin. In honorable respect to political authority, though much to their disappointment, the Nvavile people gave up their justified claims, and the whole matter was hushed up.

The consequences were manifold. No further pressure being brought on him, Anaman not only escaped the penalty of the overdue seduction fee but could not be induced to marry Awiane. He could also not be forced to carry out his duties toward his own child, first of which being to name him; in four years little Kwasi had no proper given name and was still known by his *ɛkɛla duma*. If in the course of the next few years Anaman still failed to live up to his obligations, the boy would be named not by his own *abusua* people but by Awiane's fathers.

The leading man of the latter group, Munda Aka, up to that time had personally taken little notice of his daughter and contributed almost nothing toward her maintenance. But now he felt offended in his paternal rights. He returned to Ngelekazo, delivered a noble sermon on sexual ethics to Awiane, and ended by having a violent row with her, in the course of which he formally forbade her to have anything more to do with Anaman.[1]

But Awiane disobeyed him, just as she had been disobeying her mother on the same matter. She went on having secret meetings

Chief wearing kente

with her lover whenever he came to Ngelekazo, and two years later she was pregnant by him once more.

On hearing this, Munda Aka was so angry that Mieza had to go to Ɛlonyi to pacify him with a bottle of gin, fearing that the offended father's *sipe* might make Awiane sick in the course of her pregnancy, or even cause the baby to be stillborn. It is well known, in fact, that a father's anger and grudge may have fatal effects on the child who has transgressed his biddings. Munda Aka's wrath was a little tempered by the gin, but all the same he declared he was henceforth giving up all interest in his rebellious daughter.

Eventually, Awiane's second delivery was as smooth as the first one, and little Kofi was happily born—a sturdy and healthy child like his brother, Kwasi. But when he was about eighteen months old in September 1971, a nasty sickness appeared. First, the child showed a certain difficulty in breathing and swallowing, and he took his mother's breast with growing reluctance. Soon he suffered from what grew to be an ugly, hard swelling between the jaw and neck. This sort of tumor is called *tii* (mumps?), or sometimes *nyila*.

Awiane and her mother tried to cure Kofi at first with native medicines. But when these proved of no avail, they took him to the Eikwe Catholic hospital. Here he was given injections twice, apparently with no results. When they took him for a third visit, the white doctor (a Dutchman) looked worried and said that the child should be kept at the hospital.

This entailed some financial difficulty. Awiane being such a young girl, her mother obviously had scarce trust in her where important matters were concerned, and she insisted as usual in making decisions for her. If the child stayed at the hospital, Awiane would, of course, have to go with him to Eikwe to nurse him and take care of him, but Nyima would have to follow them in order to look after Awiane. Complicated calculations were made by the family and discussed at length, and the total cost of the transportation and sojourn of Kofi, Awiane, and Nyima at Eikwe for a few days was finally evaluated at ¢5.

While the issue was being debated, Anaman came to Ngelekazo and was asked to contribute. But he took a detached attitude, remarking that these childhood diseases were better cured by native medicine, and they were women's concern anyhow, not men's. Besides, ¢5 is a substantial figure, a sum he could not possibly afford, as his monthly salary as a teacher only amounted to ¢30, barely sufficient to keep him alive.

At this stage, the Italian anthropologist living in nearby Beyin, who, as a friend of Mieza and Nyima, was regularly visiting them and had become apprehensive about little Kofi's alarming condition, intervened by giving Mieza the required ¢5. The financial problem thus being solved, it was decided that Kofi, escorted by his mother and grandmother, would be taken to the German sisters' hospital the next morning. To save time, the anthropologist himself would come to Ngelekazo at dawn with his jeep and drive them all to Eikwe.

The decision could not be put off any longer, because the child's condition had by this time taken an obvious turn for the worse. The swelling on the neck had reached monstrous proportions and was almost entirely preventing the poor child from swallowing any food. Even his breathing was impaired, to judge by the strange gurgling, gasping noises he made.

But the next morning, when the white man arrived punctually at the Ngelekazo compound as planned, Nyima called the whole thing off. She had consulted Azira the fetish priestess on the previous night, and Azira had instructed her to wait for another week before moving the child. Hearing this, the white man was not only astounded but indignant. Though having no specific medical knowledge of childhood or other diseases, he felt fairly sure that Kofi was bound to die unless promptly treated by a knowledgeable doctor; he bluntly told Mieza as much. This created friction between Mieza, who was inclined to follow his white friend's advice, and his sister Nyima, who did not intend to disobey the priestess's order. Nyima's will prevailed. The disappointed and angry anthropologist drove back alone to Beyin, fearing the worst for little Kofi's life.

The refusal to take Kofi to the hospital by no means meant that the child's *abusua* people remained idle. Their first and main concern was to ascertain the real cause of the sickness.

An obvious source of potential danger, pointed out by Azira the *kɔmenle*, but of which the family had long been aware, was Suhɔne, a goddess from the Ezinlibo area, who twice already had been connected with their branch of the Nvavile clan. A very long time ago, this goddess had chosen as her priestess one of the family ancestors called Avo Ahwia, who was thereafter known as Suhɔne Ahwia.[2] When this woman died, presumably in the early years of our century, all her ritual paraphernalia, such as beads, dolls, bells, fly-whisks, and other trinkets, had been buried with her. They should not have been. The goddess apparently interpreted this as an impediment to the continuation of her worship, and she caused several lineage members to die. When the initial blunder was discovered, in the early 1930s, the clan people went to Ahwia's grave and unearthed the objects. They had barely finished filling up the grave again, when one of the Nvavile girls present was possessed by the goddess, who thus plainly showed she had chosen the priestess she had long been waiting for. This girl was Ahɔba—Suhɔne Ahwia's "great-granddaughter" (sister's daughter's daughter's daughter), Nyima's full elder sister (by the same mother), and therefore little Kofi's "grandmother." Ahɔba died, probably in or around 1954, after having served Suhɔne as a mouthpiece and caretaker for more than twenty years. At that time, the *abusua* people went to Ezinlibo to honor (or, in the customary vernacular, to "purify") the goddess with the offering of a sheep, hens, and eggs. But they had not been back since, and from that time Suhɔne had had no priestess in the family. The goddess had good reason to be annoyed, and Kofi's present ailment could well have been a warning to the family.

A second and more direct cause could be found in the fact that Awiane had suffered from the *asonwu* as a child. Her parents, Munda Aka and Nyima, were at the time living in Asuwe, on Jawe Lagoon in the Ivory Coast. Their first three children had died in the first weeks of life. The fourth, a male baby, they named after the great god Tanoɛ with the intention of placing him under the god's protection; he survived. Two years later, Nyima was once again pregnant, and Awiane was born. Precautions were naturally taken to protect her, and the advice of a local medicine man called Ewule Aka was sought. But this did not prevent the baby from falling seriously ill at the end of her first year of life.

This was in 1954, a time when a great tide of children's diseases and high infant mortality attributed to the *asonwu* (goblins) was sweeping across Nzemaland in Ghana and the adjoining lagoon area of the southern Ivory Coast. The couple decided to leave Asuwe and returned to Ezinlibo, in Ghana, which for several generations was the hometown of Nyima's lineage. Here they took the sick baby to a local *kɔmenle* called Namua, who had acquired a reputation for healing *asonwu* illnesses. This priestess made the necessary earthenware figurines, set up a shrine at the outskirts of town, and succeeded in pacifying the *asonwu* so that little Awiane was saved.

A few years later, Munda Aka and Nyima divorced and left Ezinlibo—he to remarry in Ɛlonyi, she to settle down with her brother Mieza in Ngelekazo. Little Awiane followed her mother and lived with her until she was old enough to attend school in Takinta, as we have seen. The shrine that had been erected for her in her infancy remained in the care of the priestess at Ezinlibo; Nyima pledged herself to go back there at least once a year and make offerings of chickens. For a few years, she kept her promise. But some time in 1967 or 1968 Namua died, leaving no successor in the professional sense of the term, nor any children except one, who was a leper. So Nyima failed to return to Ezinlibo, and the shrines set up by the priestess were abandoned and fell into disrepair. This may well have caused displeasure among the *asonwu*, and consequently their attack on Awiane's child.

A third possible source of danger, according to Azira, lay in *sipe*, both by Munda Aka, who was offended and grieved because of Awiane's disobedience, and by Nyima, who had recently had a violent quarrel with her daughter. Awiane, at a time when Kofi's sickness had already manifested itself, at the end of September 1971, had once more run away to meet her disreputable lover.

From the very beginning of Kofi's illness, Nyima, Mieza, and Mieza's wife, Afo, had been aware of these impending threats to the child's health. But they didn't know which threat was the real cause. When it became apparent that Kofi's life was in danger, and when the suggestion of taking him to the white man's hospital was finally rejected, the need to solve these doubts by means of authoritative diagnosis could no longer be postponed. After long and thoughtful debates in the family circle, on 8 October 1971, an appointment was made for the following morning with a Beyin *ɛsɔfɔ* by the name of Kanra Noma. On October 9, at daybreak, Awiane, with little Kofi gasping and crying on her back, accompanied by her mother, walked from Ngelekazo to Beyin to obtain a response. The anthropologist living at the Beyin fort, who had taken a friendly interest in the child's case, was duly informed at the last minute. Thus he was able to attend, with three of his European assistants and a concealed tape recorder, the séance that followed at 7 A.M. in the *ɛsɔfɔ*'s inner parlor.

Kanra Noma, usually called Kanroma for short, was not really a follower of the Twelve Apostles, or *awa*, sect, as people thought and as the title of *ɛsɔfo* could lead one to believe. She was a church-attending Methodist, and her divining abilities, according to her own admission, were not based on the intervention of superhuman beings of any kind. They were based on her personal *sunsum* (spirit) made clairvoyant by the will of almighty God and under His inspiration, as befits a sincere Christian. Her diagnostic and divining technique consisted in casting cowries into a common iron basin, examining the pattern they formed after each cast, and at the same time questioning the patient and/or others present. She addressed and answered the cowries as if they were human beings with whom one could argue, and intermittently she invoked God's help.

In previous days, Kanroma had no doubt discreetly contrived to collect as much information as possible on the present customers and on their actual problem; but at the opening of her séance, she proceeded to investigate all aspects with the utmost care. She questioned the cowries.[3] She questioned Nyima. She even succeeded in establishing a brief dialogue with little Kofi, in which she understandably provided the answers as well as the questions. On the basis of the items of knowledge thus assembled, she directed the investigation along a line of which Kofi's relatives had not thought. Which midwife had assisted Awiane at the time of her first delivery, of Kwasi? Had this woman, whom Nyima remembered well, again been consulted and employed when Kofi's birth was expected? No, the person in question—Koafo Amoa, a priestess at Takinta—was traveling during that period and could not be located. But had agreements with her, by any chance, not been reached two years before, to the effect that Amoa would again be called as midwife at Awiane's following deliveries? And if so, had she perhaps not felt offended for not having been informed of Kofi's expected birth? And, considering how dangerous a priestess's resentment can be, could not Kofi's present ailment be attributed to Amoa's wrath for what she took as an offense? Sure of her excellent memory and perfectly self-assured, Nyima excluded such a possibility. No engagement of the sort had been taken with Amoa, so there was no conceivable reason she could be offended.

Reassured on this point, Kanroma discarded the hypothesis, which was openly scorned by Nyima both before and during the séance, that attributed Kofi's trouble to his grandparents' *sipe*. Kanroma now returned to the alternative explanations already suggested by Azira. She clearly saw the *amonle*, or "spell" or "dangerous thing," pressing against the child's swollen neck and identified it with the unsatisfied *asonwu* of Ezinlibo. Kanroma recommended that Nyima appease immediately the little monsters with libations and offerings. She did not overlook the possible interference of the family goddess, Suhɔne, suggesting that Nyima should strive to obtain Suhɔne's forgiveness. As she put it, "Suhɔne is all the time coming and going in your compound." She also dictated with meticulous precision the recipe for the remedy to be smeared on Kofi's tumor: a poultice of ground *sisiwolodo* and *ɛkpolokɛ* leaves mixed with shea butter and minced, well-chewed palm kernels. Then the cowries, speaking through Kanroma's mouth, gave the reassuring announcement that Kofi would not die. As soon as Kofi's recovery was complete, Kanroma added after a pause and a few more cowrie casts, Awiane should, to be on the safe side, pay a visit and offer thanks and a small gift to Amoa the midwife-priestess, taking both children with her. The rest would be taken care of by God Almighty, to Whom prayers should now be addressed by all present.

The consultation had lasted well over two hours and presently came to an end. When they stood up to take leave, the choking and gasping child's condition appeared more alarming than ever. But his relatives looked highly relieved. Filled with hope, they undertook the long return walk to Ngelekazo.

Their confidence, which was by no means shared by the participant observer, proved in the end not to be unfounded. For two days after the meeting at the *ɛsɔfo*'s place, other engagements prevented the anthropologist from returning to Ngelekazo. But he was told that already on the next morning after the séance, Kofi's conditions had shown a slight improvement. A visit to that compound three days later confirmed the good news. The swelling was receding, and the child breathed more normally and was once more taking, though with some effort, his mother's breast. The anthropologist was now aware of the responsibility he had hastily taken a few days earlier by his interference with the family's decisions. He began to suspect that he had been wrong when he had insisted that the child be treated at the white man's hospital. By the time the team of Italian researchers left Western Nzema, at the end of October, little Kofi had completely recovered. In the years to follow, he was seen to have developed into a sturdy, healthy little boy.

There is a lesson to be learned from the facts.

The simple, naive document represented by the story of Kofi's tumor acquires its cultural meaning and its logic in light of a whole series of traditional norms and orientations in Nzema society that the episode itself illustrates and confirms. I shall here attempt to summarize some of the significant ones, far more extensively and systematically discussed in my main work on this nation.[4]

1. The child's matrilocal residence reflected an unusual, though not exceptional, situation. As a rule, children are born, grow, and are brought up in their paternal home. The anomaly of this case derived from the fact that Kofi, born outside of official wedlock, had no legal father.

2. Public opinion strongly disapproves of men who fail to take care of their offspring, whether legitimate or not, and in particular who fail to contribute financially to maintenance and to carry out the paternal duty of naming the child.

3. Failure by the genitors to perform these duties has become in recent years a more common phenomenon and a serious problem. This is on account of the growing frequency of premarital relations and a high divorce rate. One of the results has been a strengthening of solidarity and mutual assistance within the matrilineage.

4. Responsibilities deriving from patrifiliation nevertheless remain relevant, as shown by Munda Aka's attitude. Though divorced and remarried in a distant town, long separated from his daughter, he worried over her troubles, tried to assert his authority, was shocked and angered when he failed, and condemned Awiane's behavior not so much as immoral conduct but as unforgivable disobedience of her father's orders.

5. For this breach of social ethics, one of the main causes of

Awiane's child's illness is at once seen as the automatic consequence of this disobedience. It provoked her father's resentment (*sipe*) and subordinately also that of her mother, Awiane having offended both.

6. The importance of friendship relations is shown by the fact that, when a momentous family meeting was called to discuss a serious matter in the august seat of the territorial chief, two strangers, who did not belong to either party's lineage, were invited to participate on the basis of a personal friendship bond.

7. Considerations of political expediency may hinder the normal course of justice. As one of the seduced girl's fathers is a colleague of the irresponsible seducer's father (both being territorial chiefs within the same state, as well as members of the same clan), Nyima's lineage renounced its legitimate claims.

8. Even in a case of serious illness, economic calculations may influence the choice of a given medical treatment. Situations of this kind naturally arise in societies on every continent and of every cultural level. But a look at the figure representing the dreaded expenditure anticipated in this case is nevertheless instructive; five cedis (¢5) even at the artificially bloated official exchange rate, corresponded at the time to no more than four American dollars.

9. Five centuries since the first contacts with Europeans, one century after the official establishment of British colonial rule, and more than half a century since the institution of permanent Christian missions on their territory, the faith and trust granted by the Nzema to the various categories of native herbalists, diviners, and healers remains practically unscathed. True, recourse to the "scientific" methods introduced by the white men is now an additional alternative in moments of crisis. But most consider it an expensive, and altogether unreliable, alternative. This applies not merely to the majority of illiterate, or semiilliterate, traditionally minded pagans but also to people and groups acquainted with the modern world, nominally converted to Christianity (and more rarely to Islam), and educated. Our friend Mɔkɛ Mieza, quoted in this and other episodes, was a Catholic schoolmaster; his sister—the late Nyima, who regrettably died in 1975—was a woman of remarkable personality and intelligence.

10. More generally and above all, the solution of the crisis emerging from Kofi's tumor is sought along the lines typical of

Akan Weltanschauung, which I have attempted to outline in the Introduction. Sicknesses, accidents, and deaths are not casual occurrences that may be explained empirically on the mere basis of a clinical diagnosis; they are dramatic events that involve not only the physiological but also the social, moral, and religious life of the person concerned and of kinsfolk and neighbors. The far-reaching causes of such events are not just—or not always—"magical," as so many superficial Western observers have insistently written and repeated; they are "cosmic." The anthropologist, who in 1971 happened to be involved in little Kofi's case, knew all this quite well. He had for years accepted the consistency of this view of the world and of human destiny, so different from his own. But then he became personally entangled in this chain of events as a "participant observer," sincerely anxious to contribute to save a child's life. At the moment of crisis, he opted without hesitation for the alternative that appeared obvious and indisputable in the frame of his own culture. He considered it his moral duty to influence the decisions of the interested parties; he insistently lavished advice; he felt indignant when this advice was rejected. In a word, he acted according to a decidedly ethnocentric pattern.

I have related this episode as objectively as I could, speaking of myself in the third person. It lends itself in the most exemplary way to stimulating reflections on the ambivalent role of participant observers, on the legitimacy of their interferences in the lives of the people they study, on the fact that—in the specific case examined—subsequent events proved the participant observer to have been wrong. (But of course, one could argue, things might have gone otherwise. Following the priestess's instructions, Kofi might also have died. Or, entrusted to the European doctor's care, he might equally have survived.) These and other considerations may lead to varying judgments on participant observers' professional and moral behavior, both in the specific case and at a general theoretical level. According to different points of view, these judgments will be validating or derogatory. But in both cases they will remain ethnocentric opinions. Precisely this is the significant lesson that the facts should teach us.

Appendix / Witchcraft: An Allegory?

A field of research in which contemporary anthropologists have remained staunchly entrenched in their Western ethnocentrism is the study of witchcraft. Well aware of the fact that one society after another, in many parts of the world, asserts a firm belief in the actual existence of witchcraft phenomena, they have unanimously taken for granted that such beliefs are illusory. Even to raise the possibility that the societies in question might after all be right in affirming the reality of witchcraft, and the anthropologists wrong in denying it, has apparently been deemed unworthy of serious scholarship.

I am using the term *witchcraft* in the usually accepted sense of "a mystical and innate power, which can be used by its possessor to harm other people" (Middleton and Winter 1963, 3), and I am not here concerned with the still largely unsolved question of the partial overlapping of this concept with the concepts of sorcery, evil medicine, and magical powers in general. Inasmuch as my main frame of reference is Africa, for the clarity of the argument I shall begin by summarizing the essential traits of the belief in witchcraft among the Nzema, the southern Akan society with which I am most directly acquainted.

Witchcraft (*ayɛne*) is an inborn spirit (*sunsum*) already present in some babies of either sex when they are in their mother's womb and which remains with them throughout their lives. It can occasionally be thrust upon adults, transmitted by succession, or "sold," but even in such cases it is acquired unwittingly. A person possessing *ayɛne* cannot take it into the nether world; before dying, he must pass it on either to another human being or to some domesticated animal, or wrap it up into a bundle, from which *ayɛne* will later emerge to "embrace" one of the witch's heirs. Though in rare cases used for good purposes, *ayɛne* normally

Reprinted with permission from *Medical Anthropology*, edited by Francis X. Grollig, S.J., and Harold B. Haley (The Hague: Mouton Publishers, 1973).

corrupts human nature; it causes its bearers to damage other people's property or to destroy their lives. Witches feast jointly on human flesh, each one of a group in turn providing a victim who is killed and devoured in the course of nocturnal banquets. The victim must be a close kinsman of the witch acting as host, usually (but not necessarily) a member of his or her segmented matrilineage. Witches perform most of their deeds at night, and their usual way of locomotion is flight; while the body lies in apparent sleep, the witchcraft spirit flies about, flapping its wings like a bat; its cry, resembling that of some night bird, can be heard up in the air. A witch is gifted with second sight: he or she can see things in complete darkness as clearly as in the daytime or watch things happening far away, and can also see gods, ghosts, or other preternatural beings who are invisible to common mortals. Witches can instantly transform themselves into snakes, bats, hogs, millipedes, or any other animals of their choice. They can work all sorts of wonders (such as, for example, tying together two palm fronds from distant places to make an aerial bridge on which they then run at fantastic speeds, or pulling out a person's eye and using it to replace a lorry's damaged headlight, etc.).

In its essential traits, this pattern corresponds to witchcraft beliefs known from other parts of west Africa, and to some extent also from different societies in other areas. In other terms, the Akan (or, more generally, the African) commoner will accept the fact that witches of this sort *do* exist and that the actions and prodigies ascribed to them, while unachievable by common mortals, do actually take place in everyday life—in a word, are *real*. To the average European of the twentieth century, on the other hand, this whole set of beliefs is bound to appear unacceptable, objectively "impossible," *unreal*.[1]

Faced with the alternative between these two positions, antithetical and at first sight irreconcilable, anthropologists have either openly sided with the latter view, or they have ignored the issue altogether, in both cases shifting their analysis to a different level—the sociocultural and functional explanation of that illusion, witchcraft.

In his epoch-making monograph on Zande witchcraft, oracles, and magic, Evans-Pritchard chose the first of the two attitudes mentioned. "Witchcraft is imaginary," he wrote, "and a man *cannot possibly* be a witch." In a following chapter, he fleetingly referred to the Azande's own attitude not toward witchcraft *per se*, but toward the "deception" and "inefficiency" of witch doctors:

> As in many other of their customs, we find a mingling of common sense and mystical thought, and we may ask why common sense does not triumph over superstition. . . . Their idiom is so much of a mystical order that criticism of one belief can only be made in terms of another that equally *lacks foundation in fact*. [Evans-Pritchard 1937, 119, 193–94; emphasis added]

The obvious implication is that, in the author's mind, Zande "mystical thought" is equated with "superstition," both being contrary to "common sense"—the latter embodying the prevalent opinion of twentieth-century Westerners shared by the author.[2]

The same position was taken years later by Gunther Wagner in his synopsis of Luyia ("Kavirondo") culture: "The charges levelled against [the witch] may be so fantastic that *they could not possibly have a factual basis*" (Wagner 1954, 40; emphasis added).[3]

Whether overtly declared, as in these instances, or—as more frequently is the case—tacitly taken for granted, the assumption that witchcraft is inadmissible runs as a red thread throughout the literature. This applies to the authors of general treatises who in recent decades have leaned more or less heavily on Evans-Pritchard's authority (e.g., Radin 1953, 144ff.; Hoebel 1954, 266ff.; Parrinder 1954, 122ff.; Howells 1962, 104–24; Lienhardt 1964, 149–58; Douglas 1967), as well as to social anthropologists who in postwar years have conducted field research on African witchcraft or have edited new studies on the subject (Middleton and Winter 1963; Marwick 1965; Harwood 1970). The issue in question is indeed hardly touched upon in the scholarly little book in which Lucy Mair has recently epitomized all relevant theories on the subject (Mair 1969). By and large, modern anthropologists appear to have concentrated mostly on the attempt to analyze the role of the witchcraft complex in given social contexts: its significance in relation to local frictions and tensions, especially in the framework of the various kinship and political systems and the like. I am contending not that this approach has not led to some fruitful hypotheses, but that it is too narrow. The issues involved are not merely social; they are moral and metaphysical and can be properly understood only in this broader framework.

Interpreted and "explained" in their mere social setting, native witchcraft beliefs lose some of their apparent absurdity, so contrary to our common sense. But it has strangely never occurred to anthropologists—with the laudable exception of Robin Horton[4]—that "common sense" is hardly an adequate criterion for the scientific assessment of the alleged phenomena concerned; that our duty is not only to verify the object of judgment (i.e., the authenticity of magic powers), but also, and first of all, to verify the validity of the *categoria iudicans* "the category being evaluated" itself (i.e., of the concept of reality). For this is the very crux of the problem: once I have ascertained that the members of the African society I am studying are convinced, say, that certain persons called witches fly at night, and since in my own society such an action is reputed to be impossible, am I justified as a scientist in assuming at the outset that the African's mind must be blinded by ignorance and superstition, while my own conviction is founded on objective truth? What is "reality" to him, and what is it to me? Am I justified in holding that the only method of assessing or rejecting the authenticity of psychic and behavioral phenomena is the experimental one accepted in our Western sciences?

Questions such as these were propounded and discussed a quarter of a century ago in a book by E. De Martino that has regularly been overlooked in anthropological literature abroad, but nonetheless remains a significant contribution to methodology. In his attempt to analyze the problem of magical powers, De Martino does not directly discuss witchcraft as such, his examples being taken from the cognate fields of clairvoyance, shamanism, fire walking, and precognition, instances of which are quoted from both ethnological and parapsychological sources. His basic criticism, nevertheless, applies equally well to our present topic:

> The very possibility of paranormal phenomena is intimately repugnant to the inner history of modern scientific trends. . . . [It] represents for science a real "sign of contradiction," a "scandal.". . . The analysis of the problem of magical powers in the history of ethnology provides us . . . with a further opportunity of realizing this: that we take for theoretical

> evaluation of the magic world what really is only practical expediency, and that we mistake for understanding what in fact is still polemic negation, emotional attitude. But once we have acknowledged this situation, by this very fact we have attained a higher historiographic perspective, we are laying the foundations for a worthier humanism. . . . The comprehension of the magic world is only possible in so far as we extend and deepen our criticism of realistic dogmatism (De Martino 1948, 69, 256–57; my translation).

Unimpeachable as De Martino's position is at the epistemological level, one must admit that his conclusions are only indirectly constructive for the furthering of anthropological research. True, the inadequacy of what he calls the "naturalistic method," the "experimental science of nature," to solve the problems raised by paranormal phenomena is blatant. True, more specifically, the general omission of any systematic attempt to check the factual foundations (if any) of alleged wizardry phenomena is largely due to the researchers' a priori skepticism. But of course this is not the only obstacle: the fact that the very societies which profess belief in witchcraft (as in other paranormal phenomena) enshrine this belief in what we call a "mystical aura" discourages empirical investigation. The gap in Weltanschauung is simply too wide.

So, while De Martino's appeal for a "higher" or more comprehensive approach on the part of the anthropologist remains essential, I suggest there is another way by which we should attempt to bridge the intercultural chasm: by a more thorough effort to evaluate the real nature of beliefs at the other end.

Scarce attention has hitherto been given to the ascertainment, along psychological and statistical lines, of the actual degree of faith in witchcraft among the societies concerned. Though the general pattern of belief certainly follows the blueprint accepted in each society and is rooted as such in the minds of most men and women of that society, its nature—to put it in Shirokogoroff's terms—is that of a "hypothesis" (a culture-sanctioned hypothesis), as contrasted with "positive knowledge." The belief may (and, among the Akan of whom I am cognizant, does) find varying degrees of acceptance in the minds of different individuals. Prevalent consensus does not imply totalitarian faith by the whole society, nor a lifetime's unwavering belief at the individual level.

A rare opportunity for a control of this type, apart from direct investigation in the field, is provided by a recent pamphlet on witchcraft written by an educated Nzema in his own language (Aboagye 1969), which I have elsewhere translated and commented upon (Grottanelli 1974), and which may be taken to reflect the opinion of today's literate, urbanized section of the Akan on the subject.

The author describes at such length and with such wealth and precision of details the faculties and deeds of witches, some of which are summarized at the beginning of the present paper, that readers are left with no doubt as to his firm belief in the reality of witchcraft. Yet a recurrent expression, which he untiringly uses in relating those alleged "facts," sheds a significant light on the nature of his belief. According to Aboagye (1969), witches actually *do* the perfidious or miraculous things he reports, but they do them "in ayɛne way." Here are a few examples from his text (my translation, emphasis added):

> The exchange of meals among *ayɛne* people is done eating human beings. . . . When the time comes, one of them takes a relative, son or daughter, father or mother . . . [and] kills this person at once *in ayɛne way,* or hangs him till he is fat before killing him (§ 18). . . . When they eat meals *in ayɛne way* they become well satisfied (§ 19). . . . If your *ayɛne* friends tell you it is your turn [to provide a human victim for the common meals], and you refuse, all together they will attack you and fight you *in ayɛne way* (§ 20). . . . If one of his relatives owns a lorry to transport passengers, the witch may sell it *in ayɛne way* . . . and keep the money for himself (§ 22). . . . A witch may invent an aeroplane, a steamer, a motorcar, a train, *in ayɛne way* (§ 95).

The contents and style of the booklet make it plain that Kwesi Aboagye did not write it for the sake of scholarship, but in order to provide his fellow countrymen with "factual" information as to the real nature and behavior of witches and with advice as to the practical means to defend themselves against them. At the same time, however, he stresses the fact that the nefarious deeds of witches are performed on a plane of reality conceived as distinct from that of profane, everyday life. This, I believe, is a way of suggesting—in terms comprehensible to the average Akan reader—that the whole witchcraft complex must be understood as a body of symbols,[5] a compromise, as it were, between naive popular belief and Western-inspired skepticism.

If this interpretation is correct, it would point to a possible rapprochement of the two antithetical positions mentioned above. A symbolical explanation of witchcraft, and more generally of magic, is by no means a novelty for Western scholars (cf. Beattie 1966, 202–12); if we are prepared to accept such an explanation, a major obstacle to our understanding of witchcraft beliefs is no doubt removed.

To illustrate the point with one more example from Aboagye's pamphlet: if we are asked to believe that a certain female witch actually transforms her unsuspecting husband into a horse at night in order to ride him, we refuse to do so. Such a metamorphosis is in patent conflict with our "scientific" mentality, so we declare it to be "impossible." But if the same prodigy is submitted to us as having a metaphorical meaning, implying that some domineering wife is constantly ordering her weak husband about, thus reducing him to mental and even physical exhaustion, then we are inclined to accept the fact as likely or even true, because we know from experience that such situations do in fact exist in almost every society. In Italy, indeed, this prepotent sort of wife may be referred to jocularly as a *strega*—"a witch."

To what extent the average illiterate African accepts and interprets such a metaphorical conception of witchcraft is of course a relevant question. When an Akan says that a witch has "stolen" such and such a man's brain, or has "cut off his head," he *knows* very well that the victim's head is still visible—we would say objectively—on his neck. When another informant tells us that a witch "flies away" at night, he is well aware that the witch's body is still in its place, asleep in bed, as anyone can see; he means it is only the unfathomable spiritual essence that flies away.[6] In other terms, he is referring to a "symbolic" flight; but in his mind the culture-sanctioned image of *ayɛne* surpasses ordinary human nature so greatly in power, knowledge, and harmfulness,[7] that the symbol overshadows profane experience and is more "real" than everyday reality. In some cases, no doubt, symbolism escapes simpler minds altogether, so that the beliefs are accepted in their literal, vulgar sense. But then we should not forget that the same is true in all societies, including Western ones. It is only a minority of the initiates that perceives the subtleties of symbolical expression in religion, art, and other sectors of culture.

Regardless of the degree of awareness of this symbolism, to the Akan the idea of witchcraft remains essentially the translation into culturally significant terms of an everlasting existential problem, the unavoidable presence of evil—more precisely, of that quintessence of evil brought into this world by the destructive hatred and envy lurking in the heart of close kinsfolk. Inasmuch as another essential trait of this particular kind of evil is its *subversive* nature (in the literal and etymological meaning of the adjective; see Grottanelli 1974), the witchcraft complex could be defined as *an allegory of social and moral subversion*.

Here again, I suggest that this definition of witchcraft can be translated in terms compatible with our own conception of this category of evil. That our own psychic balance, our vitality, and our very physical health are constantly being impaired and undermined ("devoured") by calamities and adversities whose final causes are often inscrutable, and particularly by the avowed or unavowed hostility of our neighbors, is an existential truth that few people in the modern "civilized" world would question. And that hostility and ill-feeling are all the more painful and destructive of our well-being and peace of mind when we detect them in our nearest kinspeople is equally undoubted. Now it is very much the same social and psychological truth that Africans try to assert when they attribute misfortune, illness, and death to *ayɛne* or similar entities, just as our own ancestors did, and indeed as some of our Western contemporaries continue to do.

If we are prepared to accept "the allegory that is witchcraft" as a formulation of existential risks to which our own society is no less exposed than are African ones, expressed in a symbolical phrasing that by its very nature eludes the requirements of experimental control, we will have gone a step further towards solving the age-old dilemma of the "reality" of witchcraft.

Notes

Introduction

1. The first British settlements along the so-called Gold Coast date to 1618. Possession of the country officially as a colony in 1821. The nation was declared independent, within the Commonwealth, in 1957. Present-day Ghana became a republic in 1960.

2. There is an extensive literature on W. W. Harris and his church. See, for example, Guariglia 1959, Rouch 1963, Haliburton 1971, and Roux 1971. For later developments of the sect in southwestern Ghana, see Cerulli 1963, Cerulli 1973, and Grottanelli 1977–78.

1. The Python Killer

1. Deaths of people struck by lightning, bitten by poisonous snakes, drowned, and murdered by a highway robber, as well as those who die by suicide or women who die in childbirth are among those grouped under the name *ɔtɔfoɔ*. They require simplified obsequies and burial, are traditionally not publicly laid out in state, and are buried not in the common cemeteries but near their place of death. In modern times this strict rule has been considerably relaxed. (See Cerulli 1977, 210–11.)

2. It is an established rule that inquiries on the circumstances and presumed causes of a person's death should exclusively be carried out by relatives of the person's lineage segment (*suakunlu abusua*).

3. Of Fort Apollonia, Lawrence (1969, 228) says, "The most ingenious and truly original design in tropical Africa was applied to the latest of the small forts, that built by the English in 1768–73 at Beyin, which they called Apollonia—a name conferred by its Portuguese discoverer, who sighted the place on that Saint's day." Partially restored at the end of World War II, the fort was kindly assigned by Ghanaian authorities as a temporary residence for the author and his assistants.

4. *Adunyi*, the string oracle, involves the manipulation of seven strings or thin leather strips, each having its own special symbol and name. The response is announced by the diviner after a series of successive casts of the strings.

5. Womb stealing, resulting in the temporary or permanent barrenness of the victim, is one of the misdeeds most frequently attributed to Akan witches, usually at the expense of young women belonging to the witch's lineage (see Grottanelli, 1974).

2. A *Wife's Curse*

1. Nzema women consider it improper to be too explicit when touching on sexual topics, especially in conversation with a male foreigner; likewise, a sensitive anthropologist refrains from asking indelicate questions. If the information reported above is correct, Asua's refusal may be accounted for by the reluctance with which Nzema women indulge in sexual intercourse in broad daylight—not out of prudishness, it was explained to me on other occasions, but because it is supposed to bring bad luck.

2. As explained elsewhere in the book, all females of a child's mother's generation within the restricted lineage (*suakunlu abusua*) are technically "mothers" to that child. Hence, the expression "the mother who brought me forth," or "my real mother," is commonly used by the Nzema for the sake of clarity.

3. These are the traditional couple of names automatically given to twins of the same sex, whether male or female. Ndakpanyi is the elder twin, and Ndakyia is the junior twin.

4. Blinya is the name given by the Nzema to the Avikam, one of the lagoon tribes of the southern Ivory Coast, living mainly in the Grand Lahou area. The Anyi call them Brinya.

5. This phrase translates as "By the mouth of the Bia [River] and [the kingdom of] Kranyabo," an oath referring to past historical events. The spelling of the two toponyms is subject to variation. Bia (the main river flowing into the Aby Lagoon just beyond the southwestern frontier of Ghana) is also spelled Bea; Kranyabo (the well-known Anyi kingdom, which the French call Krinjabo) is also spelled Kranyuabu or Kenlanwiabo, as well as in other ways.

6. *Ɛkɛla ɛhwanlɛ* is an elaborate rite performed in the forest by a *kɔmenle*, preferably the one reputed to be the caretaker and mouthpiece of the local god, with the power to retrieve the soul of a dead person believed to be imprisoned or held as hostage in the god's abode. To be successful, the rite must be preceded by offerings and prayers to appease the god.

3. *The Jealous God*

1. "Quarm" is merely the anglophone version of Kwame ("Saturday-born"), one of the seven *ɛkɛla aluma* attributed to every male baby at birth according to the day of the week on which it was brought forth. These automatic "soul names," as well as their seven female correspondents, may, however, become proper "given names" if the child's father later decides to assign one of them to his son or daughter in remembrance of some revered ancestor, relative, or friend. On personal names in general, see Grottanelli 1977.

2. Like among other minor or peripheral tribes of the great Akan group, Twi, the language of Asante, is understood and spoken in Nzemaland by the better-educated people.

3. The same term, *suanu agyalɛ,* is used to indicate a quite different type of marriage, that among cross-cousins.

4. My informant James E. Quarm, to be sure, took a firm stand also against the arch-destroyer of fetishes, Mabie (also known as Dix-sept). In doing this he was not only following the attitude of all official Christian churches, which from the start were strongly suspicious of the so-called prophet's preaching, but he expressed his personal disapproval of the man on moral grounds. Mabie had, indeed, publicly disgraced himself in 1954 by having committed adultery with the wife of the Enkyi *ɔmanhene*'s chief linguist, and by being stupidly found out. Positive evidence of the prophet's immorality lies to this day in the possession of Quarm's lineage; his uncle, who sat at the time on the Adahonle stool in the village of Mafeɛ in the southeast of the Ivory Coast, still has in his locked bɵx Mabie's golden headband or crown, left in pawn by the prophet because he did not have the cash to pay the adultery fee.

5. See note 1, chapter 1.

6. *Ndane,* "oath" or more correctly "heavy word," is a short conventional sentence, referring to some memorable (historical or personal) event of the past, solemnly and loudly uttered in grave circumstances or in serious disputes. It is spoken, for example, to affirm one's innocence, to contradict an adversary's lie, or to proclaim an important truth denied by others. At the same time, it invokes divine punishment on the swearer if the oath is false. There are state oaths, town oaths, and personal oaths.

4. *The Quarrelsome Rivals*

1. This chiefly name, in various spellings (Adualo Kwajan, Andualo Whajah, etc.) goes back to that of the supposed founder of the Ngelekazo chieftainship, Andualu Kwagya I. In the absence of reliable written documents, the date of this founding remains conjectural.

2. A chief's residence is traditionally called a "palace" even if it consists, as almost invariably is the case in Nzemaland, of a few huts with corrugated-iron or thatched roofs surrounded by a fence, very much like the dwellings of the chief's subjects.

3. The naming ceremony is usually postponed until the time when the parents have a reasonable expectation that the child will live. Until that day, the child is known by an *ɛkɛla duma* or "soul name"—that is, the name each person automatically acquires at birth, depending on the day of

the week of birth. Kabenla merely means "Tuesday-born." He was only sixteen months old when he died.

4. It appears that Ama Bomo's kinsfolk did not particularly object to her somewhat loose sexual behavior. They would have preferred her to remarry, but they considered that the important thing was for her to bring forth children for her lineage, whether in legal wedlock or not, because she was the only female of childbearing age within the whole segment of her *suakunlu abusua* at the time.

5. These are the exact terms my main informant used at this point of his report. Just as men on the eve of an impending battle sharpen their cutlasses and knives, he explained, so women grind *dazia* (black pepper) to throw into their enemies' eyes.

6. The Ghanaian currency is called the cedi, the symbol for which is ¢, which precedes the denomination (e.g., ¢20); each cedi is further divided into one hundred pesewas. At the time of the stories related in this book—the late 1960s and early 1970s—the official exchange rate for the cedi, on average, which was a somewhat inflated figure, was one cedi equaling about eighty U.S. cents to one dollar or about ten British shillings (now fifty pence). In 1987, however, the value of the cedi had dropped to about one American cent.

7. According to common belief, which is not challenged or contradicted by the ministers of the Twelve Apostles sect, the tutelary ghosts of a compound founder and of its early inhabitants continue to hover about the compound irrespective of the religion of the present occupants, even if the compound is turned into the cultic seat of an *awa* priest or priestess.

8. The traditional treatment for convulsions, epileptic attacks, and similar violent disturbances is the "water from the roof." Its main feature involves placing the patient under the eaves of a hut and throwing the contents of one or more bucketfuls of water onto the thatch, thus allowing the water to trickle down onto the person's body.

9. Permanent bachelors are rare among the Nzema and considered with a shade of disapproval and mistrust. But to understand Ama Bomo's hesitation and final refusal to marry Bile Kɔkɔlɛ, a special reason should be pointed out that made this man appear an unwelcome suitor. When a very young man in Ngelekazo, before leaving for Wassaw, where he was to spend most of his lifetime, Bile Kɔkɔlɛ had taken a local girl called Nyima as a concubine and allegedly begotten a daughter by her. But when this child was born, he refused to give any money for her and for her mother, so that the girl, as they say in the vernacular, "remained for the *abusua*"; in other words, Nyima's close relatives within the lineage had to provide all the financial support for her and her baby. This stinginess was resented and

remembered, and surely even after many years it did not recommend Kɔkɔlɛ as a good prospective husband. It is just as bad as if you marry and divorce too many women in quick succession; the next girl will refuse you.

5. A *Clear Diagnosis*

1. The custom of inscribing short sayings in Twi or in English on the body of trucks and buses is well known throughout Ghana, the Ivory Coast, and other West African countries. Ghanaian examples are "God Is Love," "The Two Friends," "Beware of Women," "Trust God," "Playboy," "Meet Me Tonight," and countless others. Painted in bold and conspicuous capitals on the sides, these mottoes make the vehicles easily recognizable, even by illiterate passengers and from a considerable distance, and make them popular along the roadside. For a recent survey, see Lebeuf 1984.

2. The Mboa Eku Society is the Ghanaian mutual aid association, specifically devoted to the financial assistance of members at the delicate moment when they are faced with the payment of costly funeral expenses.

3. The category of *nyangonle mmalɛ*, "God-given children," includes the eighth-born (Nyamekɛ) and ninth-born (Nyɔnra) children of every mother, as well as twins of all kinds (*ndalɛ*). A special shrine is usually erected in their honor in their parents' courtyard, to which yearly offerings are ritually made.

4. Such cases are surely rare, but they exist. My friend Adayi Kwame from Twinɛne once provided me with convincing information about an episode, which I shall perhaps some day publish, in which a fetish god took vengeance on a guilty lineage forty years after the sin committed by one of its members.

5. The limitation of this gift to only one-half of the required sum should not be attributed to the foreign anthropologist's stinginess. Rather, it resulted from strong doubt, since I am a Christian and had scarce reliance in the actual usefulness of the rite for the dead man's soul.

6. *The Wavering Christian*

1. Bile is a very common personal name among the Nzema. In colonial days it was commonly anglicized in spelling as "Blay." It was, incidentally, also the name of the paramount chief or king of Eastern Nzema in the 1960s and 1970s.

2. *Ahɔne* is the fetish dance, which is accompanied by drumming and music. In the course of the dance, the *kɔmenle* is expected to enter a trance and to act and speak in the name of gods or other spiritual beings.

3. Agyeba should not have been pregnant at this time. Customary

morals strongly discourage a mother's new pregnancy until she has definitely weaned her previous child.

4. The boy was named Wangala (The Nzema spelling of Wangara) after a well-known tribe, the Mande-speaking Dyula or Dyulanke tribe in northern Ghana, which are traditionally despised as inferior and uncivilized by the Akan nations. Wangara is given as a contemptuous personal name to children some of whose elder siblings have died supposedly at the hands of evil spirits or deities. People believe that hostile supernatural beings will disregard a child bearing such an illogical and despicable name, and refrain from harming it.

5. When I first met Nyanzu in Ɛlonyi, he was grinding palm nuts for oil at a neighbor's primitive oil mill just outside town. On a later occasion, he told me his ambition was to become a truck driver, but he had failed to obtain the necessary license.

6. As is regularly the case when a wicked or disapproved action is attributed to a person in the course of a conversation, but cannot be safely proved, the name of the girl in this incident was never disclosed. The same applies to the elderly woman claiming her coconuts, mentioned in the first part of the chapter.

7. Fetish gods (*awozonle*) are credited with preternatural knowledge of what they are going to be told or asked by mortals in the near future. Tutelary ghosts (less numerous), such as Kɔkɔ, are reputed to be less powerful, but very useful in other specific cases, such as (*a*) in assisting a patient who is allegedly being attacked by another ghost, (*b*) when it is disclosed that a deceased person in Hades needs some property left behind in this world, or (*c*) when an object, stolen from the deceased during life, has to be returned to the ghost to pacify the dead owner and to allow the living thief to recover from the illness believed to be the retribution for the theft. Azira showed me the two fine fetish dolls representing Ayisa and Kɔkɔ, which were usually kept locked in the private shrine in her Ɛlonyi compound. They were made for her by a Baule sculptor, as the Nzema are not nearly as clever as the Baule at wood carving.

7. *The Rich Uncle's Coconuts*

1. Even the most meticulous informants openly admit that obtaining complete Nzema genealogies is extremely difficult. Usually the genealogies omit individuals who died in childhood, and sometimes even those who attained adult age but had no offspring. Thus, it is often practically impossible to ascertain the number of children actually begotten or brought forth by any old (or deceased) person.

2. Bile Kaku's refusal was justified according to traditional custom. If a person dies in a town or village where a branch of the *suakunlu abusua* is

settled, it is normal that the deceased be buried there, unless there are special reasons for taking the body back to the person's hometown.

8. *The Man Who Fell from the Roof*

1. Nzulezo, the most beautiful village in Western Nzema, is situated on the banks of an inland lagoon north of Beyin and built entirely on platforms on piles above the water.

2. *Ezumule* means thatch, made of palm fronds plaited and bent so that they hang on only one side of the stem. It is usually prepared weeks beforehand and strewn on a sort of raffia lattice to dry before being used in the actual roofing.

3. The official receptacle of a deceased person's movable properties—often a suitcase, a trunk, a cupboard, or for important or wealthy people a locked cabinet or room—is, in popular anglophone jargon, always referred to as "the box."

4. A man's lawful successors are his "brothers" and (if there are no surviving brothers) his "nephews"; a woman's successors are her "sisters" and "nieces," always within the matrilineal family, or *suakunlu abusua*. They are nominated by the lineage assembly in the course of funeral obsequies, though their identities are usually known much earlier. Preference is traditionally given not to the closest brothers (by the same mother) but to the descendants of the eldest female member of the dead person's lineage belonging to the same generation of the deceased, hence senior "brothers" or "sisters" of the deceased. Therefore, every death within the lineage, and every consequent choice of the successor, involves a careful reconsideration of the genealogical relationships existing at the time within the whole lineage. For every male lineage member who dies, three successors are nominated. This is wise because the first legal successor, and possibly also the second in his turn, may be difficult to reach or have left the country altogether; or for personal reasons of his own he may be unwilling to accept the succession. Whenever possible, the three men are chosen, in hierarchical order of seniority, as representatives of distinct segments of the lineage. In the vernacular, the first successor is referred to as "the one who sits on the stool (of the deceased)"; the second, "the one who sits on the knees (of the first successor)"; the third, "the one who breaks the fronds (or leaves)"—that is, the one who performs the respectful task of fanning (or refreshing and honoring) the two senior successors.

9. *The Ghost, the God, and the Goblins*

1. Even two decades after the independence of the neighboring Ivory Coast, most Ghanaians continue to refer to that country as "French."

2. On the *asonwu* (pronounced *asongu*), see Grottanelli 1961.

3. Kyapum is Tiapoum on the French maps. It lies on the southeastern branch of the great Aby Lagoon.

4. The expression "completely dead" is used by the Nzema with regard to final, definitely ascertained cases of death, in contrast to the not infrequent cases of apparent death. For one of these, see chapter 16, "The Widow Who Asked to Die."

10. The Vindictive Ghost

1. The mother who brought both Nyima and Mɔkɛ Mieza forth was Bomo Bonya; but, of course, according to the Akan kinship terminology, Ɛba was equally their "mother."

2. The snake-bite treatment of incising the affected part with a cutlass or knife, causing abundant bleeding, and sucking the poison out of the wound has recently been adopted by the Nzema, probably following the advice and example of Europeans. It was not practiced in this case.

3. See note 1, chapter 1.

4. See note 6, chapter 2.

5. This statement, made by my informants at this juncture, does not correspond to general Nzema belief. Thursday, if anything, is the day dedicated to the Earth goddess, Azɛlɛ Yaba (the Thursday-born Earth). In this particular case, incidentally, Bomo Bonya was a Yaba herself, while her sister Ɛba was an Abenlema, or Tuesday-born.

6. *Afɔtɔ* is a thick porridge made of mashed plantain and palm oil, with the occasional addition of egg yolks, considered the most suitable vegetable food for gods and ghosts.

12. The Little Boy Whose Soul Flew Away

1. By coincidence, Avola's full name was Eduku Avola, the name Eduku being her father's.

2. See note 4, chapter 9.

3. He was thus named, Nyanzu Ekyi ("little Nyanzu"), not after his homonymous father but after his father's foster father in posthumous gratefulness.

13. The Unremitting Goddess

1. People are supposed to marry or remarry in the next world, and not necessarily with the same spouses they had in this world. The phrase "while she was alive" is therefore not superfluous in an Akan context.

2. When the phrase "church-attending" is used to describe the Nzema of most Ghanaian villages, one must understand that this refers more to

good intentions than actual practice, since these villages often have no church or chapel of any denomination.

3. Individual land property is an institution foreign to Nzema tradition; land belonged to the various *abusua*, to be distributed by each responsible lineage head to lineage members according to their needs and rights. The "ownership" attributed to the Twea woman in question must be understood in this limited sense. I later discussed with qualified informants the question of whether a landowner of this type would be justified if offered one-third of the crop (as in Alua's case) by the person who has been using the farmland. There seemed to be no fixed rule; it depends on the agreements reached by the two parties at the outset. Each party will choose one witness, who will be present when the verbal preliminary arrangements are made. The witnesses may later be called to testify in case of dispute, and they may even be summoned to *ahemfi* (court) if the matter is serious, and asked to testify under oath. For this reason it is often difficult to find people prepared to act as witnesses in land contracts. Generally speaking, a share of one-third for the person (or lineage) lending the plot is considered fair. But if the plot is badly tilled by the lessee, the crops will be poorer than the landowner reasonably expects, and a complaint that the one-third share is unsatisfactory may then be justified. Individual land ownership is a recent and controversial introduction based on the European example and connected with the modern development of cash crop cultivation, especially coconut and cocoa.

4. Successors of a deceased person are always nominated by the *abusua* assembly, three for a man and two for a woman. (For more detail on succession, see note 4, chapter 8.)

5. See note 3, chapter 8.

14. The Promiscuous Bride

1. This is an unusual situation. Although clan exogamy is not (or is no longer) compulsory among the Nzema, in practice men seldom choose their wives from their own clan. In the present case, father and son also belonged to the same lineage. This fact, even more unusual, did not, however, imply any infringement of the strict rule of lineage exogamy; Akatia had, in fact, married a known descendant of a slave woman formerly adopted into his lineage. This type of marriage, *suanu agyalɛ* or *suakunlu agyalɛ*, is legally permitted and quite legitimate.

2. Ɛkɔla was an Anyi. But her indoor shrine—as described to me in detail by the informant—with its several wooden dolls, bottles, calabashes containing white clay, fly whisks, and other trinkets, placed on a low table concealed behind a curtain of white calico, was strongly reminiscent of

Nzema shrines. These two neighboring Akan nations culturally have much in common.

3. It is not surprising that the news of this intriguing *munzule* should soon have reached the faraway hometown of these Ghanaian migrant laborers. But the informant, a Catholic who tended to be skeptical about divination and pagan rites in general, was in this case astounded at the priestess's knowledge of facts (the purification rites performed in Etikɔbɔ no. 1), of which the Kwabile people were at the time not informed, but that were later shown to have really taken place in that distant little town.

15. The Wrong Sacrifice

1. See Grottanelli 1977–78, 2:364.

2. *Amonle*, a common term of the Nzema lexicon, means "charm," "amulet," and by extension in some cases also "curse," "oath," "ordeal test" (see Aboagye 1968, 24). The peculiar assonance of the word with the English *amulet* and Portuguese *amuleto* may be quite coincidental, but may on the other hand present an interesting problem to linguists. Cardona (1977, 138–41) has recognized a significant little list of Nzema words demonstrably derived from European languages, notably Portuguese and English. In this context, it is worthwhile to note that the Portuguese word *feitiço*, first heard and memorized by natives of the Guinea coast in the late fifteenth century, is still used to this day in its variants by anglophone and francophone West Africans when referring to their "fetish" cults.

3. Individual food interdicts in general, and especially those derived from a deity's prescription, are usually inherited and observed by the direct descendants and heirs of persons from whom the particular interdict originated. This did not apply to Afo, who provided me with the details about Nyima's taboos, because she considered herself a Catholic, and as such not expected to follow pagan practices. In her childhood, in fact, Afo was not brought up by her mother, who followed at the time the Twelve Apostles' church; Afo's father Ekpale Ekyi, who was a Catholic, took her and left her for a few years in an *adanelilɛ* fashion with his own beloved twin sister, also a nominal Catholic. This is the religion to which Afo decided she would belong, especially after she married Mɔkɛ Mieza, who was also a Catholic, though to my knowledge she never criticized her mother for becoming a *kɔmenle*.

4. On account of this god's acknowledged preference for dog meat, more dogs are bred to this day in Ngelekazo than in most other Nzema towns. The god is said to prefer black or dark-brown dogs rather than yellow or white ones, but in fact most of those one sees in town are piebald. A male animal is preferred to a bitch; if a bitch is chosen for sacrifice, it

must be one that has delivered at least three times; no pregnant bitch can ever be offered. Unlike sheep and fowl, dogs are not killed by slitting the throat. While two men keep the animal down by holding its legs, a third man slits it between the ribs on the left side and extracts the heart, which is offered to the deity together with the lungs and head. Before this, the god receives an offering of *afɔtɔ* made with *banna anyilɛ* (a small variety of plantain). The rest of the dog's meat is eaten by the men, and reputed to be a delicacy. It is cooked in a soup or stew with salt and pepper, but with no onions and no tomatoes. Women are neither allowed to eat dog meat or cook it.

5. See note 1, chapter 4.

6. The reconstruction of this dialogue is admittedly conjectural, because Afo was not actually present, and no other reliable earwitness could be found.

7. Nana Andualu Kwagya II died shortly after the episode of the sacrifice we have related, at the end of 1968. However, considering that his illness long antedated that event, it did not occur to people to connect the causes of his death to those of Kanra's. He was in due course succeeded on the Ngelekazo stool by another Twea, a classificatory brother of his, ruling under the name of Nana Andualu Kwagya III; he still held the chieftainship when I was last in Nzemaland.

8. The name of the stream, Ekyia Ɛkɛra, means "If in need, you will come."

16. The Widow Who Asked to Die

1. See note 4, chapter 9.

17. The Contended Acolyte

1. Most Nzema marriages conform to the *alie nwo agyalɛ* pattern ("courtyard marriage" or "outer marriage"). However, the Nzema have eleven traditional types of marriage, depending on the kinds of spouses, forms of bridewealth payment, wedding ceremonies, promissory pacts, religious allegiance, and so forth (see Grottanelli 1977–78, 1:61–67). It should be mentioned at this point that in recent times, and especially in the 1980s, an increasing number of couples live and procreate together without having submitted to any of the social formalities required by legal marriage.

2. In connection with my query whether it was right for Azɛmɛla to remarry and have children after her leprosy had manifested itself and had become a matter of public knowledge, the causes and risks of this malady were discussed. My Nzema friends thought there was no harm in a leper marrying; the disease cannot be transmitted by sexual contact, although of

course it can be caught if one uses a leper's sponge, soap, and towel. Leprosy, I was told on this occasion, is ultimately caused by the *kokobɛ ngɛkɛba*, tiny insects like worms, who live in the stomach and vomit their poison; but there are other widespread explanations (see Grottanelli 1977–78, 2:262–64). It was most unfortunate, my Sanzule informants pointed out, that Azɛmɛla could not avail herself of an excellent medicine that only a few years before her time had succeeded in healing another leper right there in Sanzule. This man, Ɛzɛnlɛnra, was the Sanzule chief's first *kpɔmavolɛ*, or spokesman; he was treated by a medicine man from Ɛlazula in the Ivory Coast, where he had gone to work on a farm. The treatment, which he continued for many months after his return to Sanzule, consisted of a poultice from several herbs pounded together, which was rubbed on the affected parts and left there as a thin layer, then washed away in a warm bath every fourth day. Ɛzɛnlɛnra was completely cured of his leprosy in the end, but alas, the recipe was lost.

3. Nana Afful III once told me that people, to get rid of an undesirable clan member, would take that person out of the (Nzema) country—say, to Asante—and sell the offender there as a slave. But this was done very rarely, when the person was found guilty of a particularly heinous offense.

4. This is done by another person lifting the animal with both hands from the ground to chin level of the person who is supposed to bless it, then lowering it down to the person's feet, so that the victim's body brushes against that of the standing offerer. No actual "embracing" is done.

5. The Nzema text is published in Grottanelli 1977–78, 2:388–89.

18. The Woman Who Was Punished for Being Too Kind

1. The Nzema recognize three levels of friendship: (1) *agɔnwolɛyɛlɛ*, or ordinary friendship; (2) *agɔnwolɛyɛlɛ kpalɛ*, or "good" friendship, which is a stronger and lifelong tie uniting two people (almost always of the same sex) with obligations of mutual assistance and collaboration of a financial nature; and (3) *agɔnwolɛ agyalɛ*, or "friendship marriage," usually between a man and a male teenager, more rarely between two women, in which preliminaries partly similar to those of real marriage are performed, partners cohabit for short periods, exchange presents, and share the same bed or mat. The latter form, eight cases of which were recorded and examined by Signorini in 1971, is now considered obsolete. The second, referred to in this chapter, still exists among the Nzema to the present day, especially in its male variety. A person rarely has more than one or two "good" friends in a lifetime.

2. For Nwoza, intercourse with Tayi would not strictly speaking have constituted *munzule* ("scandal," "dangerous act"), the kinship relationship between the two being one that even permits lawful marriage. It

was the personal aspect of their social relation up to that time, as well as the difference in age, that made the proposal appear shocking to Nwoza. Her reaction is one more testimony to her virtuous character, considering that most other middle-aged Nzema women would have been flattered by a young man's offer, and favorably receptive to it.

19. The Two Priestesses' Husband

1. Mpataba (simplified colonial spelling for Mgbɔtɛba) lies on the main inland highway almost exactly at the same longitude as Nzulezo. The forests around Mpataba are remembered as the haunts of the nineteenth-century Nzema king Kaku Aka, famous for his courage in war but above all for his bloodthirstiness.

2. All the children begotten by Ɛzonle's late brother who were not yet fully grown and married—not only Hɔma's but also Afiba's more numerous lot—were adopted, as we would say, and brought up by Akpɔ in his own compound. By his two wives Akpɔ had eight children himself, six of whom were alive at the time and yet unmarried. So one must admit that even by Nzema standards Akpɔ ranked as a generous father and a remarkably able provider.

20. The Sick Child and the Participant Observer

1. It is always the legal father who has the first, and often final, word on the subject of his daughter's marriage, even if the two have long been separated, as in the present case. Owing to Awiane's promising good looks, many well-to-do men had approached Munda Aka and asked to marry her, even long before she reached puberty. He had told them to wait. But when they returned after she had reached the age, they found her pregnant. In such a situation a suitor becomes wary. It is not the girl's lost virginity that matters, nor does the still-unborn or newly born baby create an impediment. The problem arises from prospective suitors perhaps thinking, "Maybe the girl is betrothed, or her lover will soon ask her to marry him, so why should I waste my time over this girl?" If they are very keen, they will wait and reconsider their proposal two or three years later. Then if they can see that the child has grown and is not being followed by others, they will say, "Why has the lass had no further pregnancies? It must be because she has broken off her relation to her lover and has not taken a new one." But during this long interval, the girl will find no immediate suitors, and it will be either for her father or her *abusua* people to keep her and pay for her maintenance.

2. Patronyms, which precede the personal given name, are often not employed in everyday use. But they are needed to distinguish people having the same personal name and living in the same environment.

Ahwia has a fairly common name, so her father's name Avo was prefixed to hers to distinguish her from namesakes—a frequent practice, whereas it is uncommon for *ahɔmenle* to use their deity's name in the same way.

3. The casual swiftness of the successive casts made in the quasi-darkness of the room, and the general attitude of the diviner who spoke almost without interruption during the whole séance, justified the observer's impression that the *ɛsɔfo* was really giving little or no attention to the cowries' actual position after each cast.

4. See Grottanelli 1977–78.

Appendix, Witchcraft: An Allegory?

1. The refusal to admit the reality of witchcraft (as opposed to sorcery) antedates by at least ten centuries the rise of anthropological science. Among the authorities who in the Middle Ages held that *strigae* (witches) were no more than a fiction of popular superstition and did not exist in reality are St. Agobardus, Archbishop of Lyons between 816 and 840, Regino of Prüm, Abbot of the famous Prüm Monastery in Eifel between 892 and 899, and Burckhard, Bishop of Worms in the first quarter of the eleventh century.

2. Some authors go as far as to lament overtly the persistence of this class of beliefs. Nadel (1951, 52) writes, "No one would dream of defending the perpetuation of a state of ignorance and superstition, of beliefs in witchcraft."

3. But for a more prudent evaluation, see Wagner (1949, 112).

4. One could now add the name of M. G. Marwick (1973), whose article came to my notice after the present paper [this Appendix] had been written.

5. Another Akan writer, a francophone Anyi from the Ivory Coast, refers to witches' alleged cannibalism as "symbolic meals" (Amon D'Aby 1960, 58, note 1).

6. Both opinions are alternatively held by African peoples: that witches fly out *in spirit* at night to do their nefarious work and that they go out *in the flesh*. According to Junod and to Stayt, the Thonga and Venda of southeastern Africa accept the former theory, while according to Schapera the latter prevails among the Kxatla (Schapera 1934, 294). Further inquiries along quantitative lines might help to ascertain how exclusive these two contrasting conceptions are among the peoples concerned.

7. Carlos Casteneda's studies of Yaqui magic (1971), a recent edition of which was translated into French in 1973 under the telling title *Voir*, have lately called our attention to the fundamental relevance of

paragnomic versus "natural" ways of seeing. Exactly like the Copper Eskimo shaman (see Rasmussen 1932, 27), the Nzema (Akan) witch is described as "one who has eyes": hence his immense superiority over common mortals.

Glossary

The spelling of Nzema terms follows the current official Ghanaian orthography. It employs the standard English alphabet plus two additional vowel characters, ɛ and ɔ; ɛ is referred to as an open *e* (pronounced as *a* in English "bad"), ɔ as an open *o* (pronounced as *a* in English "tall"). The sound *ng* (as in "sing") was formerly rendered by ŋ, but since 1961 this sign has officially been replaced by *nr* in front of a, ɛ, e, and i, and by *nw* in front of ɔ, o, and u. So, for instance, *kanra* ("slave") should be pronounced "kanga," *asonwu* should be pronounced "asongu."

abusua clan, lineage
adanelilɛ fostering, child rearing
adiema brother, sister
adunyi string oracle
afɔtɔ a special porridge for ritual use
agɔnwolɛ friend, friendship
agyalɛ marriage
ahɔne fetish dance
akpetekyi illicit gin
amaneɛ exchange of news (a traditional meeting formality)
amonle charm, spell
awa calabash (symbol of the Twelve Apostles sect)
awozoa nephew, niece
awozonle pl. of *bozonle*
awuvonyi mother's brother
ayɛne witch, witchcraft
azebɛla mother-in-law
azɛlɛ earth; the Earth goddess
bayivolɛ witch
belemgbunli chief, king
bozonle fetish god or goddess
bulu ten, tenth child
ebia stool
ɛbolɔ netherworld, Hades
egya father
ɛkɛla soul, life principle
ɛsɔfo priest, priestess
evinli pollution, impurity
ewiade (the present) world; world of the living
ewule disease, death
ewuole white clay
kanra slave
kɛnlamo Muslim
kokobɛ leper, leprosy
kɔmenle fetish priest or priestess
kpanyinli elder, senior
kpɔmavolɛ chief's spokesperson
kundum new year festival
kyibadeɛ taboo, food taboo
mgbɔnla concubine
mmotia mythical dwarf
mota person with no offspring
mralɛ children (pl. of *ralɛ* = child)
munzule abomination, scandal
nana grandmother; epithet of respect for a [male] chief

ndalɛ twin
ndane oath
ninsinli herbalist, healer, diviner
nwomenle ghost
nyɛma string, leather strap
Nyamenle sky deity, God
nza palm wine
ɔmanhene paramount chief, king
ɔmɔ mother
ɔtɔfoɔ bad death
ɔmɔ mother
ralɛ child
raalɛ woman
renyia male
sipe enmity, grudge
sua house
suakunlu chamber, inner room
saukunlu abusua one's direct lineage
sunsum spirit, soul
tufuhene headman, former military chief

References

Aboagye, P. A. K. *Nzema nee Nrelenza edwɛbohile buluku*. Accra and Tema: Ghana Publishing Corporation, 1968.

______. *Ayɛne*. Accra: Bureau of Ghana Languages, 1969.

Amon d'Aby, F. J. *Croyances religieuses et coutumes juridiques des Agni de la Côte d'Ivoire*. Paris: Larousse, 1960.

Beattie, J. *Other Cultures*. London: Cohen and West, 1966.

Bosman, W. *A New and Accurate Description of the Coast of Guinea, Divided into the Gold, the Slave, and the Ivory Coasts*. London: Knapton and Midwinter, 1705.

Busia, K. A. "The Ashanti of the Gold Coast." In *African Worlds*, edited by Daryll Forde. London: Oxford University Press, 1954.

Cardona, G. R. "Profilo della lingua nzema." In *Una società guineana: gli Nzema*, edited by V. L. Grottanelli, vol. 1. Turin: Boringhieri, 1977.

Castaneda, C. *A Separate Reality*. New York: Simon and Schuster, 1971.

Cerulli, E. "La setta dei Water Carriers." *Studi e Materiali di Storia delle Religioni* 34, no. 1 (1963): 27–59.

______. "I Water Carriers nove anni dopo." *Religioni e Civiltà* 1 (1973): 69–124.

______. "L'Individuo e la cultura tradizionale: Norma, trasformazione ed evasione." In *Una società guineana: gli Nzema*, edited by V. L. Grottanelli, vol. 1. Turin: Boringhieri, 1977.

Christaller, J. G. *Dictionary of the Asante and Fante Language Called Tshi (Twi)*. Basel: Evangelical Missionary Society, 1933.

Christensen, J. B. *Double Descent among the Fanti*. New Haven, Conn.: Human Relations Area Files, 1954.

Danquah, J. B. *The Akan Doctrine of God*. London: Lutterworth, 1944.

______. "Akan Society." *West African Affairs* (1951).

Debrunner, H. *Witchcraft in Ghana*. Accra: Presbyterian Book Depot, 1961.

De Martino, E. *Il mondo magico*. Turin: Einaudi, 1948.

Douglas, M. "Witch Beliefs in Central Africa." *Africa* 37 (1967): 72–80.

Evans-Pritchard, E. E. *Witchcraft, Oracles, and Magic among the Azande*. Oxford: Clarendon Press, 1937.

Grottanelli, V. L. "Asonwu Worship among the Nzema: A Study in Akan Art and Religion." *Africa* [London] 31 (1961): 46–60.

———. "Leben, Tod und Jenseits in den Glaubensvorstellungen der Nzima." In *Réincarnation et vie mystique en Afrique Noire, Colloque de Strasbourg*, 69–86. Paris: Presses Universitaires de France, 1965.

———. "Nzema High Gods." *Paideuma-Mitteilungen zur Kulturkunde* 13 (1967): 32–42.

———. "Gods and Morality in Nzema Polytheism." *Ethnology* 8 (1969): 370–405.

———. "La stregoneria Akan vista da un autore indigeno." In *Demologia e folklore: Scritti in memoria di G. Cocchiara*. Palermo: Flaccovio, 1974.

———. "Witchcraft: An Allegory?" In *Medical Anthropology*, edited by F. X. Grollig and H. B. Haley, 321–29. The Hague and Paris: Mouton, 1976.

———. "Personal Names as a Reflection of Social Relations." *L'Uomo* 1, no. 2 (1977): 149–75.

———. ed. *Una società guineana: gli Nzema*. 2 vols. Turin: Boringhieri, 1977–78.

Guariglia, G. *Prophetismus und Heilserwartungs-Bewegungen als völkerkundliches und religionsgeschichtliches Problem*. Vienna: Verlag Ferdinand Berger, 1959.

Haliburton, G. McK. *The Prophet Harris: A Study of an African Prophet and His Mass Movement in the Ivory Coast and in the Gold Coast in 1913–15*. London: 1971.

Harwood, A. *Witchcraft, Sorcery, and Social Categories among the Safwa*. London: Oxford University Press, 1970.

Hoebel, E. A. *The Law of Primitive Man*. Cambridge, Mass.: Harvard University Press, 1954.

Horton, R. "African Traditional Thought and Western Science." *Africa* 37 (1967): 50–71, 155–87.

Howells, W. *The Heathens: Primitive Man and His Religions*. Garden City, N.Y.: Doubleday, 1962.

Lawrence, A. W. *Fortified Trade-posts: The English in West Africa, 1645–1822*. 2d ed. London: Jonathan Cape, 1969.

Lebeuf, J. P. "Noms de véhicules automobiles en Afrique noire." *Journal des Africanistes* 54 (1984): 115–19.

Lienhardt, G. *Social Anthropology*. London: Oxford University Press, 1964.

Mair, L. *Witchcraft*. London: Weidenfeld and Nicolson, 1969.

Manoukian, M. *Akan and Gâ-Adangme Peoples in the Gold Coast*. London: International African Institute, 1950.

Marwick, M. G. *Sorcery in Its Social Setting*. Manchester: Manchester University Press, 1965.

———. "How Real Is the Charmed Circle in African and Western Thought?" *Africa* 43 (1973): 59–70.

Middleton, J. and E. H. Winter, eds. *Witchcraft and Sorcery in East Africa*. London: Routledge and Kegan Paul, 1963.

Murdock, G. P. *Theories of Illness: A World Survey*. London: Oxford University Press, 1980.

Nadel, S. F. *The Foundations of Social Anthropology*. London: Routledge and Kegan Paul, 1951.

Parrinder, E. G. *West African Religion*. London: Epworth Press, 1949.

———. *African Traditional Religion*. London: Hutchinson's University Library, 1954.

Radin, P. *The World of Primitive Man*. New York: H. Schuman, 1953.

Rasmussen, K. *The Intellectual Culture of the Copper Eskimos*. Copenhagen: Gyldendale, 1932.

Rattray, R. S. *Religion and Art in Ashanti*. 2d ed. London: Oxford University Press, 1954. (Originally published in 1927.)

Rouch, J. "Introduction à l'étude de la communeauté de Bregbo." *Journal de la Société des Africanistes* 33 (1963): 129–202.

Roussier, P. *L'établissement d'Issiny, 1686–1702*. Paris: 1935.

Roux, A. *L'Evangile dans la forêt: Naissance d'une église en Afrique Noire*. Paris: 1971.

Schapera, I. "Oral Sorcery among the Natives of Bechuanaland." In *Essays Presented to C. G. Seligman*, edited by E. E. Evans-Pritchard, R. Firth, B. Malinowski, and I. Schapera. London: Kegan Paul, Trench, Trubner, 1934.

Shirokogoroff, S. M. *Psychomental Complex of the Tungus*. London: Kegan Paul, Trench, Trubner, 1935.

Signorini, I. "Agɔnwolɛ Agyalɛ: il matrimonio tra individui dello stesso sesso degli Nzema del Ghana sud-occidentale." *Rassegna Italiana di Sociologia* 12 (1971): 529–45.

Soppelsa, R. T. "*Assongu:* A Terracotta Tradition of Southeastern Ivory Coast." *Africa* (London) 57, no. 1 (1987): 51–73.

Tauxier, L. *Religion, moeurs et coutumes des Agni de la Côte d'Ivoire*. Paris: Paul Geuthner, 1932.

Twumasi, P. A. *Medical Systems in Ghana*. Tema: Ghana Publishing Corporation, 1975.

Wagner, G. *The Bantu of North Kavirondo*. Vol. 1. London: Oxford University Press, 1949.

———. "The Abaluyia of Kavirondo (Kenya)." In *African Worlds*, edited by D. Forde. London: International African Institute, 1954.

Welman, C. W. *A Preliminary Study of the Nzima Language*. London: Crown Agents for the Colonies, 1925.

Index